W9-BOA-631

Culture and Customs of Brazil

Map of Brazil. (Darin Grauberger, University of Kansas Cartographic Services)

Culture and Customs of Brazil

ᛒᚱᛒ

Jon S. Vincent

Culture and Customs of Latin America
and the Caribbean
Peter Standish, Series Editor

GREENWOOD PRESS
Westport, Connecticut • London

Library of Congress Cataloging-in-Publication Data

Vincent, Jon S.
    Culture and customs of Brazil / Jon S. Vincent.
        p.   cm.—(Culture and customs of Latin America and the Caribbean, ISSN
    1521–8856)
    Includes bibliographical references and index.
    ISBN 0–313–30495–5 (alk. paper)
    1. Brazil—Civilization—20th century.   2. Popular culture—Brazil—History—
    20th century.   I. Title.   II. Series.
    F2537.V73   2003
    306'.0981—dc21   2002044841

British Library Cataloguing in Publication Data is available.

Copyright © 2003 by Jon S. Vincent

All rights reserved. No portion of this book may be
reproduced, by any process or technique, without the
express written consent of the publisher.

Library of Congress Catalog Card Number: 2002044841
ISBN: 0–313–30495–5
ISSN: 1521–8856

First published in 2003

Greenwood Press, 88 Post Road West, Westport, CT 06881
An imprint of Greenwood Publishing Group, Inc.
www.greenwood.com

Printed in the United States of America

The paper used in this book complies with the
Permanent Paper Standard issued by the National
Information Standards Organization (Z39.48–1984).

10 9 8 7 6 5 4 3 2 1

Contents

Illustrations

Series Foreword

"CULTURE" IS A problematic word. In everyday language we tend to use it in at least two senses. On the one hand, we speak of cultured people and places full of culture, uses that imply a knowledge or presence of certain forms of behavior or of artistic expression that are socially prestigious. In this sense large cities and prosperous people tend to be seen as the most cultured. On the other hand, there is an interpretation of "culture" that is broader and more anthropological; culture in this broader sense refers to whatever traditions, beliefs, customs, and creative activities characterize a given community—in short, it refers to what makes that community different from others. In this second sense, everyone has culture; indeed, it is impossible to be without culture.

The problems associated with the idea of culture have been exacerbated in recent years by two trends: less respectful use of language and a greater blurring of cultural differences. Nowadays, "culture" often means little more than behavior, attitude, or atmosphere. We hear about the culture of the boardroom, of the football team, of the marketplace; there are books with titles like *The Culture of War* by Richard Gabriel (Greenwood, 1990) or *The Culture of Narcissism* by Christopher Lasch (1979). In fact, as Christopher Clausen points out in a recent article published in the *American Scholar* (Summer 1996), we have gotten ourselves into trouble by using the term so sloppily.

People who study culture generally assume that culture (in the anthropological sense) is learned, not genetically determined. Another general assumption made in these days of multiculturalism has been that cultural differences should be respected rather than put under pressure to change.

But these assumptions, too, have sometimes proved to be problematic. For instance, multiculturalism is a fine ideal, but in practice it is not always easy to reconcile it with the beliefs of the very people who advocate it: for example, is female circumcision an issue of human rights or just a different cultural practice?

The blurring of cultural differences is a process that began with the steamship, increased with radio, and is now racing ahead with the Internet. We are becoming globally homogenized. Since the English-speaking world (and the United States in particular) is the dominant force behind this process of homogenization, it behooves us to make efforts to understand the sensibilities of members of other cultures.

This series of books, a contribution toward that greater understanding, deals with the neighbors of the United States, with people who have just as much right to call themselves Americans. What are the historical, institutional, religious, and artistic features that make up the modern culture of such peoples as the Haitians, the Chileans, the Jamaicans, and the Guatemalans? How are their habits and assumptions different from our own? What can we learn from them? As we familiarize ourselves with the ways of other countries, we come to see our own from a new perspective.

Each volume in the series focuses on a single country. With slight variations to accommodate national differences, each begins by outlining the historical, political, ethnic, geographical, and linguistic context, as well as the religious and social customs, and then proceeds to a discussion of a variety of artistic activities, including the press, the media, the cinema, music, literature, and the visual and performing arts. The authors are all intimately acquainted with the countries concerned: some were born or brought up in them, and each has a professional commitment to enhancing the understanding of the culture in question.

We are inclined to suppose that our ways of thinking and behaving are normal. And so they are . . . for us. We all need to realize that ours is only one culture among many, and that it is hard to establish by any rational criteria that ours as a whole is any better (or worse) than any other. As individual members of our immediate community, we know that we must learn to respect our differences from one another. Respect for differences between cultures is no less vital. This is particularly true of the United States, a nation of immigrants, but one that sometimes seems to be bent on destroying variety at home, and, worse still, on having others follow suit. By learning about other people's cultures, we come to understand and respect them; we earn their respect for us; and, not least, we see ourselves in a new light.

Peter Standish
East Carolina University

Preface

WHEN INVITED TO write this book, Jon Vincent launched enthusiastically into the task of accounting for the culture of Brazil, a country he loved and knew so well. Sadly, he had completed some two-thirds of the manuscript when he succumbed to cancer. This book appears under his name and in tribute to him. It has been supplemented with the helpful contributions of some of his fellow Brazilianists, and the good offices of his lifelong friend and colleague, George Woodyard, at the University of Kansas.

Introduction

God is a Brazilian.

—Popular saying

THIS BOOK IS a greatly expanded version of a lecture I developed over the years entitled "Everything You Always Wanted to Know About Br**il But Were Afraid to Ask." The lecture went through different incarnations to accommodate different audiences. Sometimes it was addressed to internationalists who were interested in different facets of the world but who probably knew very little about Brazil. At other times, it was aimed at undergraduates who were likely studying Spanish but who had not yet learned anything about Brazil. Once, I even had the honor of the presence of a number of senior staff officers from the Brazilian military.

Brazil is so vast and complex a country that it is difficult to determine what a good starting point would be in a general introduction. But perhaps that vastness and a series of other things of magnitude might serve as a logical place to begin, since bigness, and indeed extravagance, are in some ways so intimately connected with the national image, accurate or not, Brazilians have of themselves and of their country. Brazil is the fifth largest country in the world (about 3.29 million square miles in area), the largest country in Latin America, and the most populous Roman Catholic country in the world. It contains the world's most voluminous river (the Amazon), the world's largest oxygenating forest, the world's largest wetland (the *pantanal*), the world's largest fluvial island, a third of the world's iron ore reserves, and the world's largest soccer stadium (the Maracanã). It has the world's largest hydroelectric project currently in operation (Itaipu), the world's longest continuous box-and-plate girder bridge (the Rio-Niterói bridge), and the largest automobile industry in the Third World. Its Rede Globo is the largest private television network after the big three in the United States. It has 12 cities of over a million in population, one of them, São Paulo, the third largest city in the world. Finally, and not at all incidentally in a country in which soccer borders on religious belief, it has won the World Cup soccer championship five times (no other country has won more than three times).

Logic would demand that any country of such superlatives also house some major deficiencies, and such is indeed the case. Brazil has one of the largest debt burdens in the world, one of the worst income distributions in the world, and until 1996 had one of the most pernicious chronic inflation problems of any nation. It has very little petroleum and is plagued with homelessness, street crime, and uncontrolled pollution. It is a country that exports food but cannot adequately feed its own population, one of the reasons that Brazilians themselves refer to their country as "Belíndia," a nifty shorthand combining Belgium and India to characterize a country with a tiny population of very well-off residents and a gigantic mass of indigents.

It is a standard cliché that Latin America is a region of contrasts, and its largest country seems to amplify that rather banal observation to a level of abundance sufficient to make it a country of contradictions. Since it is such a big country and since it embodies so much paradox, the safest strategy to adopt would appear to be simply to exercise caution and not say anything rash. But I think that Brazil does have a character, and I think there are avenues of approach that allow for some understanding of this fascinating and contrary culture.

My approach in this book is to assume that most readers will know almost nothing about Brazil itself but will have at least a nodding acquaintance with Latin America, especially Mexico. Since Mexico is the only country in the region with which we share a border, it is the country Americans are likely to know most about and the country from which we derive most of our stereotypes of Latin Americans. I will on occasion refer to such stereotypes, if only to correct them, but I will also refer to Brazil in the context of Spanish America in general, since I am assuming it is likely that most readers will be at least somewhat familiar with such dramatic events as the conquest of the Aztec Empire in Mexico and the spread of the Spanish Empire in the Americas. I also make comparisons with our own history and geography.

Very few Americans can claim sufficient expertise on all aspects of Brazil to hold forth without occasionally overstating or understating a detail, but I have made every attempt to ascertain that the factual content of this book is as accurate as possible. I have been fortunate to have lived and worked in Brazil, and I am thus sufficiently conversant with the language and culture to be able to operate in it without appearing to be an alien. But it is difficult in many social situations not to let on that you are a foreigner, and thus much of the time I operated in Brazil between cultures, as a person who spoke the language but was still not a Brazilian. Another minor difficulty in dealing with anything as complicated as a national culture is the fact that it is practically impossible to discuss a single facet of the society without taking other matters into consideration. It is impossible to talk about race in Brazil without addressing class, and it is unjust to discuss the excellence of Brazilian cuisine without mentioning the problem of hunger.

One way to open a discussion of Brazil and the Brazilians is to start with the stereotypes held of Brazilians. Given the biases of stereotypes, this may not appear to be a very good idea, but the very fact that Latin Americans appear even to possess such a notion may tell us something about this unusual country, because such notions of national character are not at all universal. Ask most Latin Americans what they think of a Honduran or an Ecuadorian and you are not likely to get much of response. But aside from the Mexican and the Argentine, who both seem to own a national image, the one nationality you can almost count on eliciting fairly consistent canned response is Brazil. And what is that stereotype? Well, someone dark-skinned, perhaps a mulatto (a person of mixed black and white ancestry), who is happy-go-lucky, accomplished with members of the opposite sex, something of a free-spender, enjoys life, and is a good dancer. For the males of the species, add that they are incredibly good soccer players. If I were offered the opportunity to contribute my two cents to this image, I would add an element that is not included by most, a trait I find one of the most endearing and a nearly universal one in Brazilians I know—a roguish and at times self-effacing sense of humor.

There is a tinge of racism in this portrait, and also a subtle note of envy, but I think it does convey at least some of the ways Brazilians are perceived, and, like many stereotypes, there is at least a kernel of truth to it. Part of what I will be doing in the course of this book is to correct the parts of this that are misleading and to attempt to explain why others are so much a part of the image of Brazilians abroad. The scope of the inquiry will not be limited to assessing the accuracy of something as superficial as a stereotype, but I hope that through a discussion of where Brazilians live, where they have been, and what they do that some more profound sense of what Brazilians are like may emerge.

Almost anyone who has spent time in Brazil comes away with admiration and affection for the Brazilians. But to feel affection for the Brazilian people does not make it any easier to write about the country. Brazil is a country which defies neat definitions, because everything seems slightly out of focus. Brazilians can be racially at once black and white. They speak a European language that is so influenced by African, Indian, and other languages that it is no longer altogether intelligible to its European forbears. It is a Catholic country in which everybody seems to have a second religion, and it is a culture which has been illiterate for most of its existence, but which has produced some of the best poetry and prose in the hemisphere. Brazilians are sometimes almost stifled by tradition but persist in being free-wheeling—when the bureaucracy or the social structure have proved too rigid, Brazilians have created imaginative circumventions. There are no bullfights in Brazil, and it is a country that has bloodless revolutions. But this culture of outgoing and friendly people has just emerged from a cruel and brutal military dictatorship that lasted almost two generations. Brazilians are casual about government except to be generally against it, but Brazil was a country which survived the nineteenth century intact by having the only monarchy in the Western Hemisphere.

Everything in Brazilian culture seems to blend, to blur boundaries of definition that seem to work everywhere else. Many books written about Brazil echo this sense of imprecision, of ill-definition, including the classic *Neither Black nor White* (Carl Degler) and *Black into White* (Thomas Skidmore), which are about race. But recent books that deal with more than race also reflect the difficulty in making tidy judgments in a country of complexity and diversity. *The Brazilian Puzzle* (David Hess) and *The Brazilian Quandary* (Marcílio Moreira) suggest that a lot remains unsolved. *Brazilian Mosaic* (G. Harvey Summ) hints at the intricacy of problems, and *The Once and Future Country* (Marshall Eaken) implies that even time does not follow the rules in Brazil. Other books raise provocative questions about the country, such as *Why Is This Country Dancing?* (John Kirsch) and *O que faz o brasil, Brasil?* (What Makes Brazil Brazil?) (Roberto Da Matta). One of Brazil's most famous contemporary composers, Antônio Carlos Jobim, once remarked that "Brazil is not for beginners," (cited in Eaken, *Brazil*, p. x.) I hope I can prove him wrong.

Publisher's Note: It proved impossible to cover the subject of performing arts, per the series format, in a timely fashion.

Chronology

1808	First Brazilian press
1815	Brazil elevated to kingdom status
1822	Brazil gains independence
1824	Brazil's first constitution, under Pedro I
1835–1845	Revolts against Portuguese control
1840–1889	Reign of Pedro II
1865	Spiritualism arises
1888	Slavery officially abolished with Golden Law
1889–1930	First Republic
1898	Filmmaking introduced
1922	First radio broadcasting, founding of the Brazilian Communist Party, the Copacabana Revolt, Modern Art Week
1928	First magazine with national circulation launched
1930–1945	Vargas regime
1942	Brazilian ships torpedoed and Brazil declares war on the Axis powers
1945–1954	Second Republic
1950	Television introduced
1964–1985	Military government
1977	Divorce law enacted

1

Geography

Brazil is a continent.

—Popular saying

BRAZIL IS NOT truly a continent, but it is almost three times the size of India, which is commonly referred to as a "subcontinent." Brazil is also more than 10% larger than Australia, which *is* a continent. It is 92 times the size of the mother country, Portugal, and larger than the lower 48 United States. One of its larger 26 states, Bahia, is larger than France, and one of its smaller ones, São Paulo, is larger than Great Britain. Marajó Island, in the mouth of the Amazon River, is bigger than Switzerland.[1]

Aside from sheer size, Brazil is a country of remarkable geographic and climatic stability. Brazilians think Americans are weirdly preoccupied with the weather, because the weather there varies so little. Brazil has no typhoons, no hurricanes, no tornadoes, no earthquakes, no blizzards, no forest fires, no volcanoes. The only phenomena that qualify as natural disasters are the cyclical droughts in the Northeast (which promote further internal migration), the occasional Atlantic storm (which often produces mudslides in Rio—one in 1966 killed over 500 people), and periodic frosts in the South (which tend to elevate the price of coffee for us). The only time Brazilians seem to really take notice of the weather is when one of them, who has spent his entire life in the tropics, enrolls in the "spring" semester and comes from balmy Rio to the frigid Midwest of the United States in the middle of January.

In order for a North American to have some idea of the remarkable differences between this continent and Brazil, it can be instructive to think upside-down. The Equator cuts across northern Brazil at about the latitude of the Amazon River, but that does not really provide a sense of the tropical nature of the country. The old city of Salvador on the northeast coast is at about the same latitude south as Managua, Nicaragua is north. Belo Horizonte, in the center of the Southeast, is at almost the same latitude as Miami, our southernmost metropolis, and Porto Alegre about that of New Orleans. A close equivalent to New York City in South America would be Bahía Blanca, Argentina, which is almost 1,000 miles south of the Brazilian border. If Minneapolis were in South America it would be located in the middle of Patagonia, and Los Angeles would be even further south than Santiago in central Chile.

But there is a hidden agenda to the geography of Brazil, something that might be called a geography of the mind. Since it is such a large country, Brazilians view themselves and others as identifiable by region of origin. Regionalism has always been an important factor in Brazilian history, and even today certain assumptions are almost automatically made by one Brazilian about another because of where he or she is from. It is not altogether different from our tacit assumptions about Texans or New Yorkers, but is far more pervasive. In Brazil almost every region has its own stereotype, and some are so narrow as to allude to specific towns or cities. The Brazilian term for this is *bairrismo*, literally excessive fondness for one's own *bairro*, or neighborhood, but it is used by extension to mean an exaggerated loyalty to a city, state, or region. *Cariocas*, the natives of Rio, for example, are thought to be carefree to the point of indolence, at least by residents of São Paulo, the *paulistas*, themselves considered by *cariocas* to be industrious to the point of boredom. *Mineiros*, those from Minas Gerais, are considered suspicious and wily, while *baianos*, residents of Bahia, are thought to be stupid, at least in the South. It is probably useful to keep this specificity of geographic origin in mind even though the real differences from region to region are not all that remarkable.

But differences do exist from region to region. Brazilian geographers have traditionally divided the country into five areas, or "macroregions," in part because the country is so big that it is impossible to make any useful generalities about topography or climate. One of the few sweeping generalities that can be made is that it is largely a tropical country, with only the two southernmost states classed as subtropical. But there is considerable variation in the tropics, and it is therefore instructive to discuss the geography of Brazil in terms of these large areas.

THE NORTH

The largest and least populated of the Brazilian regions is composed of the states of Acre, Amazonas, Rondônia, Pará, Roraima, Amapá, and Tocantins. To give some idea of its size, it is almost ten times the size of California or over six times the size of Texas. Amazonas and Pará have been states since the nineteenth century and Acre since 1962. Rondônia, Roraima, and Amapá are former territories which became states in the 1980s and 1990s, and Tocantins was separated from the state of Goiás in 1988. This region covers over 45% of the area of Brazil and contains less than 7% of its population.

One glance at a map of Brazil will suggest even to the untrained eye that two major river systems, the Amazon in the North and the Paraná in the South, are dominant features of the Brazilian landscape. The Amazon itself is a study in superlatives. Although the Nile is slightly longer (4,145 miles versus 4,007 for the Amazon), it is not much more than a trickle by comparison. The average discharge at the mouth of the Nile is about 34,000 cubic feet per second (cfs), that of the Amazon a whopping 7,100,000, or more than 200 *times* that of the Nile. Even compared to our "mighty" Mississippi, the outflow of the Amazon carries a volume of water over 10 times that of North America's largest river. It is also something of an anomaly in relation to the terrain it traverses—the Nile rises at about 7,000 feet, the Mississippi at a puny 1,467, the Amazon rises in the Andes at an altitude of over 18,000 feet—but in its final 1,900 miles to the sea it drops an altitude of only about 270 feet.[2] Since it carries so much volume, it would be logical to speculate that it is both wide and deep, but both vary a great deal. Its depth varies from 60 to 460 feet and its width from several miles to a mere mile at the strait of Óbidos, about 350 miles from the mouth. To put that into perspective, consider that a contractor estimates each story of a building to be 10 feet, so at its shallowest the Amazon would cover a six-story building, and in an average place you could cruise a battleship over a sunken building of 30 stories and not touch it. Six of its tributaries are over 1,200 miles long and three are over 1,800 miles long, not too short of the length of the Mississippi. Two of those tributaries, the Negro and the Madeira-Mamoré-Grande, in fact, are among the ten largest rivers in the world. One of the reasons the Amazon has such a large volume of water is its unique position. The main stem of the river runs within 4° of the Equator, and thus, unlike most rivers, it has not one but two flood seasons annually—one from October to January, fed by its southern tributaries and one from March to July, fed by the tributaries which rise in the Northern Hemisphere.

Until large-scale burning of the forest began in recent years, almost the entire area was covered with tropical forest vegetation, interspersed with occasional small sections of wetland and a few areas of scrub vegetation called *campos*. The climate is hot, but probably not as hot as people are likely to think—annual mean temperatures of 77° are high, but they rarely exceed 81°—which means that it is always hot but never reaches the 100° range as it does in the United States in the summer. The area's reputation for stifling heat is probably due to the minuscule variation from the hottest to the coldest months. A typical example is the city of Belém do Pará, located at the mouth of the Amazon, where the mean temperature in the hottest month, November, is 79°, while in the coldest, February, the mean temperature is 76°. Rainfall is abundant, with an annual mean of about 60 inches, with precipitation of almost 100 inches a year near the mouth and in western Brazil. The only American cities which have precipitation surpassing 60 inches a year are southern cities such as Miami, Florida, and Charleston, South Carolina, but none has more than 80 inches a year. Although the population of the area has mushroomed with the discovery of gold deposits and the relocation of population from other parts of Brazil under government settlement programs, it still has a population density far sparser than in the South. At the turn of the century the entire region had only about 700,000 inhabitants, a number which grew to an impressive 10 million by about 1990; this sounds like a lot but it still gives a population density of less than 1.5 inhabitants per square mile. The fact that those former territories are now states is one indication of rapid population growth, but even that is relative, since some other areas of Brazil have also had extremely rapid population growth.

THE NORTHEAST

The Northeast comprises nine states—Maranhão, Piauí, Ceará, Rio Grande do Norte, Paraíba, Pernambuco, Alagoas, Sergipe, and Bahia, with a total area about four times the size of California or two and a half times the size of Texas. This region is a good example of how difficult it is to make generalities about climate in a large country, because it contains four distinct and quite different microregions. The first is a fairly narrow coastal strip on the Atlantic coast which runs the entire length of the area. This is another clearly tropical zone which was once forested like the Amazon but which has been slowly deforested since the colonial period, mostly for the planting of sugar cane, and, in the southern part of the state of Bahia, cacao. The soil is productive and the rainfall averages between 60 and 80 inches a year. The second zone, called the *agreste*, is another narrow band, this one a transition zone between the humid coast and the arid interior. This area is utilized

Oxen (*boi*), often used for riding on muddy terrain in the rural northeast. (Author photo)

largely for small to medium agricultural plots, mostly for the cultivation of beans, corn, and cotton. Rainfall in this region gradually decreases from east to west until reaching the third region, the arid *sertão*, a broader band of terrain which includes much of Piauí, most of Ceará, most of the interior of Bahia, and the western parts of the other states. This is the so-called "polygon of drought," where the annual rainfall rarely exceeds 20 inches and in parts of which it may not rain at all for extended periods. The term *sertão* in Portuguese is actually a kind of generic term for any remote or forbidding place, much as we might use the terms "backlands" or "boondocks," but in this context it refers to a sizable and inhospitable tract of land in which the vegetation is either scrub thorn (the so-called *caatinga*) or little more than low scrub and cactus. Surprisingly enough, this area is utilized mostly for raising cattle, although not the sleek Herefords and Angus we think of as beef cattle, but a cross-bred animal derived from the zebu of India which is more heat and drought-resistant than other breeds. The cowboys of this region do not look much like the romantic image we have, since the spiny vegetation requires head-to-toe protective covering, which is made of leather. Even the horses are protected by a leather covering. The final microregion of this area is called the Mid-North, which occupies the state of Maranhão and the Parnaíba Valley in Piauí. A transition zone to the Amazon, it is

Mercado Modelo, the former city market in Salvador, Bahia. (Author photo)

notable for the abundance of babassu and carnauba palms, both of which are exploited for construction materials, oil (babassu), and wax (carnauba). The main economic activity in this area is traditional agriculture, including cotton, sugar cane, and rice.

The Northeast amounts to about 18% of the area of Brazil and holds a little over 28% of its population. It was the first area exploited by the Portuguese in the colonial period, and thus the techniques used in agriculture and the social structure are traditional almost to the point of atavism.

THE CENTER-WEST

This region includes the states of Goiás, Mato Grosso, Mato Grosso do Sul, and the Federal District, Brasília. It covers an area just slightly larger than the Northeast. Since it is located centrally, it is defined by the two major river systems which drain it, the Amazon in the North and the Paraná in the South. The Paraná is part of the Plate drainage, itself the world's sixth largest river. This region is dominated by the central plateau, which ranges in altitude from about 650 feet to around 3,000 feet. The northern portion is part of the Amazon Basin and has a climate corresponding to that region, and the southwest contains the *pantanal*, a gigantic wetland which is inundated during the wet season but which is nevertheless extensively utilized, mainly as pastureland. This area is part of the Paraguay River drainage. The southeastern sector contains the major tributaries of the Paraná River.

The Center-West amounts to about 19% of the area of Brazil and has less than 7% of its population. The entire region has a tropical, semi-humid climate with mean temperatures from 70° to 79° Fahrenheit and rainfall from 40 to 120 inches a year. The Mato Grosso plateau in the North has the highest mean temperatures and highest rainfall, which makes it not much more than an extension of the Amazon region. The Goiás Plateau and the Pantanal itself have slightly less rain and slightly lower mean temperatures. Only a small slice of the northern edge of the region is forested, the dominant vegetation being grassland punctuated by *capões*, which are occasional stands of trees. This is obviously a prime setting for cattle grazing, which is the major economic activity.

THE SOUTHEAST

This is the smallest microregion in the country, but it is also the most populous. It is a little over 10% of the area of the country, but it contains almost 44% of Brazil's population, including the three largest cities. It is also the industrial hub of Brazil, accounting for almost 80% of its wealth.

The Southeast includes the states of Espírito Santo, Rio de Janeiro, Minas Gerais, and São Paulo. Only the interior of Espírito Santo and the northern part of Minas Gerais remain in a state of underdevelopment comparable to other parts of the country. The northern boundary of this region coincides almost precisely with a normal temperature line of 75° and the southern with a line corresponding to 65°. Except for a narrow coastal band running south and west of Rio de Janeiro, where annual rainfall is 80 to 100 inches a year, rainfall in this region averages from 40 to 60 inches a year. The vegetation in the northern part is mostly grassland in the northern half and a mixture of hardwood forest and mixed pine forest in the south. Outside the cities, almost all these types of vegetation are being transformed into agricultural use, which has immediate ecological implications. In the more mountainous areas of Minas Gerais and the state of Rio de Janeiro there are numerous small cities which have become famous as summer retreats for coastal residents. The most famous one is Petrópolis, in the state of Rio, where the Emperor Pedro II (1840–1889) had a summer palace.

THE SOUTH

The South consists of only three states—Paraná, Santa Catarina, and Rio Grande do Sul, which amounts to only about 7% of the surface area of the country. It has about 15% of the population of Brazil. If any region in Brazil can claim to be different from the others, it is this one. Only in northern and coastal Paraná does the tropical climate typical of the rest of Brazil obtain. Over most of the region annual temperatures are in the 60° to 65° range, and in the southern part of this region the daily average may be only 50° in the coldest month (July). Rainfall is regular and abundant, with about 50 inches a year on average. Snow may occur on occasion in the higher elevations. The northern half of the region is dominated by pine forest and the southern half by *campinas*, better know to us as the pampas, a relatively treeless plain which is ideal for pasture. This is the only part of Brazil in which the more delicate breeds of cattle such as Hereford and Black Angus are raised. Because the soil is fertile, much of the pine and tropical forest has been cleared for agricultural use. Again, some crops are temperate rather than tropical (wheat and soybeans), though the climate is mild enough to permit the cultivation of other crops common in Brazil (such as sugar cane, beans, and rice). This is also the only area in Brazil with a climate appropriate for the growing of grapes, and Brazil has recently become an exporter of excellent wines.

WHERE BRAZILIANS LIVE

One of Brazil's first historians, Vicente do Salvador, criticized Brazilians for living "like crabs, stuck on the beaches."[3] Until very recently, this observation has proved to be a remarkably durable one. There are now 12 metropolitan areas of over a million in population. In the United States there are only eight. In the 1960s in Brazil there were only two—São Paulo and Rio de Janeiro, and even in the 1970s there were only six—the previous two plus Recife, Salvador, Belo Horizonte, and Porto Alegre. What is notable about that is the fact that all the major cities in the country, until very recently, were located either on the coast itself or within about 200 miles of it.

The process of urbanization has been extraordinarily rapid in Brazil. The first towns did not arise until the gold rush in the eighteenth century, and real urbanization did not begin until almost the end of the nineteenth. Prior to that period the number of Brazilians living in cities barely reached 10%. It is in this century that real urbanization has taken place. The number of Brazilians living in urban areas reached about 30% in 1940, 45% in 1960, and about 75% in 1990. In the 2000 census it was a bit over 80%. In most developed countries urbanization has been gradual and has proceeded along with industrialization as new jobs were created. As in most Third World countries, urbanization in Brazil took place independently from industrialization. As a result, urbanization in Brazil is deceptive, because large segments of the new urban population may actually be marginalized from the money economy and may lead lives which are not in a meaningful way different from what they experienced in a rural setting. Much of the population growth of all these large cities is a result of internal migration, in which great numbers of people despair of the dead-end existence of trying to eke out a living in an economically backward and physically trying rural working situation. They move physically to an urban area, but many are unable to find decent work, and much of this recent migrant population is unemployed or underemployed. All these cities have large *favelas*, as slums are usually called in Brazil.

But because such a large percentage of Brazilians now lives in cities, a brief survey of the major ones can provide insight into the recent movement of people and their economic activity. In the North, the two largest cities are Manaus and Belém. Manaus is the capital of the enormous state of Amazonas.

Aerial view of São Paulo's major *favela* (slum) of Heliópolis. (AP Photo/Dado Galdieri)

It was for hundreds of years not much more than a village, populated largely by Indians and *caboclos* (of mixed Indian and white blood). Not until the rubber boom in the last years of the nineteenth century did it experience a real spurt of growth. It was during this period that running water, paved streets, and the famous Manaus Opera House were brought to the city. But it was not until the Brazilian government established a Free Trade Zone in Manaus in 1967 that new industries, including electronics and small machines, came to the area. Those industries, along with the thriving fluvial port activities for the export of Amazonian products and the recent construction of railroads linking Manaus with the South, have all contributed to rapid population growth. Belém, capital of the state of Pará, was established in 1616 as a fortress to protect the Portuguese colony from French, English, and Dutch pirates. As the major city at the mouth of the Amazon it also benefited from the rubber boom, and like Manaus it has very recently enjoyed the advantage of new rail and highway construction. Today it is the principal port for the transshipment and export of such products as rubber, Brazil nuts, leather, foodstuffs, and aluminum.

The Northeast has three cities of over a million population—Fortaleza, Recife, and Salvador. Fortaleza was founded as a fortress to counter the French presence in the Northeast. The fort was destroyed by Indians and

Long, narrow fishing boats (*saveiros*), used for transporting foodstuffs. (Author photo)

rebuilt by the Dutch during their incursion. It began to grow rapidly when abundant electric power from the Paulo Afonso hydroelectic plant on the São Francisco River became available. Today it is a major port city for the export of sugar, carnauba, and textiles, including the beautiful hammocks for which Ceará is noted. Part of its rapid growth can be attributed to waves of migration from the interior, which in turn creates unemployment problems. Recife began as a humble fishing village. When the Dutch took nearby Olinda, Recife was part of the mini-renaissance that took place, housing the zoo and botanical gardens the Dutch built, as well at the first European observatory in the Americas. Recife has grown very rapidly since the 1960s with the growth of metallurgy, textiles, and chemicals. Like Fortaleza, it is a port city and a haven for migrants. Salvador was Brazil's first royal city. Founded in 1549, it was for most of the colonial period the principal port of entry for the millions of slaves brought from Africa, and it is still Brazil's most African city. Salvador ranks as the fifth fastest-growing of the world's cities in a study that projects population growth. An excellent natural port, it is an exporter of sugar, textiles, tobacco, leather goods, vegetable oils, and cacao. It is also the site of one of the first oil refineries in Brazil and has a major industrial center, Aratu, on its outskirts. Like Fortaleza and Recife, it is also an increasingly popular destination for tourists. Its beautiful colonial buildings and white beaches stand in contrast to the Alagados, the largest stilt slum in the country.

The two largest cities in the Center-West are Brasília and Goiânia. Although the idea for a new capital had existed since at least 1789, Brasília was built only recently, during the administration of Juscelino Kubitschek. The jury for the selection of a city planner was headed by Oscar Niemeyer, the principal architect of Brasília's famous buildings. The planner selected was Lúcio Costa, who designed a city to accommodate a population of 700,000 (it currently has almost two million). Brasília was built by a work force of 30,000 men, who in the late 1950s toiled for 41 months to complete the major buildings of the new capital.

One item not included in the plan was where all those workers would live while construction went on. An instant *favela*, called the Cidade Livre and looking much like a frontier town from a Western movie, sprang up on the outskirts of the city proper. Since its inauguration in 1960, Brasília has been the seat of the government and a constant magnet for migrant populations. Located on a plateau 3,000 feet above sea level, it is eerily beautiful but very un-Brazilian in both appearance and "feel." Goiânia is another planned city. Completed in 1942, it, like Brasília, has far exceeded its projected population. A commercial hub for agricultural products such as rice, cotton, and vegetable oils, it also has thriving industries including ceramics and furniture. Its rapid growth in recent years can be attributed at least in part to its proximity to Brasília.

The Southeast contains the three biggest cities in Brazil—São Paulo, Rio de Janeiro, and Belo Horizonte. Founded by Jesuits in 1554, São Paulo was not much more than a village until the nineteenth century, when the cultivation of coffee and the onset of industrialization began. It experienced another population boom after World War I, and since 1950 has been the premier destination for immigrant populations. Today the third largest city in the world (after Tokyo and Mexico City) and projected to be the tenth fastest-growing, it contains the largest and most varied industrial park in Latin America, with refineries, petrochemical and electronics industries, and a thriving automobile industry. The economy of the state of São Paulo, in fact, is larger than that of any *country* in Latin America except Brazil's. The city is also a major financial and cultural center, with some of the largest and best-known museums and universities and a vibrant theater. Because of its rapid growth and sprawling industrial park, it also suffers from underemployment and severe air and water pollution, and it has slums commensurate with its bigness in other areas.

Rio de Janeiro. (© Richard T. Nowitz/
CORBIS)

What is today Rio de Janeiro was actually settled first by the French, who
constructed a fort there in 1555. In 1560 a Portuguese expedition routed
the French and destroyed the fort, and in 1565 a more or less permanent
Portuguese colony was established. Although a major sugar port in the sixteenth century, Rio grew slowly until the gold rush at the end of the seventeenth century, and in the eighteenth century the shift of the economic
axis of Brazil made Rio a natural site for its second capital. It was capital of
Brazil from 1763 to 1960. When the Portuguese court moved to Rio in 1808
the city underwent one of its many transformations. At independence in
1822 it had a population of about 100,000 and by 1920 its population
reached a million. Shortly after the proclamation of the republic the "Old
Tunnel" through one of Rio's many mountains was completed, making the
now-famous "southern zone" boroughs of Ipanema and Copacabana accessible. A major sanitation project completed in 1906 finally made Rio a livable
city for the first time. Known as one of the most beautiful cities in the world,
Rio is, like São Paulo, a major cultural and publishing center. Unlike São

Paulo, its slums are located not on the outskirts of town but on the mountains that push up all over the city, which makes them uncomfortably visible.

Like Brasília and Goiânia, Belo Horizonte is another of Brazil's planned cities. It was designed as the new capital of the state of Minas Gerais and completed in 1897. It functioned almost exclusively as a political and administrative center until 1930, when the government of Getúlio Vargas launched Brazil's industrial revolution. Today Minas Gerais is home to four of the most important steel mills in Brazil, and Belo Horizonte itself has major metallurgical, electrical, and textile plants. As industrialization progressed, the government financed the construction of new highways linking Belo Horizonte with the other major cities of the Brazilian South. Today Belo Horizonte has far exceeded the dimensions of its original plan and is not only an industrial hub but also one of the major sites for national and international banking in Brazil.

The South has two fairly recent entries to the million-plus list, Porto Alegre and Curitiba. Porto Alegre was one of the few cities in Brazil colonized by couples. In 1752, 60 couples from the Atlantic islands of the Azores settled in what is now the capital of Rio Grande do Sul. Principally a commercial center, it began rapid growth in the nineteenth century with the arrival of large numbers of immigrants, notably from Germany, and with the Germans came a new industry, beer production. Consistent with the country's fondness for the gigantic, it is today the home of two of the ten largest breweries in the world. In the early part of the twentieth century Porto Alegre became the southern terminus for new roads and highways and in 1920 authorities finally authorized a major dredging operation in the port to compensate for the loss of shipping to ports such as Montevideo, which could accommodate large vessels. After World War II major industrial growth took place in the region, including petroleum refining. Porto Alegre is another port city, exporting such items as metal goods, leather, and textiles.

The area around Curitiba, capital of the state of Paraná, was settled by gold prospectors in the seventeenth century. When news of the discoveries of gold and diamonds in Minas Gerais reached the area, many of its inhabitants left, and the area remained a remote outpost on the mule and cattle trails that went from Rio Grande do Sul to Minas Gerais. In 1820 there were only 200 houses in Curitiba. In the nineteenth century large numbers of immigrants, mostly from Italy and Poland, began to arrive, and soon Curitiba was the center of a large agricultural region. With the growth of the coffee industry Curitiba prospered, and in the twentieth century industrialization added to that growth. Industries in Curitiba include metallurgy, chemicals,

Big house (*casa grande*) on a dendê palm fazenda near Nazaré, Bahia. (Author photo)

and furniture. One of the most prosperous cities in Brazil, it is also known as a pioneer in urban renewal, with innovative transport systems, recycling plans, and urban renewal projects.

It is probably unwise to draw too many conclusions about Brazilian perceptions based on the grandeur of the country and of the grand endeavors of its people, but it would not be excessive to assume that they naturally regard Brazil as an extraordinary place, which would imply that other countries are somewhat less so. In a country with so many monumental things, both natural and man-made, any comparisons with its immediate neighbors make the neighbors look pretty puny. Indeed, several of Brazil's neighbors are very small countries and even some of the larger ones are quite poor, which tends to magnify the differences. The lone exception is Argentina, which for a time looked as if it was destined to be the regional power in South America. Brazilians probably don't spend much time thinking about the rest of the continent, probably in part because those other countries seem so insignificant. In a less generous people this kind of attitude could easily turn into arrogance, but in the Brazilian case it is likely not much more than a cavalier attitude, itself softened by the Brazilian tendency not to take anything all that seriously.

NOTES

1. In part because of its huge size, Brazil ranks very high in a number of categories. But it is also a country of notable characteristics for other reasons. An interesting and provocative book compiled by Russell Ash, *The Top 10 of Everything 2002* (New York: DK Publishing, 2001) has Brazil popping up in a number of categories, both expected and unexpected. Among them: Brazil ranks fifth among the largest countries in the world, and third as a country with the most neighbors. It is second among countries with the largest area of forest and first among those most rapidly deforesting; it is eighth among countries with the largest protected areas. It comes in third among countries both with the longest road networks and with the longest inland waterways; it is ninth in the number of daily newspapers. Brazil was fifth among countries to make seat belts compulsory, but it ranks eighth among countries with the highest number of road deaths. It was the fifth country in the world to have television and ranks fifth in the world in the number of VCRs its citizens own. It is fourth among beer-producing countries, sixth in iron production, tenth in salt production, second in sugar production, and sixth among sugar consumers. Brazil ranks sixth among countries with the most workers, fourth in terms of consuming alternative power, and ninth among electric consuming countries. Of the countries with the top 10 Internet users, Brazil ranks ninth. The statue of Christ overlooking the city of Rio is the seventh tallest free-standing statue in the world. A circus fire in Niterói in 1961 is listed as tenth among the worst fires at theater and entertainment venues, and a fire in the Joelson bank and office complex in São Paulo in 1974 is rated as the seventh worst commercial or industrial disaster in the world. Brazil ranks tenth in the number of dollar billionaires, and finally, it is ranked as number one of the countries most in debt.

2. Jere Van Dyk, "Amazon, South America's River Road," *National Geographic* 187, no. 2 (February 1995): 3–39 (chart is on p. 13).

3. Frei Vicente do Salvador, *Historia do Brasil, 1500–1627*, nova edição revista por Capistrano de Abreu (São Paulo and Rio: Editores Weiszflog Irmãos, 1918), p. 19.

2

Race, Ethnicity, and Class

Brazil is hell for negroes, purgatory for whites, and paradise for mulattos.
—André João Antonil, *Cultura e Opulência do Brasil*, p. 160

THE ETHNICITY OF RACE

THE CONVENTIONAL WAY of viewing the question of race and ethnicity in
Brazil is to see the country as some sort of fusion of three ethnic groups—
white, black, and American Indian. That is in a very general sense the case,
but the notion is complicated by the great variety of ethnicities that exist in
each of these three groups. The Portuguese themselves were certainly not
purely white in the way that term is construed in a racist society such as ours.

The original inhabitants of the Iberian Peninsula were called Celtiberians,
a group of unknown ethnicity. Phoenicians began to visit what is today
Portugal as early as 1100 B.C., the Greeks around 900 B.C., and the Car-
thaginians about 535 B.C. In about 200 B.C., Rome began a slow conquest
of the peninsula, eventually naming present-day Portugal the province of
Lusitania (whence the prefix "Luso-" for "Portuguese"). In 400 A.D. the
country was invaded by Visigoths, a Germanic people who remained there
until 711 A.D., when the peninsula was again invaded, this time by Moors
from northern Africa. In Spain the expulsion of the Moors (called the "reconquest") was not completed until 1492, the year Columbus made his first
voyage. Although Portugal's reconquest was much earlier (1249), it is clear
that various ethnic groups, including those mentioned as well as Berbers,

Jews, and Romanies (Gypsies), had contributed to the gene pool in Portugal. In addition, by the year Brazil was "discovered" by Europeans in 1500, it is estimated that nearly 10% of the population of Lisbon was composed of African slaves from Portugal's various outposts on that continent.

The Africans brought to Brazil as slaves were as ethnically varied as the Portuguese themselves and spoke a variety of languages. The indigenous populations of Brazil, Amerindians, also were genetically diverse, so to view the present population as simply an amalgam of three identifiable racial or ethnic groupings is a great oversimplification.

The three basic ethnic groups were also unequal in terms of relative numbers. There were perhaps a million Amerindians in Brazil, but that number was drastically reduced first by warfare with Europeans and more importantly by European diseases, against which Indians had never developed an immunity. Others have gradually melted into the population biologically, so that today perhaps one-fifth of the original number is ethnically identifiable as Indian. The four million or so African slaves brought to Brazil also contributed to this blending, and almost that many European immigrants in the nineteenth century added yet another important element to the ethnic palette.

The conquest of Brazil was undertaken by adventurers and *degredados* (persons who had been expelled to the colonies from Portugal for a crime). Unlike the Spanish, who found high civilizations of great population, the Portuguese encountered fairly sparse populations of Amerindians. Unlike the English, the Portuguese did not colonize in family groups, so a Portuguese-Indian hybrid was characteristic of the early colonial population. The Portuguese also brought African slaves to the Americas in astonishing numbers. Of the roughly six million Africans who survived the Atlantic crossing, almost two-thirds went to Brazil. Only about a half million were brought to the present United States.

With the arrival of Africans slaves, all three groups blended, and by the end of the colonial period it would have been difficult to identify a single individual in Brazil who was genetically purely European.

Some ethnic populations virtually vanished by admixture. In the 1776 census about one-third of the population of Brazil's southernmost state, Rio Grande do Sul, was estimated at almost one-third Negro and that of Minas Gerais in central Brazil as half Negro (Mörner 1967, 72). European immigration would have contributed to some reduction in the percentage of black population, but today the black population of Rio Grande do Sul is minuscule and that of Minas about 10%, meaning that a large part of the reduction of the black population in both states must have been through a purely biological process.

IMMIGRATION

Beginning early in the nineteenth century the British exercised their considerable political (and naval) influence on Brazil to end the slave trade, and when slavery in any case became less and less economically viable, the Brazilian government embarked on a program to encourage immigration. Although Brazil was considered a less than ideal destination because of the notion that the tropics were an enervating environment, immigrants did arrive in large numbers, because Brazil was still considered a place of some opportunity. Although the government never publicly admitted it, preference was given to European immigrants in an attempt to whiten the population, in keeping with the racist theories in vogue at the time.

Since the waves of European immigrants began coming in the early nineteenth century, the population of Brazil has become markedly whiter than it was in the colonial period. Immigrants came in largest numbers from Portugal, Germany, and Italy. The preponderance of these new Brazilians went to São Paulo, with somewhat lesser numbers going to Paraná, Santa Catarina, and Rio Grande do Sul. Some smaller groups went to Espírito Santo and even Amazonas. Among the other countries contributing new Brazilians were Switzerland, Spain, and Poland. There are also numerous descendants of Syrians and Lebanese today, and beginning in 1908 a large Japanese population, the largest in the world outside Japan, has settled in the city of São Paulo and the surrounding municipalities and in the Amazon, where they were one of the few successful immigrant communities in the area. Although less numerous, Brazil has also received Czech, Polish, Russian, and Ukrainian immigrants. In 1934 the Vargas government imposed a quota system on immigration, but Brazil has still received recent immigrants from Korea and even from neighboring South American countries. In the 1980s, for the first time, Brazilians began to emigrate to the United States, Europe, and Japan because of the difficult economic and political situation.

All these ethnic groups assimilated into Brazilian culture, some more quickly than others, and all have intermarried to some degree with the already mixed Brazilian gene pool. When Brazil joined France and Britain against Germany in World War I, there was considerable internal tension, because there were completely unassimilated populations of monolingual Germans in the South. Brazil confronted the problem by requiring that Portuguese be the language of instruction in all public educational institutions (German and other languages could still be studied as foreign languages), which considerably attenuated the "German problem" when Brazil again sided with the Allies in World War II. Brazil faced a similar problem with the unassimilated Japanese population when World War II broke out, but even the Japanese population became gradually Brazilianized, at least after the second generation, and ethnically Japanese Brazilians began to intermarry as well. When some Japanese Brazilians returned to Japan in the 1980s, they encountered varying degrees of rejection and culture shock, since even those who spoke Japanese still *acted* like Brazilians, which made them conspicuous and even offensive in such a circumspect culture.

Discrimination without Segregation

Brazilian society is far from achieving the ideal of a "racial democracy," the term itself ringing somewhat false in a society so pervaded by inequalities, and it is also short of the truth to attribute what visible prejudice there is to class alone. But it is at least a society in which physical attributes alone are only one factor in determining exactly where an individual fits into a hierarchy of values. It is also a culture which takes a certain pride (sometimes hypocritically so) in being a place where various ethnic groups have commingled to an extraordinary degree. If this falls a bit short of the rather more exalted ideal of the national mythology, it stands in sharp contrast to the institutionalized racism of the United States or South Africa or the equally violent and degrading ethnic conflicts in the Middle East and Eastern Europe.

Historically, the racial and ethnic composition has always been characterized by admixture, first of the Portuguese and Indians, later with Portuguese, Africans, and Indians mixing to such an extent that it became almost impossible to identify a person by race alone. But the rapid decline in the Indian population and the relatively few Portuguese immigrants means that the continued importation of African slaves made the population largely black and mulatto for almost two centuries—in 1818 the population of Brazil was 60% black. The waves of immigrants which came in the nineteenth and early twentieth centuries were composed largely of Europeans, but many also came from the Middle East and the Orient. The great influx of immigrants has ended, and the ethnic makeup of the population has been relatively stable for the last three censuses. The census figures give some indication of the present composition of Brazilian society but are no means absolute. When the census is taken individuals are asked to what ethnic group they belong. If an individual does not like the ethnic group to which he thinks he belongs he is free to identify himself as belonging to another, and many probably do not really know to which group they belong. The other problem is that the census allows only five categories, which has a rigidity many Brazilians resent. Given those limitations, the 2000 census results indicate roughly the following breakdown:

white	54.0%
pardo (brown)	38.5%
black	6.0%
yellow	0.5%
indigenous and undeclared	1.0%

Although there is considerable historical similarity between Brazil and the United States with regard to race—relatively low indigenous population, importation of African slaves, large-scale European immigration—there is a marked contrast between them today. One revealing contrast is in the terminology used to designate racial admixture between black and white. In English, such terms as mulatto, quadroon, octoroon, and high yellow have become archaic, since in past century the United States adopted a strictly binary system in which individuals are thought of as either black or white. In Brazil, however, a gamut of literally hundreds of terms ranging from *branco fino* ("fine white") to *negro retinto* ("very dark black") is used. Intermediate terms include *branco da Bahia* or *branco da terra, moreno, sarará, mulato claro, pardo, mulato escuro, escuro, cabo verde, cabra,* and *preto* or *crioulo,* roughly on a white to black continuum. There are also terms for white/Indian mixtures (*mameluco*) and black/Indian (*cafuso*).[1] Some anthropologists have theorized that this proliferation of terminology is as much a function of social class as of racial discrimination, but there is evidence to support the assertion that discrimination, while veiled, in fact exists in Brazil.

One reason that it is difficult to prove that racism exists is that Brazil has never had the kind of institutionalized racism that existed in the United States—Brazil has never had separate facilities for different races, and there has never been a race riot in Brazil. A law passed in 1951 and a clause of the 1988 Constitution specifically prohibit racial discrimination. But the virtual nonexistence of blacks in the general ranks of the military, the diplomatic corps, and the Naval Academy, and their majority status in such occupations as laundress, porter, and dock worker is a clear indication that barriers to upward mobility, however invisible, exist on the basis of race. Whites outnumber nonwhites in the professions by a ratio of three to one, while half the population working in agriculture and domestic service is nonwhite. And though public education is provided in Brazil through the eighth grade, the average number of years of school for whites at age 25 is 2.3 years more than for blacks of the same age, a huge difference in a country in which the general average is six years of study.[2] Blacks, mixed-bloods, and, recently, Indians have, however, been elected to congress or otherwise made a mark in Brazilian society, particularly in the arts. Some notable examples are the mulattoes Machado de Assis, probably the best novelist in the Americas in the nineteenth century; Lima Barreto, also a canonical writer; the black Symbolist poet Cruz e Souza, and the mulatto sculptor Aleijadinho.

The lack of institutionalized discrimination gives Brazilians a sense of comfort or even superiority as regards race. An important element of the national mythology is the notion of a "racial democracy," an idea so pervasive that the average Brazilian never questions it. "Racial democracy" is a concept based on the myth that slavery in Portuguese America was somehow milder and more humane than that in the Spanish colonies, an idea clearly refuted by the existence of colonies of runaway slaves (*quilombos*) in the colonial period, slave rebellions in the nineteenth century, and various forms of racial protest in the twentieth, especially in the 1920s and 1930s. A corollary is the concept of "whitening" or "bleaching," which is based on the hypothesis that the Brazilian population will gradually blend itself into racial homogeneity, itself undoubtedly a construct of the ruling white elites. That race remains an important issue in Brazil is further upheld by the existence of a magazine called *Raça Brasil* ("Race (in) Brazil," subtitled "the magazine of Brazilian blacks"), which began publication in the late 1980s.

Racism is further evident in the ideal of feminine beauty shared by Brazilians. For many years the Brazilian "Misses" who were candidates for "Miss World" or "Miss Universe" were uniformly blonde and often blue-eyed, racial characteristics not easily encountered except in the three southernmost states. Another good example is Xuxa (SHOO-sha), the blonde marketing phenomenon of Brazilian television, a kind of grotesque combination of Madonna and a female version of Mr. Rogers.

Brazilians will at times admit to their racist attitudes when speaking to white Americans, probably on the assumption that if one is white and American he or she is automatically a racist. If pressed to provide more information about the existence of racist attitudes in such a racial democracy, Brazilians will usually fall back on the misleading belief of class, not race, as the determinant. In fact, Brazilians are somewhat bewildered by the thoroughness of the binary system which exists in the United States; for example, by the election of Andrew Young as head of the NAACP—first, because he does not look black enough to be called a black in Brazil, but also because he has held elective office and wears a suit, both of which disqualify him as a black in Brazil. The adage in Brazil is that "money whitens," which is another charming half-truth.

SOCIAL CLASS

The pervasiveness of racial and ethnic prejudice in Brazil has produced a society in which the upper classes are the whitest and the lower classes are the darkest. This is not an absolute rule—Brazil has no caste system. But neither is it an open system like that of the United States, in which social mobility is the norm. For members of the lower classes there have not until recently existed many avenues of upward mobility, which means essentially that persons born in one class are destined to remain in that class indefinitely.

Traditional Class Structure

In Brazil's plantation society social class was of an almost feudal character. There were basically two classes, the aristocracy of the planter class, which was created by the acquisition of land and property, and the peasants who worked for the wealthy. The relationship between these two classes was one of the absolute dependence of the poor on the rich. Members of the lower class were either sharecroppers or debt peons. They rarely owned any property, were generally illiterate, and subsisted on a diet of rice, beans, and manioc. To survive, they needed the protection of a *patrão*, a person of wealth and prestige, and this often involved the *compadrio*, a very old system of ritual kinship in which the person of power becomes a *compadre*, or godfather. A peasant who convinced a powerful *patrão* to be his child's baptismal godfather gained protection for himself and some kind of guarantee for the child if he should die. Members of the lower class were neither politicized nor organized except in this very personal client relationship. There are still many areas of rural Brazil in which this antiquated structure remains virtually unchanged from the colonial period. In some areas the structure remains but the lower classes have become better organized and are taking steps to transform the society into a more egalitarian one. Remnants of the planter class, especially the sugar barons, still exist today, though their absolute power remains in force only on their own turf. Industrialization and the growth of cities have made them something of an anachronism, though many of the old family names are still important in politics. But they are a rural class, and Brazil is no longer a rural country.

The Transformation of Traditional Class Structure

The rapid urbanization of Brazil and the fundamental transformations in the economy have had a profound impact on class, though there is still a sharp contrast between the wealthy and the poor. The new upper class is composed of bankers, industrialists, exporters, and entrepreneurs. Until the middle of the twentieth century Brazil's export economy was principally one of unfinished goods (mainly sugar, coffee, and cacao), but by 1990 finished goods (automobiles, appliances, arms) and services were worth over twice as much as raw goods. The most radical transformation in the export sector has been the growth in the export of technology, mainly to less developed countries. Brazilian technicians have built numerous dams, bridges, and highways abroad, and it was Brazilian engineers who designed the Baghdad subway system.

The creation of this new class of privilege has been accompanied by the growth of a new urban lower class and by changes in the old rural lower class. The new urban lower class is really more than one class, because it includes the real proletariat—those who work for wages, usually in factories—and a marginal lower class of recent migrants to the cities, who are really very much like the old rural lower class but who now live within the boundaries of a city. Many of them are part of the "informal" economy, which means that they actually operate at the margins of the capitalist economy of the cities. The urban proletariat has become a kind of elite in the lower classes. They earn enough money to buy houses and appliances, and they have become a force in local and national politics. Workers in such industries as automobiles, appliances, chemicals, and metallurgy are, unlike their rural counterparts, organized and politicized. But the new migrant populations of urban poor, those who do not participate directly in the economy on a regular basis, are rarely organized and indeed lack many of the basic necessities of life.

This marginalized sector of the urban poor often resides in slums, which are omnipresent in Brazilian cities. In 1987 the Brazilian Institute of Geography and Statistics estimated the number of Brazilians living in slums to be over 25 million, or slightly more than the population of Peru. The most famous and most visible urban slums are those of Rio de Janeiro, because there the poor live on the hills and the rich live on the lowlands, a reversal of the usual pattern. Rio's slums are called *favelas*, after the first slum in Rio was created, ironically by an urban renewal project which was undertaken early in the twentieth century. Several tenements were razed by the municipal government and its inhabitants forced to leave. They went to a hill originally called Providência, which was later renamed "Favela" after the name of a hill in Canudos. In Pernambuco these slums are called *mocambos*, in Bahia they are *alagados*, and in Rio Grande do Sul *vilas de malocas*. The *alagados* in Bahia (the word means "swampy") are built on stilts out into the Bay of All Saints and are the largest stilt slum in Brazil. Fortaleza, capital of the northeastern state of Ceará, has over 200 slums, housing perhaps a one-fourth of the population of the city.

Brazilian slums are generally built on land owned by someone else. They usually have no running water, sewers, or electricity. In some, city services such as electricity are pirated by running illegal lines to a power source, often to power television sets. The houses of the residents are made of cardboard, sheeting, zinc roofing, discarded lumber, and anything else that can be used to construct a crude shelter. In Bahia new slums are created by an *invasão* (invasion), in which squatters identify a piece of unoccupied land and organize a quasi-military expedition, usually at night, in which the invaders erect from a dozen to as many as fifty *barracos* (shacks). When dawn breaks the owner of the property, whether the state or a private individual, is faced with a complete community where yesterday there was nothing. Such invasions have often been seen as an excuse to resort to violence against the squatters. Since 1986, however, the government, recognizing the national scope of the problem, has enacted laws to help *favelados* acquire title to the land they invade, especially if the terrain has been historically underutilized.

The Middle Class

Because of rapid industrialization and the concomitant growth in the service sector and the growth of government, Brazil's middle class has grown very rapidly in the latter half of the twentieth century. Traditionally, government service, including military careers, have been among the few avenues for a person of the lower class to edge into the middle class. Now, however, the growth of sophisticated industrial enterprises and the boom in technology has created a demand for professionals in many fields. Scientists, technicians, engineers, and specialists of all kinds are in high demand, and most of these are members of Brazil's new middle class. Like members of the middle class in many countries, middle-class Brazilians tend to be rather conservative socially and politically, and they share more values with the upper class than with the lower class. They also tend to live a bit beyond their means. Unlike the middle class in most countries, middle-class Brazilians generally have domestic servants.

Access to the middle class necessarily entails access to higher education.

There were no institutions of higher education in Brazil until the nineteenth century, and only in the twentieth century did higher education in Brazil become available to a large part of the population. Since the 1920s the federal university system has grown very rapidly—in 2002 there were 43 federal universities in Brazil. To enter the system, which guarantees a virtually free education, students have to pass the dreaded *vestibular*, a national entrance examination. The *vestibular* is administered over a four-day period, and students are required to select beforehand the field of intended study. In some areas there may be 50 or 60 candidates for a single vacancy, so thorough preparation is essential. Although this exam appears to be a democratic one, the competition is so fierce that to pass it in one of the more attractive fields a student almost has to take a private (and expensive) preparatory course called a *cursinho*, which virtually eliminates the democratic factor. This system has been under fire for some time, and Brazilian educators are now considering replacing it with another type of examination, though exactly what kind has not been decided.

The level of competition for few vacancies clearly means that the higher education system in Brazil is in crisis. A great many Brazilians get degrees in higher education in other countries, especially the United States, but that is an avenue open only to the very wealthy or to the lucky few who get scholarships. Of the 871 institutions of higher education which existed in Brazil in 1988, only 83 were categorized as universities, in contrast to the roughly 2,300 in the United States.[3]

Despite the growth of the middle class and the increasing educational and political sophistication of the urban lower classes, Brazil is still a country in which the income disparity between the wealthiest and the poorest is among the worst in the world.

NOTES

1. Thomas M. Stephens, in his *Dictionary of Latin American Racial and Ethnic Terminology* (Gainesville: University of Florida Press, 1989), 255–367, includes 112 pages of ethnic terminology for Brazil alone. Since some of these terms are historically or regionally restricted or listed as variants, the absolute number is probably high, but at an average minimum of nine entries per page, there would be between 900 and 1,000 viable terms.

2. *Almanague Abril 2002* (São Paulo: Editora Abril, 2002), p. 141.

3. *Brasil A/Z* (Larousse Cultural) (São Paulo: Ed. Universo, 1988), p. 278; *The World Almanac and Book of Facts, 1997* (Mahwah, NJ: K-III Reference, 1996), pp. 258–282.

3

Language

Life didn't reach me through newspapers or books
but came from the mouth of the people, bad speech of the people
good speech of the people
because it's the people who speak Brazilian Portuguese with gusto
while we
all we do is
imitate, monkey see, monkey do
the language of the classics

—Manuel Bandeira, "Evocation of Recife,"
trans. Candace Slater, p. 85

IT MAY SEEM odd to some readers that an introduction to Brazilian culture includes a chapter on language, but language is to Brazilians a very important part of their identity, whether or not they consciously think of it. Yes, the national language of Brazil is Portuguese, a fact known to so few Americans that questions about it are raised on popular game shows. Part of the problem is that, aside from the United States and Canada, Brazil is the one massive country whose language does not appear in the name of the country. The Russians speak Russian, the Chinese speak Chinese, and the Brazilians speak—Portuguese. Portuguese has an imperialistic nature. In eastern Paraguay, northern Uruguay, and in parts of Bolivia and Colombia, Portuguese, not Spanish, is the *lingua franca*. Part of this is due to incursions of Brazilian settlers, but it is also due in part to Brazilian television, which blankets the airwaves of the neighboring countries with its fascinating *telenovelas* (soap operas), and in part because of the economic importance of the language. The Portuguese spoken in Brazil is also markedly different from that spoken in Portugal. The vocabulary, syntax, and pronunciation of Brazilian usage contrasts sharply with the Portuguese. It is probably fair to say that the difference is even greater than the one between "received" British usage and American English.

The fact that Brazilians speak Portuguese and most of their neighbors speak Spanish endows them with a sense of otherness—they are in this very concrete way different from their neighbors. In fact, Brazilians will sometimes talk about "Latin America" as if it were a space on another planet, not an area of the world with which they can identify. There seems to be an unconscious notion in Brazil that Latin America is in reality Spanish America and that Brazil is some other thing and is located in some other place. But in addition to the otherness implicit in speaking what many regard to be an exotic tongue, the language also confers, by its very strangeness, an unusual sense of national identity. In one large linguistic sense, Brazilians are not after all so different from their neighbors in Spanish America. They both live in verbalistic cultures, in which the art of rhetoric is still cultivated and in which what is said is often less important than how it is said. In the 1950s Brazilians were still reciting poetry, and sometimes prose, at public gatherings. The ability to recite well and to do it with emotion and conviction was still highly esteemed. This admiration for speaking well is still a major attribute for politicians, and it might be argued that some recent losers in national elections might not have lost if they had spoken better and created a better image. A rally for a mayoral candidate in Bahia illustrates this. The candidate was young and handsome and very well dressed, in rather striking contrast to his constituents. He spoke with a formal elegance seldom heard on the streets, and when he finished he was rewarded with a thunderous round of enthusiastic applause. At this point a rather shabbily dressed man in front, still applauding, said, with a smile, "I don't have any idea what he said, but, boy, was it beautiful."[1]

It may surprise some readers to learn that Portuguese, with almost 200 million speakers, is the world's seventh (or eighth, depending on whether nonnative speakers are included) most widely spoken language. The inclusion or exclusion of nonnative speakers obviously affects some languages more than others. English, for example, which is probably the most important commercial language in the world, jumps from fourth place to second place if nonnatives are included. Russian, probably for political reasons, goes from eighth place to fifth if nonnatives are included. Portuguese lacks both the commercial and political importance of English or Russian, but it is the official language of seven countries and is an unofficial language in several enclaves in China, India, and North America.

Portuguese was declared a "critical language" by the U.S. Department of Education in 1958, meaning that it was among the six languages singled out by the U.S. government as a language of political, economic, or cultural importance but which was spoken by few Americans. This designation was intended to encourage the study of the languages in U.S. colleges and universities, and indeed the government offered the added enticement of providing fellowships for the study of Portuguese and other critical languages. Sadly, now American institutions of higher education enroll a bit over 1% of the number of students of Portuguese as study Spanish, and even students in Italian, German, Japanese, and Hebrew outnumber students of Portuguese by large margins. An odd by-product of speaking a language few foreigners study is that both Brazilians and Portuguese are remarkably tolerant of the mistakes made by foreigners when they try to speak the language. In fact, most Portuguese speakers are so delighted that a nonnative is trying to speak their language that it is almost impossible to get them to correct errors. Because Brazilians are so verbal, in fact, it is altogether possible to learn a few fill phrases, such as the equivalents of "I see," and "Indeed," and come away from a conversation with the Brazilian lauding your alleged fluency in the language.

Spanish speakers like to say Portuguese sounds like baby talk to them, but in fact Portuguese is considerably more complex than Spanish. It has phonemic open and nasalized vowels, unknown in Spanish, and several structural complexities which have either disappeared from Spanish (such as the future subjunctive) or are simply nonexistent (such as the personal infinitive). Indeed, Brazilians can understand their Spanish American neighbors better than those neighbors can understand them. A Brazilian can understand about 60% of an educated Spanish speaker's speech but a Spanish American can only understand about 40% of a Brazilian's speech. One of the reasons for this is that Spanish has a remarkably tidy vowel system with only five vowels, the variations of pronunciation being so minuscule as to be largely unimportant when learning the language (one of the reasons Spanish sounds "fast" to nonspeakers is that the syllables are of roughly the same length). Portuguese, for starters, has thirteen vowels. In addition, it has a vast vocabulary (among the major European languages only English surpasses it), in part because Brazilian Portuguese has never been afflicted by notions of linguistic purity (European Portuguese speakers are considerably more rigid). Unlike the Real Academia Española or the Académie Française, there is no educational body whose mission is to purge such barbarisms as "drugstore" from the tongue. Brazil has an Academy of Letters which meets periodically with the Academy of Sciences in Lisbon, but the purpose of these meetings is not to ensure linguistic purity but to reach an agreement on a universal spelling of Portuguese (they get closer every time but still have not reached a full agreement). It is, then, very much like American English, a language which relishes new inventions but is also lexically so porous that borrowings from other tongues regularly appear in italics for a few years and are then quietly absorbed into the lexicon as ordinary words. Portuguese has a predictably high number of words derived from Latin (Portugal was called "Lusitania" when it was part of the Roman Empire) and Arabic (Portugal was occupied by the Moors until 1250), and it has also borrowed numerous items from the European languages, especially Spanish, English, French, and Italian. And since the Portuguese were the first Europeans to have contact with many other linguistic groups, it contains many words from India and the Orient, including everything from dialects of Chinese to Tamil to Malay to Japanese to Sinhalese to Hindi, and most of these words now exist side by side with Latin-derived forms as normal parts of the lexicon. Paradoxically, linguists consider Portuguese a "conservative" language because it retains such features as the initial "f" in words like *ferro* ("iron," from Latin *ferrum*, which is *hierro*, with a silent "h" in Spanish). Oddly, it also hangs on to many words of Arabic origin, even though Portugal was rid of Arabic speakers over 200 years before Spain (a couple of examples are *açogue* ["butcher"] and *alfaiate* ["tailor"], both of which have Latinate forms in Spanish). Although it does maintain many archaic features, borrowings have been responsible for major changes in the lexicon.

Two other sources of borrowing became extremely important in the New World—Tupi and African languages. Tupi is a shortened form of Tupi-Guarani, which is not a language nor even a language family but a super-family. To illustrate roughly what is meant by a super-family, you might think of Romance languages, all derived from Latin, as a language family, while the Indo-European languages, which include Germanic, Celtic, Greek, and Slavic, would be a super-family. A linguistic map of indigenous languages in Brazil at the time of contact would look like a political map of a European country in the twelfth century—hundreds of tiny fiefdoms, each discrete and quite separate from its neighbors. Because there were dozens of languages spoken in Brazil which did not even belong to this super-family, the linguistic variety of colonial Brazil was truly astonishing.

It was especially astonishing if you consider that the political leaders sent to Brazil were charged with uniting the populace and the missionaries were charged with catechizing the populace. If you could walk for two hours and find a population speaking another language, how could any such control be achieved? Contrast this situation to the two jewels in the Spanish crown in the colonial period, New Spain (Mexico) and Peru. In Mexico there was not only an advanced culture but an empire, consisting of a capital and dozens of tributary city-states which had to pay fealty (and communicate with) their Nahuatl-speaking lords. A similar situation obtained in Peru, with Quechua as an imperialistic language. Dominance and instruction are easily carried out when there is an imperialistic language already in place, but the Portuguese faced a much different situation. Not only did the indigenous peoples speak dozens of unrelated languages; their population was sparse and many groups were not sedentary, so when the Portuguese attempted to force the natives to perform labor for them, those who survived the onslaught of the European-introduced diseases, to which they had no resistance, simply faded into the forest. So the Portuguese needed a language which would allow them to communicate with their reluctant subjects, not only for labor but for the aims of the Roman Catholic Church. The first missionaries in Brazil were Jesuits, perhaps the most scholarly of orders, and it must have been a combination of an exceedingly frustrating linguistic situation and the cleverness of the missionaries that led them to do a very Jesuit kind of thing—they invented a language based on the phonology, vocabulary, and structure of the languages they found most widespread and used this language as an intermediary language for political and religious control. Actually, there were two languages, both called *língua geral*, or general language, because the gross features of the frequently contacted language groups varied a good deal from north to south, but at any rate this unusual linguistic solution became not only the language of religious instruction for the native population but the language of survival for the colonists. These two dialects constituted the dominant linguistic medium for the entire colonial period and were spoken not only by the clergy and the converted Indians but by the Portuguese colonists as well.

In the nineteenth century, after Brazil became first the seat of empire and then an independent nation, a wave of anti-Portuguese sentiment swept the country. Societies called *mata-galego* (literally, "kill the Galicians," a pejorative term for Portuguese) arose. At their meetings they served indigenous foods and in general spoke ill of the Portuguese. It is altogether likely that they also told amusing stories in which the Portuguese were the butt of the joke, a practice which can still be observed in Brazil. There was even a movement to bring back the *língua geral* as a national language, but by this juncture Portuguese had somewhat silently taken over as the national tongue and the disappointed Brazilians discovered that their nifty invention had literally died out.

Although a nativistic language was no longer a viable option, Brazilians did manage to reject at least one feature they thought of as an imperialistic relic—the rather rigid system the Portuguese had imported regarding given and family names. Even in modern Portugal there has existed an extremely inflexible set of rules for names. My son was born in Lisbon during the Salazar regime. As the son of two American citizens, he was entitled to American citizenship and an American passport, but he first had to be registered in the Portuguese Civil Registry. I took the necessary papers to the Registry, where the clerk cautioned me that not only did all the names I assigned to my son have to be Portuguese and Christian, there was also a limit on the number of names I could use. I don't recall offhand if it was seven given and five family or the reverse, but the numerical limit was nevertheless twelve. Brazilians, having achieved independence, felt burdened by an unneeded and capricious system of nomenclature, and they felt that even if they could not have their own language they could have their own names. The first source of names was classical antiquity, and it is thus not unusual to meet Brazilians whose given name is Aristóteles or Praxíteles. A second source was in Tupi-derived names, especially those that had been used in the Romantic Indianist fiction of the late nineteenth century. Iracema and Ubirajara are fairly common names today, and one of Brazil's famous pop singers, Cauby Peixoto, has a given name taken from another romantic character. The final step was a most Brazilian one. If they could use the classics or fiction for names, why not other sources? The end result is that although there exists in theory a system for surnames in Brazil, it is almost universally ignored, and given names can be gleaned from virtually any source. One fairly important source are the names of the founding fathers—of the United States. Hamilton and derived forms (Enilton, Airton) are common, as are Washington (the given name of a twentieth-century president of the Republic), Franklin (or Francolim), and Jéferson. But Brazilians also name their children after their favorite soccer team, a trademarked shoe or soft drink, or on the basis of whimsy. Many names can be viewed as merely the product of a slightly anarchic and certainly droll turn of mind. The names of trees are common surnames in Portuguese, but such inventions as "Um Dois Três de Oliveira Quatro" (literally "One Two Three of the Olive Tree Four") and "Último de Carvalho" ("Last of the Oak Tree") surpass the conventional inventiveness of naming.[2]

Brazilian Portuguese also borrowed a vast number of words from African languages and from various Tupi dialects. Among the African languages contributing large numbers of words to Brazilian Portuguese is Kimbundu, a Bantu language of northern Angola. Words of African origin are common especially for foodstuffs, in African-derived religious ceremonies, and for the numerous musical instruments of African origin still used in Brazil. Tupi words are very common for flora and fauna and in toponyms, but Brazilians often use other Tupi words such as the word *guaçu* ("big") for humorous effect. Although the effect may be comical, the meaning is universally understood.

Finally, if a linguist were to juxtapose the two major dialects of Portuguese, the European and the Brazilian, several interesting contrasts emerge, and they all point in the direction of a hypothesis for Brazilian Portuguese as a creolized language. A creole language is a pidgin or blend of two languages which has become the native language of a population, as in the case of Haitian Creole, a blend of French and African languages which is now the national language. One of the most interesting characteristics of Brazilian Portuguese is the palatalization of "d" and "t" before "i" (the "d" is pronounced as the "j" in "jeep" and the "t" as in the "ch" of "cheese"), a feature which is found in only one other dialect of Portuguese, the Creole of the Gulf of Guinea. In fact, one linguist claims that at least one-quarter of the Brazilian population speaks a true Creole, and using his criteria for creolization it would appear that even standard Brazilian Portuguese lacks only two principal features to be so designated.[3] In addition, the lexicons of the two dialects of Portuguese are so different that numerous bilingual (European-Brazilian) dictionaries exist, further evidence that, without really having tried, the Brazilians ended up having their own language—if not the *língua geral*, a novel and extremely plastic version of the mother tongue.

GESTURES

Gestures are part of what linguists call "paralanguage," which refers to parts of the communicative act that are not usually considered language per se, such as tone, loudness, and speed. One paralinguistic feature of Brazilian Portuguese most foreigners take note of almost immediately is space, since Brazilians, like most Latin Americans, tend to move much closer to the person addressed than we are accustomed to. Most English speakers have an invisible but nevertheless real space before them for conversation, and Brazilians in a sense violate this space, leaving foreigners intimidated or even frightened by this incursion. When they perceive that they are not being understood, Brazilians also have a tendency not to speak more slowly but to speak louder, which can worsen a bad situation.

They are also, to us, inordinately fond of gestures. At times the use of gestures can make it easier to understand what the speaker is saying, but many Brazilian gestures either do not exist in English or mean something else, so it is a good idea to know something about Brazilian gestures. Some think that the Brazilian fondness for gestures is a result of the Italian influence on Brazilian culture, since our stereotype is that Italians alone use gestures constantly—as in the old joke about the ship that foundered, the only passengers to swim to shore being two Italians. When asked how they reached shore so quickly, the answer was simply, "Parlando, parlando"—"Talking, talking." But Brazilians from areas of the country with little or no Italian influence use gestures often. Such common expressions as "more or less," "excellent," and "I doubt it," can be expressed entirely without verbal clues, so that there is at least a rudimentary sign language which operates on a national level.

The problem gestures are those that do not travel between cultures. One which American males use a lot, especially when they are waiting around for something to happen, is to idly rap a palm on the other fist, one above the other, which is obscene in Brazil (it means "screw you"). The "hook 'em horns" gesture used by Texas football fans is an indication of cuckoldry in Brazil. Another is the "AOK" sign made by holding the index finger against the thumb and raising the hand, which in Brazil is another equivalent of the middle finger. Needless to say, American movies about pilots are extremely popular in Brazil, because every time the pilot enters the cockpit and gets ready to take off, he makes an unmistakably gross gesture to his ground crew.

Brazilians also strike Americans as affectionate beyond the limits of decency. Men routinely embrace each other when they meet, and women often offer ritual kisses as a greeting. Brazilians of both sexes touch a lot when they are talking and sometimes when they are not, hold hands, or grab an arm in situations in which Americans would have no contact whatsoever. The fact that we do not, and the fact that our personal space is so large, are two reasons Brazilians have for thinking us cold.[4]

NOTES

1. Author's observation.

2. These and hundreds of others can be found in Mário Souto Maior's *Nomes Próprios Pouco Comuns* (Rio de Janeiro: Livraria São José, 1974).

3. See John A. Holm, *Pidgins and Creoles*, vol. 2 (Cambridge: Cambridge University Press, 1988), p. 299; and John A. Holm, "Creole Influence on Popular Brazilian Portuguese," in *Pidgin and Creole Languages*, ed. Glenn G. Gilbert (Honolulu: University of Hawaii Press, 1987), pp. 406–429.

4. A good introduction to gestures and paralanguage in Brazil is Phyllis A. Harrison, *Behaving Brazilian* (Rowlay, MA: Newbury House, 1983).

4

History

Brazil is the country of the future—it always has been, and it always will be.

—Popular saying

THE FOLLOWING OVERVIEW of Brazilian history attempts to include the events that constitute a grammar of Brazilian culture, the singular events which make Brazilians think about themselves and about others in a particular way. One could think about these events as formative of the national character. Portugal's claim to at least a part of what is modern Brazil had its foundation in one of the most extraordinary acts of chutzpa in the history of the world. In 1493, Pope Alexander VI, Rodrigo Borgia, father of Cesare and Lucrezia Borgia, acceded to a request by the Spanish crown to grant Spain title to the lands Christopher Columbus had discovered by issuing a vaguely worded bull granting such title. A later bull clarified the demarcation by granting Spain title to lands west of an imaginary line 100 leagues west of the Cape Verde Islands. João II of Portugal, loath to cede title to possible Portuguese discoveries, threatened war with Spain, and in 1494 his representatives met with Ferdinand's in the little town of Tordesillas in northern Spain and signed a treaty moving this imaginary line to 370 leagues west of Cape Verde. That the pope and then two monarchs could simply sit down and draw a line running from pole to pole and agree that one kingdom owned what lay east and the other what lay west is an indication of the remarkable power of both the papacy and the two seafaring nations.

Portugal had already taken two islands, Madeira and the Azores, and in 1488 Bartolomeu Dias rounded the Cape of Good Hope, opening the way for a sea route to India, which Portuguese explorer Vasco da Gama would reach in 1498. But Columbus, who maintained to his death that he had reached the Orient, reported his landfall in the "Indies" in 1492, which was sufficient reason for the Portuguese to seek to guarantee at least a piece of the potentially lucrative pie in the New World. In 1500, Pedro Álvares Cabral led a fleet of 13 ships with a heavily armed crew of a thousand men west from Lisbon. Advised by Vasco da Gama that for ships to round the Cape of Good Hope it was necessary to sail as far west as possible to catch favorable winds, Cabral's fleet made an unexpected landfall in late March, and on May 1 Cabral had his cannoneers fire a salvo as he took possession of this new land, which he called Ilha da Vera Cruz (Island of the True Cross).

Historians have long disputed whether or not Cabral's discovery was an accident, and some even think that the Portuguese designated the new territory an "island" to deter the interest other nations might have in the area, though the first exploratory expedition to Brazil in 1501 landed a good 200 leagues (roughly 700 miles) north of Cabral's landfall. But Cabral's mission in India was clear and he shortly proceeded to carry it out. And if the Portuguese thought it was an island, they must have known that it was an uncommonly large one. Brazil was of only marginal interest to Portugal, at any rate. Fortunes could be made, and were, in the lucrative commercial empire that the tiny country was forging, and Brazil offered very little of interest to a mercantile nation. One of the few things of interest was a commercially viable dyewood called *pau-brasil*, or brazilwood, so called because it produced a brilliant red dye the color of a glowing ember (*brasa*). In less than a decade the Island of the Holy Cross was being called *Terra do Brasil*, and that name appeared on a map as early as 1511.

EARLY DEVELOPMENT, 1500–1530

In 1501 an expedition led by Italian explorer Amerigo Vespucci and Fernando de Noronha explored a portion of the northeast coast of Brazil. Vespucci published a map of his explorations in 1507 and serendipitously became the christener of two entire continents—North America and South America. Within two decades two *feitorias*, a kind of trading post based on the ones the Portuguese operated in Africa, were established in Brazil. The first was founded by the so-called New Christians, former Jews who had at least nominally become Roman Catholics. These trading posts were essentially bartering sites where the Portuguese traded baubles and mirrors for the scarlet wood that gave Brazil its name. This brazilwood cycle was the first in a series of economic cycles that would characterize the Brazilian economy for the entire colonial period. The first cycle was economically primitive, because it consisted solely of an extractive industry which eventually produced revenue for the Portuguese in Europe. This early period, lasting about 30 years, was also marked by the beginning of race mixing (the Portuguese brought no women) and by the Jesuits' efforts to devise some sort of communication system so that the indigenous peoples could be catechized. The Portuguese also had to take defensive measures at an early date, because the French and English both appeared to be interested in this new colony. In 1526 one of the principal colonizers, Cristóvão Jacques, seized three French vessels at Bahia.

By any standard, this is a remarkably low level of activity for a European power with ambitions of empire, especially given the presumed legality of the Portuguese claim to Brazil. By 1530, Spanish conquistador Hernán Cortés had already conquered and plundered Tenochtitlán and a good portion of the Aztec Empire, and Francisco Pizarro was on his way to Peru to do the same to the hapless Incas, but in Brazil no more than a few dozen Portuguese were involved in a fairly marginal barter arrangement which might have been lucrative for them but which promised very little in terms of wealth for the Portuguese crown. In fact, Brazil's existence was given very little import in Lisbon, first, because there was no high civilization worthy of plundering and second, because the Portuguese Empire was based in the Orient, not the Americas. The Spanish Empire was one of conquest and plunder, but the Portuguese Empire was largely a commercial operation, and it seemed pointless to pay much attention to a jungle full of naked savages when Vasco da Gama's expedition in 1499 repaid the cost of the venture to the tune of a sixty-to-one ratio. In fact, the Portuguese crown paid very little attention to Brazil until the middle of the seventeenth century, and then only because circumstances changed. This is not to say that Brazil would have necessarily benefitted by having a more doting motherland, but it is worth keeping in mind that in the context of Portuguese commercial activities, the truly lucrative market was the Orient.

THE CAPTAINCY SYSTEM, 1530–1549

The brazilwood period, also known as the "period of neglect," ended in 1530, when a Portuguese noble, Martim Afonso de Sousa, was named by the king to reconnoiter the coast, drive out the French, and lay claim to the territory by the planting of stone markers. Members of this expedition also planted the first sugar cane in Brazil, which would become the basis of the next economic cycle. The Portuguese, who had planted sugar in the Madeiras as early as the 1420s, were among the few Europeans who had learned the technology for the raising and processing of sugar cane, and they found much of the Brazilian coast ideal for this crop, which would soon surpass brazilwood as the principal export commodity. As a means of securing the rest of the colony for Portugal, King John III then decided to implement the *capitania* (captaincy) system the Portuguese had used on the Atlantic islands. As a system purported to ensure the defense and colonization of a vast territory, the arrogance of this system approaches that of the Pope's drawing of the famous Tordesillas line. Brazil was divided north to south into 15 captaincies, each of which was "donated" by the crown to a *donatário*, or donee. This single individual was in essence the governor, principal judicial official, tax collector, and general big shot of a parcel of land that was 50 leagues (150 miles) wide and theoretically extended westward to the Tordesillas line, meaning that those that extended the farthest east (on the hump of Brazil) would be 1,000 miles long, for a total land area roughly the size of the state of Montana—or over four times the size of Portugal.

The donees had vast powers, including the right to choose a successor and appoint judicial officials, as well as the right to make smaller grants of land within the captaincy (*sesmarias*). They also had considerable responsibility, including defense. Colonizing this vast new land was not without its perils, aside from Portugal's somewhat lukewarm enthusiasm for the venture. Some of the donees never went to Brazil, others gave up in the face of hostile Indians, and at least one donee ended up as dinner. One group of colonists reportedly starved to death. After two decades only six of the fifteen captaincies were functioning at all, and only two of them were anything approaching successful.

The Portuguese quickly learned the need for an expanded labor force. In the Iberian tradition, they were reluctant to do manual labor themselves and had always managed to conscript others into doing the work for them. But the Indians were few in number (between one and two million at first) and unreliable. Most of the Indians in the coastal area were semi-sedentary and those of the interior were tropical forest peoples without fixed residence. Many engaged in armed resistance at Portuguese attempts to enslave them; others simply disappeared into the forest. In addition, Portuguese law was ambiguous about the enslavement of Indians, and before the end of this period the Portuguese began to import slaves from Africa, which they had been doing in Portugal for almost a century. The native populations, decimated by disease and warfare, suffered a massive population reduction. African slaves became the principal source of labor in Brazil—the Portuguese would bring between three and six million Africans to Brazil before the traffic was banned in 1850. These two groups also contained the only women available to the Portuguese, and within a very short time the population of Brazil began to become a multi-ethnic one.

CROWN COLONY, 1549–1580

This somewhat mixed success prompted the crown to consider other alternatives. And, although the Brazilian colony was not a first priority in the context of the empire, it is well-known that nothing makes something more attractive than another's covetousness, and the French interest in Brazil was high indeed. In 1548, João III bought back the captaincy in Bahia, and in 1549 the first crown expedition was sent to Bahia to establish the Captaincy General of Bahia, an enterprise of the Portuguese crown. The expedition, with over 1,000 men, was the largest to that date in Brazilian history. Its commander and the new governor-general was Tomé de Souza, a loyal soldier who had served the king in Africa and India. Sousa brought with him instructions to set up the bureaucracy thought needed to govern the colony, including a justice system administered by the *ouvidor-mor*, a treasury administered by a *provedor-mor*, and a defense system coordinated by a *capitão-mor-da-costa*. Perhaps more importantly, Tomé de Sousa also brought with him six Jesuits, who would eventually play a major role in both the conversion of Indians and the education of the Portuguese during the entire colonial period.

By 1580 a system of town government was established, the French had been driven out, and both the secular and regular churches were functioning. The Jesuits had already begun establishing *aldeias* (literally "villages") to catechize the Indians, a task the secular church had been notably remiss in carrying out. Rio de Janeiro was established as a royal captaincy in 1567, and several other coastal towns were prospering, mostly on the basis of sugar production. At this point there were about 17,000 whites in Brazil and about twice that many black slaves.

THE BABYLONIAN CAPTIVITY, 1580–1640

The year 1580 is not an arbitrary date but one which was to have considerable importance in the eventual growth of the colony, not because of anything momentous in Brazil but because of events in Europe and Africa. In 1557, João III, who had not yet reached the age of 60, suddenly died of a heart attack. Although he had sired 11 children, they had all died before he did, meaning that the rightful heir to the throne was his three-year-old grandson Sebastião. A regency was established to run the country until he reached majority. But as soon as he reached the age to ascend the throne, the romantic young king decided on a quixotic crusade in Morocco. Leading a force of about 20,000 men, he foolishly pursued the Moors into the desert, exactly as the enemy had hoped. They finally attacked and not only routed the Portuguese force but also killed the young king.

The repercussions of this tragic episode were numerous. The first was that the logical claimant to the throne was Sebastião's uncle, already in his late sixties. Eventually, no fewer than seven pretenders emerged, among them Philip II of Spain, who not only had a vague blood claim to the throne but also commanded one of the largest military forces in Europe. He used his troops to legitimize his claim, and in 1580 began the 60-year "Babylonian Captivity" with a Spanish monarch on the Portuguese throne. A second and less expected result of the episode was that since none of the young king's men actually saw him die in battle, a folk belief soon arose that Sebastião would one day return to save his country when it was in peril, a notion that eventually grew into a generalized belief throughout Luso-Brazilian culture and would eventually be at least marginally responsible for numerous messianic movements in Brazilian history. A third and even more important result was that since the monarch of Portugal was also the monarch of Spain, the Tordesillas Line dividing the New World territories of the two countries became technically nonexistent.

A major complication of this arrangement was that Portugal also inherited Spain's enemies, which during this period included France, England, and the Netherlands. Part of the impetus for expansion in the colony was to combat the encroachments of these states, especially France, although there were also altercations with the English, including at least one case of piracy by English freebooters. But the colony also needed timber and more land, since sugar was a crop that depleted soil quickly. In addition, Indian slaves were also in demand because, although they were held as less than ideal workers, they were virtually free for the taking in contrast to the high expense entailed in importing slaves from Africa. The first line of Portuguese expansion was through Paraíba and Rio Grande do Norte into Ceará, where Fortaleza was established by a royal expedition in 1610. The second was in response to a French incursion in Maranhão, which was finally repulsed in 1616. The third and perhaps most important was the advance into Pará, where the Portuguese established a fort in 1616. This fort, at present-day Belém, would be a key factor in the expansion of Portugal into the Amazon, because no other European power made an all-out effort to control this important waterway. Because the other European powers were preoccupied elsewhere and in part by reason of Portugal's skillful handling of its Indian allies, the eventual control of the vast territory of the Amazon would rest with the small but opportunistic Portugal. To this point the entire colony was called the State of Brazil, but in 1621, in order to guarantee control of this potentially important area, the Portuguese created the State of Maranhão, which included the entire northern sector of the colony.

Although most of Brazil's population remained in the sugar-producing area in the northern coastal region, a smaller but similar expansion was taking place in southern Brazil, where the *bandeirantes* were carrying out slaving expeditions to provide labor for the burgeoning agricultural crops of the area around São Paulo. Brazil also experienced its most serious foreign incursion in this period. The Spanish had been at war with the Netherlands off and on for a number of years, and Philip finally decided to close Spain and Portugal to commerce to protect his economic interests. In retaliation, the Dutch first founded a Dutch East India Company (1602) and then a Dutch West India Company (1621) in order to undermine Spanish and Portuguese commerce in the Orient and in the New World by conquest. The Dutch chose Brazil as a first target for invasion on the assumption that it was the most poorly defended of Spain's New World territories, an assumption that seemed to prove true. In 1624 a fleet of 26 vessels, carrying over 3,000 men, attacked Salvador. The city seemed to be well-enough defended, as it had several imposing forts amply armed with cannon, but the Portuguese had miscalculated the range of their artillery, and the Dutch took the city without much difficulty by simply landing *between* the forts, out of range of the Portuguese weapons. Philip, fearing that with such a foothold in South America even Bolivia might fall to the invaders, assembled a fleet of 65 ships and retook the city only two weeks after it had fallen. But the Dutch were tenacious, and in 1627 the famous Dutch pirate Piet Heyn took the Spanish silver fleet off Cuba, resulting in a declaration of a 50% dividend for the Dutch West India Company. They then looked to Recife, which was probably richer and even less well defended than Bahia, and in 1630 a fleet of 65 vessels took that city. Again, the Spanish and Portuguese relied chiefly on sea power to attempt to regain control of Recife, but several inconclusive sea battles and the perversity of the prevailing winds thwarted their attempts. The Dutch would remain in Recife for 24 years, and the foothold would eventually extend from the São Francisco River clear into Maranhão.

The Dutch were extremely efficient managers, and by the 1640s, Recife alone was producing more sugar than the rest of Brazil. They also took several important cities in Africa, including the capital of Angola, in order to ensure a steady supply of slaves. They established the first representative government in South America, and for a time cultural life flourished in this little Dutch island in the tropics. The Dutch improved the city of Recife by constructing canals and establishing public gardens, and they also appeared to be the first Europeans to demonstrate any scientific interest in the flora and fauna of the tropics. The governor of Dutch Brazil, Johan Maurits, the Count of Nassau, took it upon himself to invite scholars and artists to Dutch Brazil, where the first notable scientific studies were undertaken and artists such as Frans Post painted Brazilian landscapes. But since it was an economic colonization, Dutch Brazil had no real roots, and when revolts occurred and concentrated military power was brought to bear, this brief Dutch renaissance in the tropics would disappear, though surnames such as Wanderley still attest to the importance of Dutch intermarriage with the local population.

PORTUGUESE REVOLT AND THE END OF DUTCH BRAZIL, 1640–1654

The Portuguese had long viewed Spanish rule as a mixed blessing, and as Spain continued to appoint Spaniards to all the choice posts and then to raise taxes in an attempt to slow the decline of the Spanish Empire, the Portuguese finally revolted. In 1640, João IV initiated the Bragança dynasty and declared independence from Spain. The Portuguese lacked the military might to make such a declaration unilaterally, but the Dutch, the French, and the English were eager to participate in anything that weakened Spain. The Spaniards, already involved in the Thirty Years' War and faced with a simultaneous revolt in Catalonia, were stretched too thinly to retaliate, and Portugal regained its independence.

The determination of the Portuguese to remain independent of Spain meant that they were not prepared to expend much effort liberating Dutch Brazil, but the Portuguese in Brazil, inspired by the revolt in Europe, rose up against the Dutch and won some major land battles against them. In 1649 the crown acceded to popular demand and established the Brazil Company, which eventually sent a strong fleet to Recife, where it isolated the Dutch and finally expelled them altogether.

PORTUGUESE EXPANSION, 1637–1750

The Amazon

The first expedition to traverse the Amazon was a Spanish expedition from Quito, Ecuador, led by Captain Juan de Palacios and a group of Franciscans in 1636. As a result of this feat, the Portuguese were spurred into action, and the following year Pedro Teixeira led a Portuguese expedition up the Amazon, formally claiming the land for Portugal, the documentation of which later held up in court. The Portuguese then began establishing frontier outposts along the Amazon, including Santarém in 1640 and Manaus in 1660.

But the real story of the colonization of the Amazon is the rivalry between religious orders and between the orders and the secular colonists. Initially, the Franciscans nominally controlled the area, but for lack of funds they eventually gave up their claim, and secular colonists dominated the area until about 1652. In that year the Jesuits were given permission to enter the Amazon Basin, and they alternated control of the region with lay colonists until 1680, when the Jesuits regained complete control. This time they agreed to allow other orders (Franciscans, Carmelites, and Mercedarians) to control the northern side of the Amazon while they controlled the southern bank. The Jesuit strategy in this mission field was to catechize the Indians by bringing them into villages, which they did with considerable success, using secular military forces to control the native populations. At the same time, Spanish Jesuits were entering the Amazon Basin from the other side, creating a two-front war in the battle for souls.

The River Plate

By the middle of the seventeenth century Portugal was losing its empire in the Far East and was heavily in debt due in large part to an expensive war with Spain and the massive dowry paid when Catharine of Bragança married Charles II of England. Recognizing that the only way to keep an empire was the consolidation of its foothold in Brazil, the Portuguese decided that it needed to colonize the subtropical and temperate parts of Brazil, and to that end they needed to establish a base in the River Plate. In addition, the Portuguese continued their so-far fruitless search for precious metals, and they created monopoly companies along the lines of the Dutch model in order to exercise close control over their interests in all of Brazil.

The colonization of the South was quite different from that in other parts of Brazil. Most of the colonists came from Rio and São Paulo or from the Atlantic islands of the Azores and Madeira. The Indian population of this area was even sparser than that in the Amazon, which meant that there was a limited labor supply, and since the crops of this region were wheat and vegetables rather than sugar, there was no need to import slaves from Africa. The result of these circumstances was that land tenure ended up being small farmholds rather than the massive plantations found in the sugar regions.

One motivation for this push into southern climes was the need for silver, which had long been traded illicitly as contraband in exchange for slaves. But the Portuguese probably had their eye on the rich mines of Potosí in Bolivia, and an outpost on the Plate was at least a step in the right direction. In 1680 the Portuguese founded Colônia do Sacramento, clearly an incursion into Spanish territory. This outpost changed hands numerous times, and the Spanish finally established a fort at Montevideo to ensure control of the region. In a kind of territorial ping-pong, the Portuguese erected other forts, establishing outposts at Rio Grande and finally at Porto Alegre. Maritime traffic between these southern outposts and the better-established colonial northern towns was complicated by unfavorable winds, and eventually a land route between Santa Catarina and Colônia was established. Along this corridor inns, which eventually became towns, sprouted.

THE GOLD MINING FRONTIER

In 1695, almost 200 years after the discovery of Brazil, the commodity that the Portuguese had sought for most of that time—gold—was discovered in Minas Gerais. The result was the same as it has been in other parts of the world—a massive influx of population, skyrocketing prices for foodstuffs, wild frontier towns, thievery and murder, and, in this case, elaborate schemes to smuggle the gold out to avoid the 20% duty the crown exacted. The discovery of diamonds shortly thereafter accelerated the boom. Most of the gold was found either in the river beds themselves, where it was extracted by panning, or in deposits less than six feet deep, which meant that promising sites were soon depleted. The shallow location of the gold contributed to a frontier that moved with surprising speed, and within a few years Mato Grosso and Goiás were the outposts of the frontier. Since no one really knew how far inland the gold was, the frontier continued to expand, since there was always the rumor of gold or at least the possibility of another major strike.

Brazil was the world's greatest producer of gold and one of the principal producers of diamonds for over half a century. Aside from the immediate effect of expanding the Brazilian frontier in a truly spectacular fashion, the gold rush produced an equally rapid population shift from the North to the South, from Portugal to Brazil, and even from São Paulo northward and westward. It also eliminated any talk about social and political reform in the colony, since it guaranteed that the nobility would retain a comfortable seat in the lap of luxury.

Several new captaincy units were created to deal with the burgeoning population—Minas Gerais in 1720, Goiás in 1744, and Mato Grosso in 1748. But gold also produced a hollow frontier. Although the Portuguese advanced inland and laid claim to a vast territory because of the gold, the mercantilist mentality of the Portuguese made gold an end in itself, and little was done to promote agriculture or manufacturing. The English in fact provided most of the manufactured goods needed—in exchange for Brazilian gold. The irony was that it is not altogether an exaggeration to say that gold extracted by African slaves from Brazilian rivers financed the Industrial Revolution in Great Britain.

Despite some internal revolts and one important French incursion in Rio in 1710, Portuguese control was greatly expanded and solidified during this period. In addition to the new crown captaincies, there were four new bishoprics established before 1750, and since the influx of people and wealth in Minas Gerais, a flourishing cultural life had developed there, with important developments in the arts, particularly architecture, sculpture, and poetry.

POMBAL AND AFTER, 1750–1808

José I ascended the Portuguese throne in 1750. One of the least distinguished of Portuguese monarchs, he was completely upstaged by his famous prime minister, the Marquis of Pombal. Pombal left a very mixed legacy in Portugal itself, his most notable accomplishments being the organization of reconstruction after the disastrous Lisbon earthquake of 1755 and his suppression of the Jesuits in 1759, but he was regarded more highly in Brazil. He envisioned Portugal and Brazil as not only developing independently of each other, but also free of British influence, a not inconsiderable ambition in the face of British commercial dominance. The expulsion of the Jesuits also brought some unexpected consequences, because the Jesuits were largely responsible for most of the education that went on in Brazil, and their departure left many schools without teachers. A fair number of Indian *aldeias* were also left without leadership, although the institution persisted for some years.

During Pombal's administration a colonial militia was established and the 11 remaining hereditary captaincies were bought by the crown. The capital of Brazil was moved from Salvador to Rio de Janeiro in 1763. Part of the reason for this move was the growing prosperity of the southern captaincies, but it was also calculated to exercise closer control over the mining industry and to protect Brazil's southern border in Colônia. This southernmost outpost changed hands between the Spanish and Portuguese several times during the latter part of the century, either through military action or by treaty, but the Portuguese finally ceded the outpost to the Spanish in 1777, the year in which José died. Pombal also abolished the state of Maranhão, creating a single state of Brazil, a united Portuguese colony in the New World.

After Pombal there was some reversion of policy, particularly in regard to the British, whom the Brazilians recognized as their most important customer, especially for cotton, which was grown in various parts of the colony, notably Pernambuco. There was also an aborted independence movement in 1789, involving a number of merchants and intellectuals and led by a dentist (his nickname, "toothpuller," is known to all Brazilian schoolchildren).

By the end of the century, Brazil had a population in excess of 2.5 million, which seems substantial unless the size of Brazil is factored in. It is also worth noting that about 60% of that number were African slaves. The most populous captaincies, in order, were Minas Gerais, Bahia, Pernambuco, Rio de Janeiro, and São Paulo, and the great bulk of the population lived in a fairly narrow strip of land on the coast. The great expansion into the interior which had taken place with the *bandeirantes* was important for the future of Brazil, but much of that expansion had been achieved in slave forays or the search for precious metals and thus had not been fully consolidated.

The Portuguese crown had been reluctant to appoint many Brazilians to important posts, but toward the end of the century many more of them could be found in judgeships and governorships. The one thing the Portuguese did well during this period was to establish an elaborate and at times confusing bureaucracy. Although it was probably never as efficient or as tightly controlled as the one created by the Spanish, the plethora of sometimes overlapping institutions was a notable characteristic of colonial Brazil. Perhaps the two most important legacies of the period for the modern state would be that fondness for bureaucracy and the notable degree of racial mixture in the population, including considerable admixture with African peoples.

FROM COLONY TO KINGDOM TO INDEPENDENCE, 1808–1822

Serendipity played an important role in the early history of Brazil. The first seemingly fortuitous event of moment was the discovery itself, still thought by some to be an accident. Even if it were not, it lacked the high drama of the Spanish discoveries and conquests. The second was the merging of the two crowns in the Babylonian Captivity, an event which certainly seemed a disaster to Portugal but which gave Brazil the opportunity to expand far beyond the frontiers demarcated by the Tordesillas Line, since that line no longer had any meaning. The third was another seeming disaster for Portugal, the Napoleonic invasion of the Iberian Peninsula in 1807.

At the time of the invasion João was regent of Portugal due to the mental condition of the real monarch, Maria I. A somewhat indecisive person, he waited until literally the last moment to put his retainers aboard ships as the French approached Lisbon. Part of the reason for the invasion had been the refusal of the Portuguese regent to seize British assets and citizens, and the British were, of course, sufficiently grateful for his inaction that they encouraged and indeed protected the passage of the royal family to Brazil. This move was a truly extraordinary one—the Portuguese were not only the only European royalty to visit their colonies in the New World; they were the only monarchs to rule their European territory from a colony. The results were probably mixed for Portugal, but truly momentous for Brazil.

One reason that the transfer of the monarchy to the colony had such impact was that part of Portuguese colonial policy had been to keep Brazil quite literally in a state of servility during the colonial period. Brazil was viewed not only as a potential threat to the integrity of the empire but also, given its size and wealth, as a potentially powerful rival to Portugal. With the arrival of João the motivation for keeping Brazil in a state of subservience dissipated, and suddenly Brazil was allowed to exercise rights which befitted the seat of empire. Brazilian commercial enterprises, previously severely restricted by the crown, were freed of control, and Brazil's ports, previously tightly controlled by Portugal, were opened to friendly commerce—which meant principally England, but the United States was also a new commercial partner.

Education had also been severely restricted in colonial Brazil. Since it had been largely the purview of the Jesuits, education had always been not only strictly religious but also limited to the secondary level. Although several thousand Brazilians attended the University of Coimbra in Portugal during the colonial period, the fact that no universities existed in Brazil was another clear indication of the rigorous control exercised over every facet of life in the colony. Within two years of João's arrival a school of surgery, a school of economics, a school of agriculture, and a school of chemistry had been established in various parts of Brazil. In addition, both a military and a naval academy came into being. Perhaps most importantly, a Brazilian newspaper was created, and the printing press finally made its debut in Brazil. João also invited foreign scholars to come to Brazil to study its flora and fauna and even its history.

FROM KINGDOM TO INDEPENDENCE, 1815–1822

Brazil was elevated to the category of *reino* (kingdom) in 1815, and in 1816 Maria died, making João the king, though he delayed his coronation

until 1818. The main reason for the delay was a separatist revolt in Pernambuco, which actually declared itself a republic in 1817, an indication that
many of the new ideas which had been seeping in from France and the United
States were now flowing with some force. His other major problem area was
the southern frontier, where another regional separatist movement was under
way. With the Spanish government in chaos due to a rebellion and the
outbreak of independence movements in the American colonies, there was
little organized resistance, and Brazil formally annexed what is present-day
Uruguay as the Cisplatine Province in 1821. In that same year João responded to his insistent government and returned to Portugal, leaving his
son Pedro in charge of Brazil.

In Portugal the ancient legislative body called the Cortes was reconvened
after a liberal revolt against the regency, but the Brazilian delegates were paid
very little attention by the snobbish Portuguese, and they finally returned
home. On January 9, 1822, the regent Pedro finally acceded to popular
sentiment and declared to the populace that he would remain in Brazil. The
only thing lacking for complete independence was a formal declaration. The
recalcitrance of the Cortes was at least partly responsible for that happening.
Pedro was traveling in the interior near the Ipiranga River on September 7
of that year when news came that the Cortes would not relent in its decision
to reduce his powers and revert to what amounted to colonial status, and
Pedro issued the "Cry of Ipiranga" declaring Brazilian independence.

PEDRO I, 1822–1831

It is probably useful to note here that Brazilian independence and the
government that was created contrast markedly with the independence movements in Spanish America. One clear difference was that Brazilian independence came about with remarkably little bloodshed, in sharp contrast to
the sometimes protracted episodes of violence in the former Spanish colonies.
The second is that instead of a liberal republic, Brazil became a monarchy.
Whether this was good or bad is less important than the fact that it was true,
because the legacy of the monarchy would make Brazil even more different
from its neighbors than it might otherwise have been.

Pedro dissolved the first constituent assembly and appointed a new one,
which promulgated the Constitution of 1824, Brazil's first. In keeping with
the form of government, it was a fairly conservative document, with an
indirectly elected Parliament and qualified suffrage. It also provided for a
Council of State, itself a throwback to the Middle Ages. Perhaps most importantly, it gave Pedro the *poder moderador*, or moderating power, allowing

the emperor to dismiss or convene the Parliament and to appoint governors and senators.

Pedro faced severe problems during his reign, not the least of which were two rebellions, one in Pernambuco and one in the Cisplatine. The first was put down with the aid of the British Admiral Cochran, who had also played an important part in the war of independence. The second was more serious and involved serious combat. Finally, at the instigation of the British, the conflict was settled in 1828 with the creation of the buffer state of Uruguay.

The British had also been influential in the creation of the government. By 1815, Portugal owed Great Britain almost 1.5 million pounds sterling, a debt which the British used as a club over the Brazilians, withholding recognition unless Brazil assumed the debt. Numerous requirements about shipping, duties, and even slavery were imposed by the British, which made Pedro's foreign policy appear dictated from abroad. He was also unpopular for maintaining ties with Portugal (he sent his daughter to occupy the Portuguese throne when João died in 1824) and for keeping a mistress. A populist revolt in 1831 demanded his abdication, and he finally relented, leaving his son, at the time only five years old, on the Brazilian throne.

THE REGENCY, 1831–1840

The regency period was marked by considerable change in the character of Brazilian society. One of the noteworthy features was the emergence of separatist movements in several provinces, signaling a desire for real independence not only from Portugal (and the omnipresent Portuguese merchants in Brazil), but also from the imperial government. Most of these revolts were of short duration with the exception of the War of the *Farrapos* ("ragamuffins") in the southern state of Rio Grande do Sul from 1835 to 1845. The regency conceded partial autonomy to the provinces, but European immigration had already begun in southern Brazil, and with it came many new and liberal ideas.

PEDRO II, 1840–1889

Pedro II was a truly extraordinary monarch. Had he not been so, Brazil might be a different country today. It might even be several countries. He had been tutored intensively since the age of five, and his teachers were dedicated to making him a truly enlightened monarch. Even when he ruled arbitrarily, it was with an eye to preparing his people for self-rule. Some called him a dictator and some called him "Pedro Banana," neither of which seems really to apply. He was schooled in philosophy and religion, and he read all the provincial periodicals. He also knew over a dozen languages, seven of which he spoke. Perhaps the most important characteristic he had for Brazilians was a purely symbolic one—he was native-born.

Several groups pressured to have Pedro's majority declared, presumably on the assumption that those who supported the move would somehow eventually benefit from it, and in 1840 he was declared an adult and ascended the throne. The woman chosen to be his bride was Teresa, a daughter of the King of Sicilies, a plain, short, and slightly lame woman who eventually mothered four children with Pedro—two sons and two daughters. Only the daughters survived to adulthood.

Since his reign lasted almost half century, it would be an understatement to say that it was eventful. What must be said is that while most of Spanish America was going through a period of tremendous social and political upheaval, Brazil was being ruled by an enlightened and at times brilliant monarch, who must be credited at the very least with bringing stability to the country in a turbulent era. Disputes between Liberals and Conservatives often escalated into war in the Spanish American republics, but they alternated peacefully throughout Pedro's reign.

Pedro II faced a number of crises during his reign, not the least of which were continued rebellions. He was fortunate to have at his disposal a very able military commander, the Duke of Caxias, who was able to bring most of them to a halt in short order. The exception was the *Farrapos* revolt, which lasted into the middle of the decade. A more serious problem existed in the always controversial River Plate. In a chronically disputed area, the fragile balance of power was being threatened by the Argentine dictator Juan Manuel Rosas, who was allied with the Conservatives in Uruguay. When the upriver provinces of Argentina revolted against him, Brazil gave him a diplomatic slap by recognizing the sovereignty of Paraguay, and then invaded Uruguay. The combined forces of the Uruguayan liberals, the rebellious Argentines, and Brazilians finally defeated the tyrant in 1852. That should have been the end of the story, but it was not.

Even though Brazil had tendered recognition to Paraguay, it was still a small, landlocked state with borders on the two giants of the continent, Argentina and Brazil. Understandably a little paranoid in such a situation, the dictator of Paraguay, Marshall Francisco Solano López, built the best and largest standing army on the continent, and when Brazil again invaded Uruguay because of continued strife there, including severe loss of Brazilian property because of banditry, Solano López decided to invade to cut off the Brazilian troops. But to do so he needed to cross Argentine territory, permission for which was denied. What ensued was a sometimes bizarre and extremely bloody war with Paraguay on one side and the governments of Brazil, Argentina, and Uruguay on the other. With these odds the outcome was no surprise. What was surprising was that it took three countries five long years to defeat the Paraguayan army and kill Solano López (1865–1870). It was also an odd coincidence that the war took place when it did, because hostilities broke out just as the United States was ending the Civil War and entering the period of Reconstruction, which left it virtually powerless to intervene even in carnage of such a scale. Paraguay lost virtually half its population and nearly half its territory in the war. For Brazil, the principal immediate outcome was what appeared to be a final equilibrium on its southern border. In the long run, though, the Paraguayan War had a much more profound effect on Brazil, because the empire emerged from the war with a large and experienced military (both the army and the navy participated) which was not beholden to the planter aristocracy.

The face of Brazil was also changing in other ways. Coffee was introduced in the eighteenth century and was gradually adopted as another cash crop. While the sugar planters were experiencing increased competition from more efficient operations in the Caribbean, Brazil initially had practically no competition on the coffee market. With the abolition of the slave trade in 1850, it also became necessary to find a substitute for the slave labor used on coffee plantations, and in a short time Brazil began receiving what would eventually become a flood of European immigrants, mostly from Portugal, Spain, and Italy, but from other countries as well—including the United States (a colony of southerners founded a town called Vila Americana in São Paulo in the 1860s because they could still own slaves there). Cotton also increased in importance as an export, especially during the U.S. Civil War, and a nascent textile industry arose. The steamship was introduced, rail and telegraph lines were laid, and the country appeared to be modernizing with amazing speed.

But the apparent modernity of the Second Empire was a façade. It was, for starters, still an empire, with all the anachronistic counts, dukes, and barons such a system implies. Second, the rail and telegraph lines were laid without much thought to building a real infrastructure, but merely as a convenience to the moneyed. Brazil was also still very much a patriarchal society, and although the crops were changing, the economics were not. It was still an agrarian society, with a minuscule planter class earning the bulk of the money and a mass of landless peasants and slaves providing the labor. The enormous income disparity that existed in the Second Empire is still a salient characteristic of Brazilian society.

Two other intertwined matters which would have a lasting effect on Brazilian culture were labor and immigration. The economic viability of slavery had been undermined by the elimination of the commerce in humans in 1850. Slaves who served in the military during the Paraguayan War were automatically freed, and in 1871 a law freed all offspring of slave women. But the actual decree abolishing the institution was not signed until 1888, marking the disappearance of slavery from the Western Hemisphere.

Brazil had been under severe pressure to abolish slavery for years, and the British were among the most intense proponents of abolition. Pedro II himself was opposed to slavery and freed his own slaves in 1840, but for obvious reasons never attempted to confront the planter class. The United States was also an important role model in this respect, and there was a growing sentiment among Brazilians themselves that slavery was not only a national humiliation but also no longer viable economically. By the 1870s there were more salaried workers than slaves working the coffee plantations, and the relatively small investment and responsibility for contract labor soon made it cheaper to hire workers than to own slaves. An obvious source of new labor was immigration, which began in the 1850s with between 2,000 and 20,000 immigrants a year. Although Brazil was not considered attractive because of its reputation as a country of enervating tropical climate, numerous entrepreneurs convinced immigrants to come. Eventually, the government got into the act and began sponsoring immigration, an activity some still regard as a racist attempt to "whiten" and thus improve the Brazilian population. In all, the number of European immigrants entering Brazil in the nineteenth century was roughly equal to the number of slaves freed by the Golden Law in 1888—between 600,000 and 1,000,000.

The end of slavery was only one of the reasons for the collapse of the empire, because of the hostility it engendered among the large landowners. There was also considerable influence, especially in the military, of the decidedly anti-imperial ideas of Positivism. And there had been a growing republican movement in the civilian population since the 1870s. Finally, Pedro II managed to alienate the Roman Catholic Church. Himself an agnostic (or "limited catholic" in the euphemism of the day), he refused to publish several papal decrees attacking the growing Masonic movement in Brazil. Although the church was never the political force it had been in Mexico or Peru, it had enough popular support to further draw support away from the monarchy. Thus, when Marechal Deodoro da Fonseca's troops surrounded the imperial headquarters in 1889 and demanded first the resignation of the Minister of War and second the abdication of the emperor, there was little reason for resistance, since there was no longer any organized support for the Empire.

THE FIRST REPUBLIC, 1889–1930

Military officers ran the government in the early years of the Republic, which were marked by considerable turmoil and even some pitched battles. Much of the turmoil resulted from conflicts between the branches of the military itself, although at least one clearly separatist movement also took place. The first civilian president was seated in 1894, and Brazil entered a prolonged period of peace and prosperity, marred by a series of messianic movements, one of them among the most bizarre conflicts in its history.

In 1897 a strange fanatic named Antônio Conselheiro gathered a substantial following of peasants in the arid *sertão* (backlands) of the northeastern state of Bahia. Conselheiro was another product of the myth of Sebastianism,[1] and though he clearly posed no immediate threat to the government, officials construed this millenarian movement to be a monarchist plot, since it refused to recognize the authority of the Republic. The governor of Bahia sent a police expedition to disband the movement, but the armed peasants, now numbering in the thousands, defeated the police. The governor appealed to the national government, which sent a large military force, which was also defeated. A second army expedition met the same fate. Finally, a third force of 6,000 men, armed with the latest weapons, including heavy artillery, stormed the village and blew it to rubble, a house at a time. All told, over 4,000 people died in the various battles. After a siege that lasted two years there were only two survivors.

Aside from the problems in the *sertão*, the period from the founding of the First Republic to the outset of World War I was a remarkably prosperous one for Brazil. European immigrants, mostly Italian, Portuguese, and German, were entering the country in unprecedented numbers, providing cheap and enthusiastic labor for agriculture. Immigration also began from Japan. By World War II, Japanese would constitute the fourth largest immigrant population in Brazil and the largest concentration of Japanese outside Japan. Coffee and cotton were the major export crops, but since the invention of vulcanization and the growth of the automobile industry, Brazil also experienced a rubber boom which was almost as excessive as the gold rush it had gone through in the previous century. In fact, Brazil enjoyed a virtual monopoly on the rubber market for a time, which created a class of rubber barons who enjoyed a lavish lifestyle. At the peak of the rubber boom an Englishman smuggled some seeds out of the country, planted them in Kew Gardens in London, and shipped the seedlings to Malaysia, where they were cultivated on plantations by coolie labor, which brought an abrupt end to the rubber cycle. A brief mini-boom occurred when the Malaysian supply was cut off during World War II, but the brief cycle that had brought such prosperity was really over by early in the century. Automobiles and streetcars were introduced, and a massive sanitation campaign finally made the beautiful city of Rio livable at last. Brazil also arbitrated its boundaries with its neighbors during this period, which finally brought to an end the squabbling that had simmered over a total of ten international frontiers.

During World War I, Brazil faced a difficult set of contradictions. The economy suffered a double blow when the war broke out, because the rapidly expanding textile industry, largely dependent on British capital, was suddenly isolated. In addition, the Central Powers had been, until hostilities began, a major client for Brazilian coffee. To make matters worse, Brazil had a large, unassimilated population of Germans in the South. But Brazilian dependency on British capital and its philosophical sympathy with France made any overt expression of sympathy with Germany unlikely. The number of recent Italian immigrants, these more assimilated, also worked against any such posture. Even more important was the size and importance of the Brazilian merchant marine, and when German submarines began sinking Brazilian vessels, the government protested and in 1917 declared war. To deal with the German communities, the government declared martial law in the South and eventually established primary schools in which Portuguese was the required language of instruction (German would henceforth be taught only as a foreign language).

The 1920s were turbulent in most of the Western world, but Brazil had an unusually hectic time preceding the crash of the world market in 1929. By now Brazil considered itself an emerging world power—at the very least it regarded itself as a major regional player. The upheavals of the Mexican Revolution and the Bolshevik Revolution had alerted the world to a whole new way of viewing the way power could be exercised in industrializing countries, and although the old oligarchy was still in control of Brazil, it viewed international cooperation as one way of making itself a player on the world scene. Brazil sent delegates to the Pan American Conference, had a representative on the Hague Court of Arbitration, and named a representative to the World Court, but when it attempted membership on the permanent council of the League of Nations and failed, it finally withdrew its membership.

More important in Brazilian society was a gradual shift of the power base. Unlike the open revolts in Mexico and Russia, what happened in Brazil was symptomatic but not yet an open confrontation. Labor was weak and poorly organized in Brazil, but in 1919 textile workers in Rio and São Paulo struck and were granted an eight-hour day. But in 1922, the Centennial of Brazilian

Independence, several events seemed to be pointing to a new realignment in the exercise of social and political power in Brazil. The first was the revolt of the *tenentes* ("lieutenants"), a group of junior officers sympathetic with the labor movement and clearly disillusioned with the rigid power structure of the military. Their quixotic stand at Copacabana Fort in Rio made no lasting change in either military or civilian affairs, but the affair did point to deep dissatisfaction within the ranks of one of the traditional bastions of power in Brazil. The second was the founding of the Partido Comunista do Brasil (Brazilian Communist Party), which, though neither large nor legal, was another arrow pointing to a reorientation of traditional politics. The Brazilian Communist Party was one of only two communist parties in Latin America whose roots were not in socialism but in anarchism, another point which was probably lost on the elites at the time. The third was an apparently apolitical event called the "Semana de Arte Moderna" (Modern Art Week), a kind of multimedia "happening" that took place in São Paulo in February. The esthetic and philosophical roots of this event are in the assorted "isms" usually associated with the revolutionizing of modern art, such as Cubism, Italian Futurism, and Surrealism, but there was in the movement a weirdly contradictory nativistic element that made it both modern and fiercely Brazilian. Most of the larger countries in Latin America had pockets of such rebels, usually isolated from the mainstream and often centered on a single artist or group of artists, but the repercussions of Modern Art Week soon took on national significance. In no other country in Latin America was such a clear division drawn between those who clung to the past ways of doing things and those who espoused the new. It was a true revolution, because it ambitioned a complete break with the past and a total remake of art in all its forms—not only in poetry and prose, but also in music, painting, sculpture—indeed in the way an artist or intellectual viewed what he did in the context of the world. That such a complete revolution was impossible seemed not to bother its participants, and though in some ways it was a futile exercise, it changed the way Brazilians thought about themselves.

The Vargas Regime, 1930–1945

Brazil was still a monoculture with most of its wealth based on the production of coffee. The textile industry was expanding rapidly, but with labor practices which might have been borrowed from a Dickens novel. In strictly political terms, it was an oligarchy dominated by two important states, São Paulo and Minas Gerais. The somewhat waggish name given to this tacit alliance was "café com leite," or "coffee with milk," since São Paulo was the leading producer of coffee and Minas the principal producer of milk products. This amusing-sounding but nevertheless unholy alliance was a kind of gentleman's agreement that the two states would alternate the presidency.

Such arrogance is, of course, an invitation to disaster, especially if the details of the agreement are not met, and the disaster was not long in coming. It came in the person of Getúlio Vargas, one of the unlikeliest strongmen in the history of Latin America. Vargas was an exception to the model because there have been so many Latin American dictators whose regimes were characterized by the shameless theatricality of bemedaled generals parading down avenues with their newly purchased tanks while the masses suffered the torture and repression such governments often utilize to maintain power. Vargas was nothing like that. Short and unprepossessing, he always wore civilian clothes (though he had had military training and presumably could have used any uniform he wished); he was a practical politician who really wanted to accomplish something other than remaining in power, and in all those senses he is in some ways the embodiment of the Brazilian notion that however much common history Latin Americans may share, Brazilians do things differently. Even their dictators are different.

Vargas came to power because the outgoing *paulista* president made the mistake of naming another *paulista* his successor (rather than a *mineiro*). Opposed by Vargas, he nevertheless won the election handily but was prevented from taking office when the vice-presidential candidate on the Vargas ticket was assassinated, whereupon the natural suspicions of the Brazilian public, and more notably the impatience of the army with all these politicians, coincided to make the change to a new regime an almost painless transition. If it was a coup, it was one the traditional politicians had asked for.

It is not an easy task to apply an ideological tag to the Vargas government. It is probably sufficient to say that his principal political opponents were the Communists on the left and the Integralists on the right, and that through most of his regime Vargas either did a balancing act between these poles or used one opposing group to thwart the other. Luís Carlos Prestes, the venerable leader of the Communist Party, who led the infamous and largely ineffectual Prestes column through the interior of Brazil during the 1920s, spent most of the 1930s in and out of jail. He was among the ideological fathers of a failed coup carried out by an umbrella group called the Aliança Nacional Libertadora (National Liberation Alliance) in 1934. Plínio Salgado, leader of the green-shirted Integralists, drew some of his political philosophy from Italian fascism, but the party never really articulated a clear national policy. Salgado was one of the three presidential candidates in the 1938 election. When Congress refused to extend the state of siege ordered in response to the 1935 rebellion, Vargas first released leftist rebels from prison and then used a fabricated plot to close Congress and declare the creation of the Estado Novo (New State), the closest he ever got to the personalist regimes of Spanish America.

Throughout his administration he played the same kind of precarious political ping-pong with other constituents. Although not really a champion of labor, he created a new Ministry of Labor out of part of the former Ministry of Agriculture and was at least partly responsible for the creation of labor unions he then used as political support. But he also made sure the big cotton manufacturers got their loans. During his tenure two constitutions were written, one in 1934 and one in 1937, but both documents were more expressions of wishful thinking than articulations of real national policy. Perhaps one of the most important things he did for the long run of the Brazilian economy was to initiate national programs for development rather than leaving everything in the control of foreign enterprises. One of the most important of these was the extraction of iron, which eventually grew into a native steel industry, allowing Brazil to produce such things as truck engines and eventually aircraft well before any other country in Latin America.

Vargas also continued the government program of valorization (essentially a government price guarantee) for the key products of coffee and rubber. The burning of vast quantities of coffee kept the internal market going, but since the foreign exchange lost in this process, which translated into reduced capacity to import finished goods, many light industries also sprang up in this period.

The legacy of the Vargas period is a complex one. The Vargas regime was one of somewhat dubious legitimacy—he was first head of a provisional government, then president elected not by popular vote but by the Congress, and in 1937 he simply seized power. Despite the marginality of his claim to popular acceptance, he was a populist who also had support in the elites. He transformed the political and social landscape of Brazil in fundamental ways.

Perhaps the most important part of his legacy is that at the end of his regime the coffee barons no longer held exclusive political sway in Brazil. The middle class and at least a part of the proletariat were enfranchised during his administration, as were at least some women (working women were given the vote in 1932). He also centralized power to a degree that not even Brazil's emperors had done, diluting the regional bossism that had always dominated the political scene and even absorbing state militias into the national military.

(In Brazil the equivalent of the Spanish term *cacique*, which refers to these regional strongmen, is *coronel*, which alludes to the real or assumed rank of a local politico in the local militia.)

Brazil's first important labor legislation was enacted during his administration, the economy was markedly more diversified than it had been, the urbanization of the population had at last begun, and the government had vastly increased its support of public education. Not all of these things took place merely because Vargas wanted them, however, and it is good to remember that he was also an authoritarian who censored the media and left as part of his legacy a secret police force not unlike that of traditional tyrannies.

The last part of his regime corresponds, of course, to World War II, in which Brazil played a more important role than any other nation in the region. Although Germany had become a major customer for Brazilian products, Brazil supported the Allies from the outset, and when five Brazilian ships were torpedoed in 1942, Brazil declared war on the Axis. Because of its location, Brazil became a major staging area for anti-submarine warfare, and many of what today are municipal airports in northern and northeastern Brazil were built as military bases with U.S. military help. Brazil also sent a contingent of its air force to Italy, and it was the only Latin American country to send combat infantry troops to the front, a contingent of 25,000 men which participated in fierce combat in the Italian campaign.[2]

The war also had an effect on the Brazilian economy. The Allies were starved for Brazilian goods, and the country exported unprecedented amounts of foodstuffs and raw materials during the war. There was also a demand for Brazilian textiles and even for manufactured goods, which Brazil exported in quantity for the first time. By the end of the war Brazil enjoyed the largest foreign exchange reserves in its history.

THE SECOND REPUBLIC, 1945–1954

The war in Europe was one of the major reasons for the downfall of Getúlio Vargas. It seemed illogical for Brazil to be spilling blood in Europe in the defense of democracy if there was no democracy at home, and Vargas was notified by both his enemies and supporters that it was time to try participatory democracy again. When Vargas abruptly fired the police chief of Rio de Janeiro and replaced him with his own disreputable brother, Benjamim, the army took it as a sign that Vargas would not relent, so it staged a preemptive coup and simply removed him from office. An interim president was named, and in the 1945 elections the former Minister of War, Eurico

Dutra, once a Vargas supporter, was elected. Vargas himself was elected senator in two states and congressman in six.

The 1945 election was the most open election to date in modern Brazilian history. Not only were previously illegal parties allowed to participate; the size of the electorate had grown immensely, not only because of population growth, but also because so many previously barred from participation were now enfranchised through Vargas' own legislation. Luís Carlos Prestes was elected a senator on the Communist ticket, and several other Communists were elected to the Congress. The new Congress was also a constitutional assembly, and in 1946 it promulgated a new charter for Brazil which enfranchised even more voters and strictly delineated separation of powers and precise limits on the executive, presumably to prevent another Vargas from abusing the office.

As in most Western countries, the beginning of the Cold War made many Brazilians slightly paranoid about the perceived Communist menace, and Dutra had been hostile to the left all along. Within two years he not only suppressed the increasingly frequent strikes instigated by the Communists but also again outlawed the Communist Party, and most of the prominent members of the party either went into hiding or left the country. The other major accomplishment of the Dutra regime was to spend all that foreign exchange earned during the war. Almost all the money went to import luxury goods. When the Dutra government realized that it had wasted all that foreign exchange, it resolved to impose rigid exchange controls on imports and exports, which had the almost immediate, and completely unintended, effect of stimulating Brazilian industrial development.

The next episode in Brazilian history seems so unlikely as to strain credibility, and to understand how it came about it is useful to comment at least briefly on a relatively new phenomenon in Brazil, the growth of political parties. Parties had long been, and in some ways still are, less ideological movements than personalistic constructs, operated by the leader or leaders of the group to rally enough popular support for a candidate so that he could get elected. Vargas was a master manipulator of both the personal and ideological elements of party politics. Elected senator by the PSD (Partido Social Democrático), he also stumped in favor of the PTB (Partido Trabalhista Brasileiro), the workers' party he himself founded. He also took advantage of Dutra's anti-Communism, because when the Communist Party was declared illegal it left a vacuum in the political left, which was immediately filled by the PTB. He also cleverly, if somewhat duplicitously, made significant changes in his speeches, depending on what he perceived to be the makeup of his audience and depending on what part of the country he was in. Essentially, what he did was to apply a coat of democratic varnish to the nationalist-developmentalist-social platform he had worked out in the authoritarian Estado Novo.

Vargas was not the first nor the only Brazilian politician to demonstrate uncanny skill in reinventing himself, but he is certainly one of the most notable. Installed by the military in 1930 and deposed by them in 1945, he returned in 1950 to win a decisive victory in the popular election and thus to become president of Brazil in no less than his fourth incarnation. We will probably never know what motivated Vargas to run in the 1950 election, but unquestionably one of the appeals was the lure of power. He nevertheless made little secret of his desire for revenge against those who had ousted him. But he faced a whole series of problems he had never had to deal with before, not the least of which was the fact that he had to operate within the rules of a constitution he had not had a hand in framing. Perhaps more serious was the emergence of new sectors of political power, which, though still nascent, would contribute to making his only term as a popularly elected president a tightrope act easily the equal of his previous political acrobatics. Urban labor, always one of his mainstays, was making continued demands, while the growing middle and industrial classes were adding a completely new spin on the political football. Many of the other problems were economic, but all were interrelated. He needed to combat the rising tide of inflation, provide leadership for the industrial future of the country, and satisfy increasingly strident political and economic factions in the process.

His greatest success during his elected presidency was probably the creation of Petrobrás, the national petroleum monopoly, but even this was dampened by the fact that Brazil was a relatively poor country in that particular resource, so it remained a political victory but not very notable in economic terms. He also instituted Electrobrás, which at least on paper would have been a similar monopoly of electrical energy. But on other matters he was again beset by fierce opposition from both left and right, and his probable involvement in attempting to silence at least one of his harshest critics, Carlos Lacerda, brought about his downfall. Lacerda, a prominent if somewhat noisy journalist, was attacked in an attempted assassination in 1954. He escaped, but his bodyguard, an Air Force major, was killed. There was sufficient evidence of presidential collusion to put the military on full alert, and it wasted no time in giving Vargas his walking papers for the last time. Vargas wrote a rambling and somewhat vindictive note of farewell addressed to the Brazilian people, and shot himself in the heart.

AFTER VARGAS, 1954–1964

A vice president and an acting president completed the term of office, and in 1955 the former governor of the state of Minas Gerais, Juscelino Kubitschek, was elected. Had it not been for a preemptive military intervention, he might never have taken office, since both he and his vice-presidential candidate, João (Jango) Goulart, were supported by the two parties Vargas had founded. Kubitschek ran on a platform of "fifty years of progress in five," and in many ways he was able to carry out this ambitious plan. He envisioned a Brazil no longer dependent on extractive foreign corporations with increased production in both industry and agriculture and a revamped infrastructure. He also envisioned a new capital for Brazil, one which would move at least some of the country's population away from the coast. The idea was at least 200 years old, but Kubitschek viewed it as more than a dream, and in 1960 he inaugurated Brasília, Brazil's third capital and the crowning achievement of his administration. It was a costly venture, since the site for the new capital was 600 miles inland, and everything from the concrete and steel to the doorknobs had to be flown in. The budgetary hemorrhaging it brought about made the administration resort to a ploy which Brazilian governments short of cash had used since the 1890s—it printed more money.

Despite the exorbitant cost of the new capital, the Brazilian economy underwent an unprecedented surge of growth during the 1950s, registering an almost 7% rate of growth annually, three times the rate of the rest of Latin America. In many ways Kubitschek was a political heir to Vargas, because his political solutions were based more on the ability to improvise than on any ideological posture. Brazilians were becoming almost rabidly nationalistic during this period, but Kubitschek quietly encouraged foreign investment. Like Vargas, he also suppressed both the right and the left, and he managed to keep labor on his side largely through the influence of his vice president, Goulart. Brasília was also useful to him as more than a dazzling national symbol of modernity. It diverted attention from the increasing social problems of Brazil, notably the worsening distribution of wealth, and the agrarian problem, about which his administration had almost no visible policy. Some of the other problems that Brasília provided a smokescreen for were the increasing population pressure, rapid urbanization, inadequate education and health care, as well as the one Brasília itself helped to cause, inflation. The amount of currency in circulation in Brazil more than tripled during his administration, and by the end of it Brazil was at loggerheads with both individual lending countries and the International Monetary Fund.

In part because of the inability or unwillingness of the Kubitschek administration to deal with the increasing social problems, the next president was one whose principal platform was a quirky kind of anti-government populism. Jânio Quadros was one of the least orthodox politicians in modern history. Nominated by the UDN (União Democrática Nacional or National Democratic Union), the party whose original reason for being was to elect anybody but Vargas, he nevertheless remained a maverick, making executive decisions virtually without consultation. His principal policies were an attack on inflation and bureaucratic inefficiency, two very real problems, but also problems which when attacked directly produced immediate casualties. Quadros also dissipated a lot of energy enacting trivial laws, such as one banning the wearing of bikinis and another outlawing the *lança-perfume*, little canisters of ether which revelers squirted at one another (and sniffed) during Carnival. But his worst mistake involved his so-called "independent" foreign policy, which led him to criticize the U.S.–sponsored Bay of Pigs invasion in Cuba. To make matters worse, he awarded the national medal, the Order of the Southern Cross, to Argentine-born revolutionary Che Guevara, a lapse of judgment that cost him a good deal of popular (and military) support.

Quadros became convinced that the country was ungovernable, because presidents could be elected by the progressive population of the industrialized South, while Congress remained in control of the reactionary rural elites. When the perennial gadfly Carlos Lacerda, now not a journalist but governor of the state of Guanabara, appeared on television to announce that Quadros was planning a coup, the president, apparently to precipitate a crisis that would resolve the problem of political inertia, abruptly resigned. His administration had lasted fewer than seven months.

According to the constitution, his successor would be his vice president, Jango Goulart, who by coincidence was on a trade mission to Red China at the time of the resignation. Goulart was widely held to be a radical leftist who, during his brief stint as Minister of Labor under Vargas, had made such scandalous proposals as a 100% increase in the minimum wage. The military considered him no less than a threat to national security, and many officers favored blocking him from office. But Congress and public opinion favored the constitutional process, so a compromise was reached—he would be allowed to assume the office of president, but the system of government would be changed from the presidential system to a parliamentary system, thus considerably diluting his power.

Stripped of the traditional powers of the presidency, Goulart spent his first two years in office attempting to establish his credentials as a respectable politician, not a leftist demagogue. He visited the United States, secured an aid package for the underdeveloped Northeast, and intervened in a strike to quell rumors of his radicalism. He gradually gained support, in part because most Brazilians recognized the need for a strong executive, and in 1963 he won a national plebiscite by an overwhelming margin and was restored to the presidency with full powers.

But even with his authority restored, Goulart faced the same problem as his immediate predecessor—the recalcitrance of Congress. This problem was exacerbated by the complete fragmentation of the political left, with his own brother-in-law Leonel Brizola, governor of Rio Grande do Sul, attempting to steal Goulart's political base by making ever more radical statements. He also faced major problems with the economy, now plagued by hyperinflation and debt. His principal political base was still organized labor, and he sought to broaden that base by catering to the military—not the officer corps, but the enlisted segment of the military. He proposed a modest land reform and a tax reform, neither of which was enacted, but each of which cost him the possible support of the rural elites (land) and the middle class (taxes). Early in 1964 he submitted a package of proposed legislation which included the vote for illiterates, legalization of the Communist Party, and expropriation of lands abutting highways and railroads. In March he publicly signed a decree including some of these reforms, and he then announced that he sought "basic reforms," a promise he reiterated to the enlisted men at a Navy and Marines meeting that had been prohibited by the Minister of the Navy. On March 30 he made a similar speech, this one televised, to the Military Police Sergeants Association in Rio.

The military had been waiting in the wings to see if Goulart would prove himself to be a radical, and this seemed proof enough; on March 31 troops marched on Rio from Minas Gerais. The troops sent from Rio to stop them joined them instead. After vainly waiting for some public show of support, Goulart fled the country on April 4.

MILITARY GOVERNMENT, 1964–1985

One of the reasons that Brazil's two emperors were able to perform the balancing act necessary to keep the government stable in contrast to the generalized chaos which prevailed in the Spanish American Republics in the nineteenth century was a provision in the 1824 Constitution granting to the emperor the special privilege of moderating power. The moderating power made it appear that the government consisted of four, not three, branches, because in addition to the executive, the legislative, and the judiciary, the moderating power was in a sense a fourth division of the government. Since, however, it resided in the monarch, it gave Brazil's emperors extraordinary authority. The emperor could dissolve the legislature, veto legislation, appoint provincial presidents, and even name ministers and bishops.

Although the military became a new major player in Brazil's political system at the end of the Paraguayan War, it was not until it acted to oust Pedro II that it assumed the mantle of principal arbiter of national government, when the military in essence usurped the moderating power, and thenceforth even considered itself the rightful and sole possessor of this remarkable privilege. Military men constituted the national government early in the First Republic, and in the twentieth century the military intervened directly to change the course of government in 1930, 1945, 1954, 1955, and 1961, but usually in ways in which a generous view would make the intervention appear to be intended as the guarantor of the constitutional process, or at least undertaken in the best interests of the body politic. In 1964 no such façade was even proposed. The civilians had failed to govern the country, and it was up to the military to put things right.

Brazil's next five presidents were all generals, and although this suggests a certain sameness, there was a constant tension within the officer corps between the so-called *linha dura*, or "hard line," and a more moderate faction. But even seemingly moderate presidents, such as Costa e Silva, were often forced by the officers of the hard line to adopt extreme positions. The military governments can be characterized as extremely authoritarian regimes which ruled by decree, repressed dissent, and which favored economic stability over development. Although a few years of the dictatorship were dubbed by the generals the "economic miracle," they were in fact a period in which the Gross National Product grew at a high rate without having any fundamental positive effect on any other sector of the economy, and which provided no benefits whatsoever for the average Brazilian. The military governments were also rabidly anti-Communist and pro-American.

The first dictator was Humberto de Alencar Castelo Branco (1964–1967), a hard-line general whose regime was recognized by the Johnson administration within hours of his approval by the Brazilian Congress. Castelo Branco initiated the practice of government by fiat by passing the First Institutional Act, which granted vast powers to the executive, including the right to declare a state of siege and the curious Brazilian institution of *cassação*, which is the power to exclude individuals from all political activity (including voting and running for office) for a period of 10 years. Castelo Branco proved his contempt for representative government by applying this despotic statute to former presidents Kubitschek, Quadros, and Goulart, firing seven governors and several thousand government employees, and ousting a number of military officers. He vastly increased the military budget (and decreased the education budget), created the Serviço Nacional de Informação (National Information Service, a typically inappropriate euphemism for a secret police apparatus), and disbanded the Peasant Leagues and the National Student Union. During his regime the Second and Third Institutional Acts were also passed, dissolving all political parties, making elections of the president, vice president, governors, and mayors indirect. To replace the parties, the government created two new ones, the Aliança Renovadora Nacional (National Renovating Alliance, or Arena) and the Movimento Democrático Brasileiro (Brazilian Democratic Union, or Modebras). A new constitution, also blatantly authoritarian, was also passed in 1967. In fact, the Castelo Branco government spent so much effort on dismantling any body of potential dissent that it did little or nothing for the economy, and by the end of his term the single accomplishment in this arena was that Brazil's chronic inflation was once again held in check.

Castelo Branco's hand-picked successor was Marshall (the equivalent of a five-star general) Artur da Costa e Silva. Costa e Silva (1967–1969) was a more bland and indecisive president, and he seemed more disposed to tolerate the existence of a political left and to entertain the idea of industrialization. But numerous public protests and several strikes forced him to suppress dissent, and in 1968 he passed down the infamous Fifth Institutional Act, which gave the president dictatorial powers, shut down both the Congress and the state legislatures, imposed censorship, and suspended the right of habeas corpus. Surely one of the most Machiavellian measures in Brazilian history, it probably encouraged rather than discouraged dissent, since anyone in opposition to the government was made to feel that the only alternatives were either complete submission or open revolt. And though they were not very numerous, there were those who revolted. They were mostly urban guerrillas, who robbed banks to finance their activities and stole weapons from military facilities. Their biggest coup was the kidnapping of U.S. Ambassador Charles Burke Elbrick in September of 1969. He was only released when their manifesto was read on television and 15 political prisoners were flown to Mexico.

Costa e Silva suffered a stroke in 1969 and was shortly replaced by Emílio Garrastazu Médici (1969–1974), a former head of the secret police. The generals decided that their policies, which consisted largely of propaganda, repression, torture, and censorship, were all working, and little was done during his administration to abate the machinery of brutality. It was during the Médici administration, in fact, that the "economic miracle," which looked so good on paper but produced little of lasting value, took place, so the military could congratulate itself that it was not only suppressing Communism but also making the economy work. Although the economy was growing, it was fueled not by internal growth but by foreign loans, which meant that the generals had figured out how to make somebody else pay for the improved economy. The presumed euphoria of this successful government led the government to the outlandish extreme of governing for a time by *secret* decree, which meant that citizens could be arrested and prosecuted for violating laws that had never been made public. But guerrillas were still active, especially in the larger cities, and in retaliation (and with the tacit approval of the government) the infamous "death squads," composed largely of off-duty policemen and military, summarily executed suspected subversives.

Médici selected as his successor Ernesto Geisel, who had once been president of Petrobrás. Geisel (1974–1979) almost immediately announced a policy of *distensão*, a gradual relaxation of authoritarian government. Despite this supposed easing of repression, he closed Congress for two weeks in 1977 and issued his "April package," a set of regulations which further weakened Congress and guaranteed the continued dominance of Arena. He did ease up on both censorship and torture, but his administration continued to be authoritarian and politically exclusive. During his administration, however, there was increasing pressure from a number of groups, some of them well-organized, for a return to democracy. The Roman Catholic Church, labor unions, students, and even businessmen began pressuring the government for a more just social and economic system. In 1978, Geisel finally abolished the hated Fifth Institutional Act, which had importance at least symbolically. More importantly, he did not consult his fellow officers on the matter of his successor, and in 1979 he selected General João Baptista Figueiredo to succeed him. Figueiredo (1979–1985) was little known and was not even sufficiently high in rank to be president (he was promoted before his inauguration), and in one of his first statements as president he issued a promise to return Brazil to democracy. He did declare a general amnesty in 1979, which not only pardoned most former political prisoners but had the long-term effect of forgiving their torturers as well. But his concept of democracy was clearly not one widely shared. Popular unrest increased dramatically during his term, however—there were more than 400 strikes in 1979 alone—and by 1983 a constitutional amendment providing for direct elections for the presidency had touched a nerve in the public mind, producing the largest political rallies in the country's history. He also faced severe economic problems—by 1981 the Gross Domestic Product declined for the first time since 1942—and the chronic reliance on debt to finance the government had reached crisis proportions. In that same year a scandal involving the military also contributed to the erosion of popular support. An army captain and a sergeant had gone to a Rio theater evidently to plant a bomb to disrupt a concert supporting leftist causes. The bomb exploded in the car, killing the sergeant and wounding the captain gravely. The government's high-handed coverup did little to convince the public that the right was again out of control. Several other financial scandals further tarnished the government's image.

Figueiredo also undertook a risky political reform by dissolving the artificial two-party system and allowing new parties to form. With the economy in a shambles and this slight liberalization of the political process, the entire apparatus of authoritarian military rule came to an end. In the 1985 elections the official candidate of the party was so unpopular that the party itself fell apart, and Brazil elected its first civilian president in over two decades, Tancredo Neves, former governor of Minas Gerais.

AFTER THE GENERALS, 1985–

In a cruel turn of fate, Tancredo Neves, popular to the point of adoration, was forced to undergo a serious surgical procedure the night before his inauguration. He died in less than 40 days, leaving his vice president, a compromise candidate who had somehow managed to avoid running afoul of the military, to complete his term.

The new president, José Sarney, faced an overwhelming task. To his credit, he legalized formerly illegal parties, passed legislation allowing direct presidential elections, and announced a daring new economic plan called the *plano cruzado* ("cruzado plan," the cruzado being the name of the new currency it created). This plan, like many similar ones in the past few decades, was an attempt to revivify the economy by freezing prices and undertaking other drastic measures to shore up confidence in the currency. Like most such plans the cruzado plan failed, in part because Brazilians have such an inflationary mentality that when prices were frozen they immediately went on a spending binge, which itself undermined most of the other provisions of the measure. Americans have difficulty understanding this mentality because we have never undergone inflation of the Brazilian magnitude. Suffice it to say that in most such plans the first operation is the removal of the last three zeros in the old currency, the equivalent of transforming $5,000 into $5 overnight.

Sarney failed in his economic plan, but a new constitution was drawn in his administration and went into effect in 1988. He also failed to bring widespread corruption under control, and by 1989 his party was fragmented and politically impotent.

Proof of the general unraveling in the political process came in the 1989 elections, in which an astonishing 22 parties nominated candidates, including a popular television star with no political experience. The slate included the loser in the 1985 election, the popular leader of the PT (Partido Trabalhista, or Workers' Party), Luís Inácio da Silva, or "Lula," who had become a national figure in the metalworkers' strikes in the Figueiredo administration. He was opposed by a newcomer, the photogenic governor of the tiny northeastern state of Alagoas, Fernando Collor de Melo. Although television had become an increasingly important medium in Brazilian politics, this is widely thought to be the first election which was decided by it. The smooth Collor, running on a platform to "hunt down the *marajás*" ("maharajahs," a Brazilian term for public servants who earn lavish salaries for little or no work), won the election in the second round. His administration was almost immediately mired in scandal, and it soon appeared that both he and his wife were engaged in skimming public funds. He was impeached in 1992 and replaced by his vice president, Itamar Franco. Collor now lives in a posh house in Miami. Ironically, one other factor that led many Brazilians to vote for him was that he was already rich and thus presumably didn't need to steal. Although this was a lamentable episode for Brazil, it was the first time in the history of Latin America that a sitting president had been removed from office by constitutional means, an indication of a new political maturity.

As for Itamar Franco, he will probably be best remembered for naming as Finance Minister a sociologist and professor, Fernando Enrique Cardoso, who had been exiled during the military dictatorship and whose books were banned by them. He was also stripped of his political rights. When the military left, he ran for governor of São Paulo and lost to the enigmatic Jânio Quadros. One of the founders of the PSDB (Partido da Social Democracia Brasileira, or Brazilian Party of Social Democracy), Cardoso devised the Plano Real, yet another in the long line of currency reforms attempted in the past decades, but this one actually worked, and Cardoso became a national hero almost overnight. In the 1995 elections he was a logical candidate for president, running against the unflagging Lula, and won handily. His administration has taken on the daunting task of privatizing many of the numerous state-owned enterprises that have proliferated in the last three decades, including one of the largest mining corporations in the world, the Companhia Vale do Rio Doce, which in the face of widespread protest was sold in 1997. The Plano Real continued to hold inflation in check through 2002. Although the *real* no longer trades at par with the U.S. dollar (as of this writing it is fluctuating between 3.0 and 4.0), the economic stability that Brazil has experienced since 1995 is unprecedented in recent times. In 1997 the Brazilian Congress passed an amendment allowing Cardoso to succeed himself, and he was re-elected in 1998. The 2002 elections brought in a socialist president, Luis Inácio Lula da Silva ("Lula"), one of the founders of the Partido de Trabalhadores (Workers' Party).

NOTES

1. Sebastianism is described in Chapter 5.

2. Not as widely known as the infantry which comprised the FEB (Força Expedicionária Brasileira, or Brazilian Expeditionary Force) was the squadron of Brazilian fighter pilots known as "Senta a Pua" ("Give 'em Hell"). This contingent of 44 volunteer pilots flew American P-47s and was responsible for the destruction of some 85% of the Axis munitions and 70% of their vehicles in the Po River Valley in 1944. A Brazilian plane also sank at least one German U-boat off the Brazilian coast.

5

Religion

Lots of religion, young man. As for me, I never miss a chance. I drink
water from any river.

—Riobaldo, narrator of João Guimarães Rosa's
The Devil to Pay in the Backlands, p. 10

ROMAN CATHOLICISM

BRAZIL HAS THE world's largest Roman Catholic population and ranks as
the second largest Christian country in the world.[1] But Brazilian nonchalance
touches every institution in the country, and religion is no exception. Historically, the institutional Church was never the monolithic mainstay of
power it became in many other Latin American countries. Although six Jesuit
priests accompanied the first royal Portuguese mission to Brazil in 1549, and
were the caretakers of most of the education during the colonial period, they
were dominant in education but never in politics. Various other orders, including the Franciscans and Dominicans, competed for control of both territory and Indians. The secular Church was always somewhat wary about the
Jesuits, and when the Jesuits were finally expelled from Brazil in 1759, it
seemed a propitious time for the secular Church to replace the regular (monastic) orders with secular clergy, but that did not in fact take place. During
the entire colonial period, Brazilian Catholics demonstrated a tolerance and
flexibility almost unknown in the Spanish colonies. The few secular priests
there were often had female companions and children and were tolerant of

both Indian and African rituals, which gave Catholicism a uniquely Brazilian character.

The Catholic Church remained relatively weak up until independence in 1822, and during the reign of Pedro II (1840–1889) it was weakened further when he refused to publish a papal encyclical denouncing the Masonic Order. When some Brazilian bishops insisted on expelling Masons from their ranks, the government pressed criminal charges. Pedro II's government finally reached a compromise with the Vatican, but the Church, already weak, was further enfeebled by these trials. Freedom of religion was written into the constitution of the First Republic in 1891, though given the tradition of tolerance of other faiths it hardly seemed necessary.

Apart from its weakness as a national institution, the Catholic Church has not enjoyed great influence at the local level. Catholic clergymen have always been in short supply in Brazil, and many Brazilians who consider themselves Catholic have had little or no contact with the clergy, especially in rural areas. Traveling priests who perform mass marriages of couples who have lived together for years were common until very recently. Almost half the Catholic clergy in Brazil are foreign-born, which in the interior results in an automatic reduction of respect. What few clergymen there are receive inadequate remuneration for their services, so it is not uncommon for priests to enter into commerce or farming as a sideline, which certainly diminishes whatever special status they might otherwise enjoy.

The Catholic tradition nevertheless persists in various forms. Politically, one proof of that has been in the absence of divorce in Brazil until very recently. The Church led organized resistance against legislative attempts to legalize divorce in 1900 and 1952, and it was not until 1977 that Brazilian politicians finally enacted a divorce law. Prior to that date the only recourse unhappy couples had was the *desquite*, a form of legal separation that nevertheless prohibited remarriage.[2]

The Church was also very active in the twentieth century in a variety of activities stemming from the movement called Christian Base Communities, which began in the 1960s. Basically it was a move away from the traditional fatalism of Catholicism and toward a more active social role for the Church; its most prominent leaders were Archbishop Hélder Câmara and Cardinal Paulo Evaristo Arns. Both were outspoken critics of the social and political policies of the military government of 1964–1985 and both were deeply involved in popular and youth movements dedicated to the reform of Brazil's archaic land tenure system and social structure. The military called them subversives, and even the conservative wing of the Church was critical of their activities. They are emblematic figures in that they show an important tendency in some sectors of the Church to respond to mundane problems and representative in that they demonstrate the difficulty in making generalizations about the position of the Church.

This kind of activism is new and even frightening to many Brazilian Catholics, to whom Catholicism is a cultural presence but not a doctrine. More typical of this kind of religion are those who go to festivals with Catholic regalia, observe holy days, and participate in the rites of the Church. Such participation is often a manifestation of what is called "folk Catholicism," in which the rituals and costumes appear Catholic enough but in which doctrine and piety have little importance. The Brazilian saying that a man needs to go to church three times in his life—to be baptized, to marry, and to die—is merely one indication of the rather cavalier attitude Brazilians have about religion.

JUDAISM AND EASTERN RELIGIONS

Although most Portuguese colonists were Roman Catholics, Jews and "New Christians" (converted or nominally converted Jews) were important in Brazil from the first days of colonization. Fernando de Noronha (who discovered the island named after him) arrived in 1503, and in Cabral's 1549 expedition there was a Jewish interpreter, Gaspar de Lemos. It is estimated that by the end of the sixteenth century some 200 sugar plantations in Brazil were owned by Jews or crypto-Jews.

The Portuguese Inquisition, though considered milder than its notorious Spanish counterpart, was responsible for forcing the conversion of Jews to Christianity, and Jews were periodically expelled or repressed throughout the colonial period. Jews enjoyed two periods of reprieve with the Dutch invasions of 1624 and 1630. The first synagogue in Brazil was founded in Recife in 1642. When the Portuguese reconquered Recife in 1654 the Inquisition continued the repression until 1773, when the Marquis of Pombal abolished the distinction between "old" and "new" Christians.

Jews were also important in the arts. An important New Christian writer was Ambrósio Fernandes Brandão (158?–162?), author of *Dialogues of the Great Things of Brazil* (1618). The Inquisition also persecuted and finally burned at the stake another prominent writer of the colonial period, the dramatist Antônio José da Silva (1705–1739), who was (probably erroneously) nicknamed "The Jew."

Brazil also received numerous Jewish immigrants in the latter part of the nineteenth century, mostly from the Middle East, Russia, and Poland. Starting in the 1930s, many German Jews also immigrated to Brazil. Most of the

Jewish population in Brazil is found either in the larger urban centers or in Rio Grande do Sul, home of one of Brazil's most prominent Jewish writers of fiction, Moacyr Scliar (b. 1937). Jews have suffered some anti-Semitism, but it seems to have abated since Brazilian Jews have followed the national tendency toward syncretism, especially with Afro-Brazilian religions. Today Brazil has both Sephardic and Ashkenazi synagogues and has the second-largest Jewish population in South America, numbering about 250,000. Only Argentina has a larger Jewish population.

There are also about a half million Muslims in Brazil, most of them from the former Ottoman Empire, which collapsed after World War I. The umbrella term used in Brazil for these immigrants is *turco* ("Turk"), which is misleading geographically because most are from any Levantine country (Turkey, plus Syria, Lebanon, Egypt, Iran, etc.) and religiously, because a number of these immigrants are Maronite Christians from Lebanon. In some cities in Brazil (Ilhéus, in southern Bahia, for example) the *turcos* are such an important part of the population that signs on stores appear in both Portuguese and Arabic.

Beginning with Japanese immigration to Brazil, there are also perhaps another half million practitioners of Oriental religions, including Buddhism and Shintoism.

CANDOMBLÉ

During the lengthy period of history in which rival orders and various factions within the Church vied for the souls of the Indians, another phenomenon that would forever change the face of religion in Brazil was quietly developing. The Portuguese slave trade in Brazil began as a solution to the labor shortage caused by the decimation of the native populations, but it was not long before African slaves outnumbered their enslavers, and Brazilian culture became increasingly Africanized until the trade was abolished in the 1850s. Although the Portuguese consciously mixed ethnic and linguistic groups of Africans in an attempt to prevent any kind of cultural cohesion among the slaves, a variety of religious practices of African origin survived. Originally confined largely to the northeast coast (where most slaves entered Brazil and where the population of African origin is highest), these rituals have overspread the entire country, and today constitute a sort of second dominant religion in Brazil. These rituals are called *candomblé* in Bahia, *xangô* in Pernambuco, *macumba* in Rio de Janeiro, and *batuque* in Pará. The most traditional ones are found in Bahia, where ritual songs are still sung in the Yoruba language. Some also have part of their rituals sung in Bantu lan-

Nosso Senhor de Bonfim, a popular house of worship and site of *candomblé* ceremonies, Salvador. (Author photo)

guages, and some use little or no African language but nevertheless derive from the same tradition. There is even a form called *candomblé caboclo*, which incorporates indigenous deities and rituals. Most forms of *candomblé* are similar to the *santería* practiced in Cuba, and even the names of the deities, called *orixás*, are nearly identical. Whatever shape these religious manifestations take, they are so pervasive on a national level that the term "cult," which is often used in reference to them, is inappropriate.

Each *candomblé* has a *terreiro*, a kind of square which is the equivalent of a churchyard, and most have a central building which is either an old house or a building created specifically for the rituals. The most traditional *candomblés* are matriarchies, where the *mãe de santo* ("saint's mother") presides over all the rituals. Some of the less traditional ones have males (*pais de santo*) as priests.

The rituals are extremely complex and follow a strict ceremonial calendar. Initiates, who will eventually "receive" the saints, go through elaborate periods of instruction and can only do so after extensive preparations have been made. Each deity has particular areas of influence, favorite colors, preferred beverages and foods, and a specific symbolic representation. Most are syncretized with Catholic saints of similar attributes. For example, Ogun, god of the hunt, is Saint Anthony, Iansã is Saint Barbara, and Xangô is Saint Peter. This double-naming might have originally allowed practitioners to pray to an African saint when it appeared they were praying to a Catholic one, but the double identities are now so ingrained that most members of these religions no longer separate the two. In fact, and this is the truly remarkable feature of these African religions, the vast majority of the faithful consider themselves to be good Catholics.

Terreiros have traditionally had at least one sponsor, or *ogan*, generally a person of sufficient wealth and prestige to be useful to the faithful financially or politically (by influencing the police not to interfere). Among the better-known *ogãs* are Donald Pierson and Artur Ramos, both anthropologists who performed the function while studying the rituals, as well as Jorge Amado (1912–2001), Brazil's most famous novelist.

The police interference alluded to is no longer a problem, but in the early twentieth century, *terreiros* were routinely targets of police harassment. Today *candomblé* is not only tolerated but celebrated, surely one of the reasons for its existence over such a large part of Brazil's geography.

SPIRITUALISM AND *UMBANDA*

Spiritualism arose in Brazil around 1865, and by 1884 there was a national organization of spiritualists called the Federação Espírita Brasileira (Brazilian Spiritualist Federation). Loosely based on the writings of the pseudonymous French writer Allan Kardek (Hippolyte Léon Denizard Rivail), it involves communication with the dead, though in Brazil the movement is diverse and seems to vary in doctrine along class lines. Middle-class and upper-class spiritualists in Brazil are more interested in extrasensory perception, while members of lower classes tend to base their practices on the study of Kardek's work and holding seances. Some spiritualists mix Kardecismo and Christianity. Yet another group has intermingled spiritualist doctrines with African and Indian ritual, producing yet another blend (called *Umbanda*) typical of Brazilian society. Although it lacks cohesion, spiritualism is so popular in Brazil that, like Catholicism, it ranks number one in the world in the number of adherents.

Although most spiritualists reject much of Catholic doctrine (heaven and hell, the divinity of Christ, the Trinity) as superstition, it is impossible to separate spiritualist doctrines completely from Roman Catholicism. Historically, in fact, spiritualism, particularly *Umbanda*, seems to have arisen at least in part because of the suppression and persecution of followers of *macumba* and *candomblé*. In this historical context, it can be seen as a way of "whitening" or Europeanizing traditional African religions. Many *Umbanda* groups base their rituals on evocations of Indian and African spirits, specifically the *caboclo* (Indigenous spirit) or the *preto velho* ("old black," or African spirit), though even on this point there is considerable divergence, because there are at least three major subdivisions of *Umbanda* doctrine—"pure," "black," and "national."

It is natural to wonder why such an eclectic religion would enjoy such popularity, but Brazilian society is a fluid and eclectic one, and on reflection it may seem a perfectly logical manifestation of the kind of free-wheeling spirit of the culture. In addition, Brazilians are drawn to such religions at least in part because traditional Catholicism seems to offer unsatisfactory answers in a society in flux. With its emphasis on the eternal, on life *after* death, and with a doctrine being advocated by a largely foreign priesthood, Catholicism seems to many Brazilians to offer few answers to more immediate concerns. A spiritualist can request a consultation from his priest on anything from a failing business venture to a problematic amorous relationship and come away with what many find satisfactory advice. The perceived failure of Catholicism to respond to such mundane problems is also one of the reasons Brazilians are attracted in ever larger numbers to other religious doctrines. It is, nevertheless, always good to remember that "Brazilians are Catholics," which may lend a special flavor even to religions of sectarian narrowness.

PROTESTANTISM

Protestantism had its origins in Brazil during the brief incursions of the French and Dutch during the colonial period, but its modern roots date from 1810, when the Brazilian government permitted the limited practice of Episcopalianism. Later in the century German immigration resulted in the arrival of large numbers of Lutherans in Brazil. At the same time the Germans were arriving, numerous missionary groups, mostly from the United States, began active work in Brazil. The first of these were Congregationalists, Presbyterians, and Methodists. Later groups include Baptists, Pentacostalists, Seventh Day Adventists, Mormons, Jehova's Witnesses, and Christian Scientists. Some of the earlier arrivals enjoyed considerable success in Brazil—there are, for example, five distinct Presbyterian branches in Brazil—but some of the more recent arrivals, notably the Pentacostalists, have enjoyed huge success. The Unification Church and Hare Krishna have also been established.

Protestantism has literally exploded in Brazil in the last few decades. There were probably only 40,000 in 1900, but by 1940 there were a million, and a decade later that number had almost doubled. Given the great accomplishments of many of these churches, especially the Pentecostals, by 2000 more than 15% of the Brazilian population belonged to a Protestant denomination. Today the fastest growing church in Brazil is the Universal do Reino de Deus (Universal Church of the Kingdom of God), which was founded by Edir Macedo in 1977 and which already has over two million members. A neo-Pentecostal movement, it emphasizes exorcism and cures and claims that success and happiness are attainable on earth.

The notion that happiness is attainable in this life is certainly one of the strong appeals of many Protestant denominations. Protestants also generally refrain from smoking and drinking, attend Church regularly, and contribute to the works of the Church. Many are also actively involved in education. Perhaps the puritanism involved in some Protestant denominations has appeal to Brazilians because they think that if they live a life of sobriety they will be less likely to incur debt, their children will be educated better, and they will not have to defer to an afterlife the fruits of their labors.

MESSIANISM

Another thread that is interwoven into the fabric of the Brazilian religious experience is messianism: the belief in a Second Coming or in the return of a savior who will bring about some version of the earthly paradise. Luso-Brazilian culture has a unique variety of messianic belief called Sebastianism, which has been at least marginally important in a number of messianic movements in Brazil. Sebastianism gets its name from King Sebastião of Portugal (1557–1578), who at the age of 20 embarked on a quixotic adventure to take Morocco from the Moors. With a mixed contingent of Portuguese troops and European mercenaries, Sebastião landed a force of about 20,000. The Moroccans at first refused to engage in battle, and by the time they did the invading troops were depleted by heat and thirst. The young king perished in the battle at Alcácer Kebir. But no one could recall having seen him die, and his body was never found, which gave rise to the legend in both Portugal and Spain that one day when things seemed darkest the young king would return to inaugurate a new utopia for his people. The political consequences of this battle initiated the "Babylonian Captivity," which had Spanish monarchs on the Portuguese throne and which allowed the Portuguese to cross the imaginary Tordesillas Line. The religious consequences have been many and varied, but three of the most famous movements connected to Sebastianism offer some insight into the importance of this folk Catholic belief.

Pedra Bonita. In 1836 in central Pernambuco a mestizo named João Santos claimed that two 100-foot rock monoliths marked the location of an enchanted country he named the New Jerusalem of King Sebastião. He attracted such a following that Church authorities had him removed, but two years later his brother-in-law João Ferreira took over the leadership of the group, leading his followers in prayer, dance, and, reportedly, sexual promiscuity. The self-proclaimed "king" made lavish promises about the new kingdom and finally convinced his followers that the only way to guarantee its appearance was through sacrifice. Thirty children, twenty-three adults, and fourteen dogs were either hurled off the stones or stabbed to death. Troops were finally sent to restore order, and the Sebastianists, believing this to be a signal of the restoration of the kingdom, attacked. Twenty-two were killed, including Ferreira.

The New Jerusalem of Antônio Conselheiro. In the 1870s, Antônio Maciel, known as "the Counselor," gathered a flock of dispossessed peasants in the town of Canudos in the interior of Bahia. Conselheiro lived on alms and preached sermons about the end of the world, and when the Republic was proclaimed and civil marriage became a reality, he became identified as a danger to the state. In fact, he probably was, because one of the targets of his preachings was the taxes the new government was levying. Although it is now conceded that Conselheiro was a sincere if misguided mystic, his movement became the target of state and eventually federal attention. When he resisted two attacks by state troops, a third and eventually a fourth expedition were sent against his stronghold, which was at last reduced to rubble.

Padre Cícero and His New Jerusalem. In the 1870s a young priest, Cícero Romão Batista, began working in the municipality of Juazeiro in southern Ceará. At first noted because of his skill at directing public works to ameliorate the ravages of drought, he also gained the reputation of local saint. In 1890 a communion wafer reportedly turned into blood in the mouth of a female parishioner, and he was soon viewed as a performer of miracles. Although the ecclesiastical commission charged with determining the veracity of the miracle did not decide in his favor, many members of the commission began to suffer assorted ailments, including blindness, which only reinforced Cícero's power. He eventually became embroiled in a complex political battle involving the clan that ruled Ceará and the federal government. His "army," which included some of the most notorious bandits of the time, finally marched on the state capital, Fortaleza, in 1914 and overthrew the state government. Padre Cícero is still regarded as a saint (and still regarded as alive) by his legions of followers, and Juazeiro is the site of an annual pilgrimage.

All of this makes the question of religion a perplexing one. Statistically, the chances that a given Brazilian is a Roman Catholic are very high, but whether he or she is a traditional conservative or a folk Catholic or socially liberal is unpredictable. The odds are also in favor of that same Catholic belonging to a *candomblé* or a Spiritist or *Umbanda* center. There is also a lesser but reasonable chance that a Brazilian might be some kind of Protestant, or a Buddhist or a Muslim or a Jew, and whatever faith is involved, if there is a faith, that an individual may have chosen to mix two or more of those elements into the curious but fascinating medley that characterizes religion in Brazil today.

Notes

1. Russell Ash, *The Top 10 of Everything 2002* (New York: DK Publishing, 2001).

2. The strange limbo created by the lack of legal divorce in Brazil gave rise to a cottage industry in neighboring Uruguay. Wealthy Brazilians would travel to Montevideo, much as Americans go to Reno, for a quick divorce. Although not recognized as legal either by Church or civil law, Brazilians with an Uruguayan divorce often remarried.

6

Social Customs

Margo Milleret

An American family arrives on a beautiful deserted Brazilian beach to
camp. Later that afternoon a Brazilian family arrives to camp at the same
beach.
Q: Where does the Brazilian family put their tent?
A: Right next to the Americans.
—joke told by an expatriate American working in Brazil

WHILE AMERICANS HERALD rugged individualism, self-reliance, and solitude
as important components of a national identity, Brazilians favor cooperation,
interdependence, and connectedness. "Life is only worth living in community" might be their motto, except that the obviousness of the statement
would make it unnecessary. Brazilians organize their lives around and about
others, maintain a high level of social involvement, and consider personal
relations of primary importance in all human interactions. In fact, being with
others is so important that they are rarely alone and perceive the desire to be
alone as a sign of depression or unhappiness.

Parentela identifies the central network of associations based on the extended family from which all other associations radiate. The image of the
large Brazilian family gathered at Sunday table is not as common as it used
to be, but it lives in the memories of Brazilians who recall their childhood
in the company of *parentela*, that is, first and second cousins, aunts, uncles,
grandparents, godparents, and servants. The importance of close extended
family connections cannot be overstated—not only because of the affection

and emotional support offered by families, but also because all other aspects of life are enhanced by the knowledge and influence of family members. From their earliest days, children build a sense of identity within a family group but they also are exposed to group identity outside the home. For example, in school a student belongs to a *turma* (class). In adulthood a *turma* becomes a *panelinha*, the term that identifies those who share and promote their common interests. (The term also can be used in a pejorative sense to describe groups whose exclusivity is detrimental to others.)

Social life in extended family groups provides both benefits and obligations. On the benefit side there is never a need to worry about having something to do. Every weekend and holiday, members gather together for at least food and drink. Events are intergenerational, conversation is lively and often passionate, food and drink are abundant, and no one worries about tomorrow. *Parentela* members help each other with personal problems, financial or work issues, and official bureaucracy. They protect and support each other with fierce loyalty. A member is obligated to try to perform all favors, to participate in the social life of the group, and to be available to the others at all times. *Parentela* is similar in some ways to the more specialized networks of churches, food cooperatives, country clubs, social clubs, and support groups in the United States.

No one in Brazil would ever make the claim of being "self-made," since everyone recognizes the need for connections to others in order to do anything. Trying to act alone for one's own benefit is folly, not only because of the intricacy of rules and regulations that govern life, but also because a group provides identity and status. Brazilian society divides along class and status lines. Therefore, without the identity and status of a group one cannot be judged to be worthy of friendship, business relations, political office, or marriage. Life in social relations is an essential component of Brazilian culture that keeps individuals thriving as human beings and that moves the cogwheels of commerce and politics, as we will see in the section on *jeitinho*.

The world of social relations divides into private and public spaces, categories that surpass the common distinction made in the United States, according to Brazilian anthropologist Roberto DaMatta. The home symbolizes the refuge for the family and *parentela* where all are honored and kept secure from the dangers and competition of the street. The home and the street are two separate social spaces that thrive by virtue of their difference. Building homes and apartments like fortresses to protect those inside from the unknown outside is not a function of increasing crime or rapid urban expansion in Brazil, although those social problems have exacerbated the existing separation. Rather, it is an architectural tradition that reflects the importance of keeping family members and their moral standards pure and safe from the villainy on the street. Inside the home family members maintain their corporate identity and receive the loyal support of their loved ones. But outside the home life is a dog-eat-dog world, arbitrary, anonymous, and cruel. When Brazilians venture outside the house the elements of the home, its traditions, food and drink, parental love, and attitudes of acceptance and forgiveness are inverted. Out on the street food can be poisonous, attentions from others immoral or criminal, and mistakes are punished by authorities. Leaving home for work and school each day requires girding up for battle and carrying as a defense the status and identity of the extended family.

Finally, social relations govern attitudes toward time. Brazilians recognize that appointments should be kept, but if a friend shows up, personal loyalty requires that the friend receive attention first even if that means arriving late for an appointment. Promptness also depends on the importance of the event and its participants. Official dinners and ceremonies involving honorary organizations or governmental bodies, for example, begin at the time printed on the invitation. However, parties, dinners, concerts, rehearsals, and even college classes may start from 30 minutes to an hour or more later than the announced time. Being delayed is acknowledged as a fact of life, not an affront, especially since public transportation, traffic, and other inconveniences can easily disrupt plans. Similarly, social events in and outside the home rarely specify an ending time no matter when they are scheduled during the week. Brazilians living in the United States are surprised by party invitations that list an ending time and report afterwards that the party was just getting good by the time it had to end. In Brazil, time must bend to the needs of people.

FOOD AND DRINK

Food and drink facilitate and enhance social relations between *amigos* (friends) and *colegas* (acquaintances). These divisions between types of social relations also govern the places in which Brazilians socialize. *Colegas* are colleagues from work or school who gather at pubs or restaurants for lunch or a cold beer after work and with whom one can share obligations and responsibilities. *Colegas* maintain cordial relations that last for years without ever becoming *amigos*. On the other hand, *amigos* usually are extended family or others who have shared years of close friendship and in whom one confides the most intimate secrets. Only *amigos* visit and are entertained in Brazilian homes. Meals prepared at home and eaten with friends offer the best opportunity for social communion and the best sign of true friendship.

Feasting on *muqueca,* an Afro-Brazilian dish with dendê palm oil, coconut milk, and shellfish. (Author photo)

Children's birthday parties are exemplary social events for extended family networks. Some birthday parties are held in the afternoon for mothers and children. But traditional birthdays involve all age groups, follow a theme that is repeated in the cake and decorations, begin with the honored child opening presents as his guests and their parents arrive, include singing "Happy Birthday" in Portuguese and English, move to cocktails with salty and sweet hors d'oeuvres, and end many hours later with dancing.

Another traditional group activity for Saturdays is eating the Brazilian national dish of *feijoada,* a heavy, black bean stew with smoked and sun-dried meats on rice, topped with toasted manioc flour, and served with sautéed kale, orange slices, and hot sauce on the side. It is usually consumed around midday and must be eaten slowly. The dish probably originated in the restaurants of Rio de Janeiro around the end of the nineteenth century and then migrated to the kitchens of other eateries in the nation's largest cities. *Feijoada* is a weekend meal that lends itself to companionship. Traditionally, it must be accompanied with beer or a *caipirinha,* a concoction of lime, sugar, and *cachaça* (sugar-cane rum) that encourages afternoon naps. Although once a week is enough for a meal like bean stew, rice and black beans are staples of Brazilian tables and accompany meats or stand alone as the main noontime meal of the day. Breakfast and supper are lighter meals that may include fruit and cheese, but usually are as simple as coffee with milk and fresh bread. Families with children typically have a snack after school because supper comes late in the day.

In addition to birthdays and special meals as times for socializing, drinking coffee also represents a special moment of social interaction during the day. Coffee introduces and maintains relations in the work world and at home. It is so important that the name of the coffee server is credited on Brazilian movies and music recordings. Office employees do not have to leave the building for coffee because the server regularly comes to each business with small paper cups of lukewarm coffee with sugar. Stand-up coffee bars dot city streets and occupy corners in many neighborhoods. Drinking coffee signals the arrival of new people to a business or government office, beauty salon, or other place of commerce. Since it is consumed in very strong but small doses, it represents a quick pick-me-up that breaks the monotony of the day. Coffee consumption requires drinkers to stop their work, come together at the coffee bar or around the coffee server, drink, converse, and then return to previous duties. Coffee is also served to visitors in the home where it functions as a prelude to conversation or it signals the end of a meal.

SOCCER

When the pope visited Brazil in 1994 he drew a crowd of 300,000 in Rio. But in 2002, when the Brazilian soccer team returned after making Brazil the only country to have won the World Cup five times, the turnout was 500,000. Rio is home to the world's largest soccer stadium, the Maracanã, where, on one occasion, over 200,000 fans crammed in to watch the most famous player of the sport, Pelé, perform one last time before retirement. From its early days in the 1890s as an aristocratic game brought to Brazil by a student returning from his studies in Great Britain, soccer has evolved into a national passion that has earned Brazil an international reputation for its energetic and creative style of play. Soccer became popular because it is an accessible game that can be played anywhere with little equipment. Brazilian cities are full of empty corner lots, streets, and beaches with young boys and adult men kicking the ball, which may be no more than a wad of aluminum foil. The game became coeducational in the 1980s with the formation of the first women's soccer clubs in Rio. Soccer clubs provide youth from poor parts of the city or state with the opportunity to develop their talent, and it is one of the few avenues that the economically disadvantaged can use to get ahead.

The fanaticism for soccer begins at the city level where soccer clubs are supported by loyal fans who wear their teams' colors, attend all the games, and discuss at length the plays and strategies of the players and the coach. In Rio, traditional rivalries between soccer clubs are similar to the intense rivalries between samba schools, and soccer games, like carnival celebrations, are wild, loud, emotional events where paper cups, food, and beer go flying through the air to the syncopated beat of drums. When a team wins a soccer championship spontaneous street parties clog the main arteries of cities with dancing and singing enthusiasts waving banners and beating drums until the early morning.

Brazil's standing as one of the greatest soccer nations is a cause for national pride and soccer players are treated like international celebrities because they bring fame and honor to their country. Possibly because they are national property, Brazilians follow the careers of soccer players closely and refer to them only by their first or nicknames. Likewise, players' first names or nicknames appear on their jerseys, rather than the more customary last names, even in international competitions such as the World Cup games. During the World Cup, employees are absent from work, the traffic in the streets disappears, and Brazilian flags hang out of apartment windows. When the World Cup team scores a goal it is cheered with long shouts and honking horns, but when the team loses a game Brazilians wear black arm bands and some weep. Conspiracy rumors abounded after the 1998 championship game in which Brazil lost to France in a lackluster performance that could only be understood in Brazil as the result of subornation by the multinational company that sponsored the team and featured its players prominently in jazzy television advertisements. The outcome of the 2002 World Cup restored Brazil's damaged sense of honor and propelled it to an unprecedented fifth championship title.

CARNIVAL

Carnival has origins in Greek Dionysian festivals, Roman saturnalias, and medieval dance macabre, but it traveled to Brazil from Portugal sometime during the seventeenth century as *entrudo*, a form of street game that involved pelting others with food. In the nation's capital of Rio it slowly evolved into a form of street dance with music, gaining its own special songs in the 1890s and, in 1929, the construction of samba schools. It is the most popular religious festival in Brazil, celebrated on the three days leading up to Ash Wednesday. During Carnival the rules of decorum and propriety are suspended, liberating Brazilians from social restraints and class divisions. Its excess of playfulness, exhibitionism, and role reversal are, in fact, just the opposite of the rules that normally govern behavior in Brazil. Each region displays it own special characteristics, but a general atmosphere of permissiveness reigns nationwide.

Although those outside Brazil often characterize it as the world's biggest party, Carnival actually belongs to the family of pre-Lenten celebrations common to all Roman Catholic areas of the world. Many associate Carnival with Rio de Janeiro thanks to the considerable amount of publicity, including glossy photos of nearly naked women, that encourage international tourists to participate in the city's celebration. Carnival began to attract large numbers of tourists to Rio de Janeiro not long after the city lost its status as the nation's capital to Brasília in the early 1960s. The city tour office, Riotur, invested heavily in the promotion of Carnival and encouraged development of an infrastructure for tourists. As a result, sun worshipers, celebrities, and hedonists began to flock to Brazil in February to join in the gaiety. Since then the number of tourists has increased as have the extravagance and pageantry of the events, and Rio de Janeiro has become forever synonymous with Carnival.

In Rio, Carnival wears at least three different *fantasias* (costumes): those of the samba schools, of the ballroom dances, and of the neighborhood street bands. Preparations for the spectacular parade of the *escolas de samba* (samba schools) actually are underway year-round not only for fund-raising, but also for sewing costumes, rehearsing dance steps to the school's song, and practicing the drum rhythms that keep the school moving. The samba schools used to parade in Rio's downtown city streets, but in 1984 the city built the *Sambódromo*, a parade grounds with specially designed seats and lighting to enhance and contain the show. The headquarters for the samba schools and their members reside in the poorer neighborhoods or *morros* on the sides of the hills that surround the city. Each school can be distinguished by its colors, its song, and its banner. When the school enters the *Sambódromo* to parade, loyal supporters increase the noise factor to even higher volumes with their cheers of support and accompaniment to the school's song. Considering that each school parades with around 3,000 members, dancers, musicians, floats, invited guests and all, it is no surprise that it takes more than an hour for one school to move through the parade grounds. Eight schools parade each of the two nights of competition, meaning that the crowds begin watching the event in the dark of evening and are still there past dawn the following day. Stamina is needed to participate as a dancer or musician in a samba school, but it is also a necessity for the partisans as well.

Rio also hosts costume balls that include competitions for the city's most opulent dressers. These individuals always appear in the Carnival report of the photo magazine *Manchete* along with snapshots of the local and international celebrities in the dancing throng. Costume balls cater to the wealthy at the opposite end of the economic spectrum from samba schools. Finally, for those wishing to participate in more spontaneous celebrations there are neighborhood bands and dancing groups called *blocos* that parade through various parts of the city in a less structured fashion. Individuals can don costumes that satirize politics, economics, or popular culture and join in the fun. Unlike the glittery, feathery excess of the costume balls and the samba school parades, street carnival often makes fun of the decorative bombast and promotes humorous self-deprecation.

In all regions of Brazil Carnival is celebrated with music, costumes, and dancing. But several cities are recognized for their own versions of this national festival. The capital of Salvador in the state of Bahia is noted for its street Carnival and for its *trios eléctricos*, flat-bed trucks wired for sound that cruise around town providing around-the-clock music for individual dancers and organized groups. Several *blocos* in Salvador are dedicated to preserving Afro-Brazilian heritage and participate in street Carnivals. The capital of the state of Pernambuco, Recife, which was home to Dutch occupation in the early history of Brazil, still preserves remnants of that presence in its *frevo* Carnival dance and costumes.

Brazil's Carnival image as chaotic, boisterous, romantic, and dangerous was apparent in the 1958 French film *Orfeu Negro* (Black Orpheus). In its reworking of the Orpheus legend into the story of a Rio samba school, the movie shows a threatening costumed figure of death that shadows and frightens the heroine. This image still looms menacingly at the edges of the festivities both because Carnival's origins were violent and because the liberation from social restrictions can go awry. With its license to play, dress up, drink, and carouse, Carnival celebrates not the ordinary and usual but the outrageous and unusual. On occasion that license has meant increased crime, drunkenness, and disrespect of people and property. As a result, Brazilians who believe that Carnival represents a risk to their security escape the summer heat of the cities for the less perilous and fresher environs of the beach.

THE CULTURE OF THE BEACH

With over 5,000 miles of coastline that is home to more than half of the state capitals and thousands of beautiful beaches, it is no wonder that the beach and its culture play an important part in many Brazilians' lives. The beach provides one of the most inviting sites for Brazilians to get together. Anyone so unfortunate as to appear on the beach alone will not feel alone

The beach at Ipanema in Rio de Janeiro (AP Photo/John Maier Jr.)

for long. Beaches are virtual beehives of activity that will absorb the individual into their movement, and they are the best places to meet and flirt. As the joke on the introductory page suggested, beaches are meant to be communal, and city beaches in particular are very crowded. Everyone goes to the beach; there are no age limits or size requirements, and it is not even necessary to get in the water. Although some beaches support surfers, most promote strolling and looking. Beaches are occupied by different age groups depending on the time of day. Mothers and mothers-to-be with children, elders, and exercise buffs are the early birds at the beach, while young people show up later. Ostensibly, going to the beach is about health—it is relaxing to play in the sand and in the water, the sun and water heal, running and working out are more enjoyable at the beach. Ultimately, though, the real reason to go to the beach is to see and be seen.

The size of most swimsuits provides all oglers with plenty to see. Men and women wear tiny suits that pretend to cover some of the tender spots on the body, no matter what size or shape of body they are supposed to fit. Moving around in such small garments requires constant adjustment, an act that has been perfected into several adroit gestures. Swimsuits in themselves are not really as important in their color or shape as the physical appearance and gait of the wearer. Looking attractive is important because it demonstrates class and status but also because it indicates self-respect. Those Brazilians who can afford it spend time and money on their looks, from minimal investments in manicures and pedicures to major makeovers with plastic surgery. Men and women also cultivate the way they walk, and women are especially aware of the grace and fluidity of their bodies. The famous bossa nova[1] song *Garota de Ipanema* (The Girl from Ipanema) describes the appearance of the tall, tan, young and lovely girl, but also the way she walks by, with her movements flowing like music, so that everyone watching her sighs.

Beach life never gets boring. If the constant parade of bodies doesn't provide enough entertainment, then the peddlers walking up and down the beach selling cold drinks, combs, or other necessities will engage both eye and ears with their calls. There are beach games, like volleyball, and even exercise classes. During Carnival celebrants sing and dance on the beach along with their own rhythm sections. Some beaches have small restaurants serving coconut juice, and larger ones that offer fresh boiled crabs and performing musicians. In January beaches host New Year's celebrations and in February the observers of Afro-Brazilian religions make offerings to the sea goddess Yemanjá. They stand on the beach or wade into the water throwing bouquets of flowers and emptying perfume bottles in the hope of receiving blessings from the goddess.

JEITINHO

Jeitinho is an adaptation for coping with society. It means a way or knack of getting something done and its frequent use in Portuguese suggests that on the one hand, life in Brazil is full of obstacles that must be overcome, while on the other, that any situation can be resolved when interested parties work on it together. *Jeitinho* can be as harmless as having paperwork done more quickly in a government office or as insidious as political corruption. When Brazilians are confronted with an awkward or difficult situation the most common response is to *dar um jeito*, that is, figure out an approach that will surmount the difficulty. Short stories, newspaper columns, and travel books provide wonderful examples of *jeitinho* that explain how it works and the great lengths to which Brazilians will go to help others solve a problem using *jeitinho*. Finding a way to solve a problem appears in this chapter on social customs because it often employs the *panelinha* (family network) to identify the right person who can intervene. In addition, *jeitinho* works when the individual trying to overcome the difficulty establishes a connection, a personal relationship, between himself and that right person. *Jeitinho* is not considered bribery and usually does not involve the crass exchange of money for favors. Rather, it is facilitating the completion of a task that at first seemed impossible to execute.

A few examples of *jeitinho* will demonstrate how this most necessary of social skills and social relations functions in Brazilian life. A group of travelers on an excursion purchases too many tickets in advance for the number of people in the group. When they arrive at their destination one member goes to the ticket booth to inquire about a refund. Company policy states that no refunds are given; however, the traveler believes there should be a way to get some of the money back. When the individual first inquires about refunds the employee states that no refunds are possible. The tour member then changes the subject to something unrelated; for example, he notes the employee is wearing a shirt with a logo of the local soccer team and he begins to talk about soccer, the soccer season, a family member or friend that plays on that soccer team or played against that soccer team. Through this conversation he is hoping to establish a friendly equality between himself and the employee so that they share some common ground or point of contact. If he is able to do this, he may bring up the refund again and this time he might ask the employee whether she can *dar um jeito*. At this point he will probably get the refund. In this example the individual is able to build a sense of connection and obligation that makes the employee feel more loyal to him than to the regulations of the company, and as a result the employee refunds the ticket price.

A more complicated use of *jeitinho* involves calling on family members or friends to help perform a task that the person cannot complete on his own. Standing in line for service at a business or governmental office is commonplace. Sometimes the employee will close down the line and all those in that line will have to join another long line and continue waiting. One way to shorten the wait is to use family connections to find someone that either works in that office or works with the individuals in that office. That person will expedite the wait by personally going with the client and taking him to the front of the line or by calling the employee to one side to take care of the client. The more people an individual knows, the broader the base of resources available to intervene in his favor. *Jeitinho* implies that Brazilians ask for help from friends and family but also provide it when asked, thus expanding the network of connections and acquaintances. This exchange of favors is reciprocal and obligatory, but no one keeps a tally. Rather, *jeitinho* builds and rewards connections between people that are beneficial on a personal, social, or professional level.

DaMatta argues that the arbitrary and authoritarian system of federal, state, and local laws; the rules and practices of most businesses; and the self-importance of office employees make the *jeitinho* necessary. Under these conditions no one worries about being fair to all customers; the concern is about finishing the transaction satisfactorily. For those with money, the situations requiring circumvention can be avoided altogether with the help of a professional known as the *despachante* (dispatcher), who employs his own set of connections to complete official transactions on behalf of his paying customers. *Jeitinho* demonstrates the value of speaking well, being able to make conversation and jokes, and of showing a real interest in others. However, *jeitinho* is not totally harmless. It enables those in positions of power to benefit disproportionately from their influence and broad networks, while leaving the less fortunate trapped in a labyrinth of documents, rules, and requirements.

POPULAR FESTIVALS

Historical and national holidays appear on Brazilian calendars and are observed, but religious festivals are celebrated, although none as widely as Carnival. The celebration in honor of Brazil's patron saint, Our Lady of Aparecida, brings more pilgrimages from the faithful to the state of São Paulo than at other times of the year, but the events surrounding the celebration do not take on a national scope. In fact, communities throughout Brazil often choose to celebrate Aparecida on a different date than October 12. Smaller towns observe the feast days of Catholic saints with street fairs and during the Christmas holiday season perform several revised versions of traditional European festivals. There are maritime battles reenacting the Portuguese wars against the Moors, known as *cheganças*, street revelers who represent the shepherds looking for the baby Jesus in *pastoris*, or who visit homes performing small plays called *reisados*. The two most important festivals in the Northeast take place during the winter months. They are the *festas juninas*, a Portuguese tradition of observing the birthdays of Saint Anthony, Saint John, and Saint Peter during the month of June; and *Bumba-meu-boi*, a former religious festival that dramatizes the death and resurrection of a prize bull.

The *festas juninas* begin with the birthday of Saint Anthony on June 12, reach a climax on Saint John's birthday, June 24, and end with the birthday of Saint Peter on June 29. In cities of the Northeast like Fortaleza, Ceará, the holidays are marked as a hillbilly festival with nightly bonfires, fireworks, special dishes made from sweet potatoes and corn, a hot drink of rum called *quentão*, and square dances or *quadrilhas*. The dancers wear patched clothes and rural dress; their performance may include a "wedding" ceremony that pokes fun at country ways.

Bumba-meu-boi began as a religious festival on the cattle ranches of the Northeast in the eighteenth-century. Eventually, it became a purely secular and folkloric festival that honors the importance of cattle to the region. The focus of the festival is the bull, represented by a costume larger than a person, made of wood and fabric with elaborate decorations and oversized horns. Keeping and wearing the bull costume represents an honor for important individuals in the community. Community members also wear costumes representing local leaders—the rancher and his wife, a cowboy or slave, the priest, a policeman, animals (a burro, a snake, and the bull, and fantastic beings)—the devil, and a mythic forest dwelling beast called the *caipora*. The audience sings and comments on the story as it is being told or acted. All performers must be able to make quick retorts to the crowd and improvise. One version of the *bumba-meu-boi* (hit my bull) story pits the cowboy or slave against his oppressive employer, the rancher. The cowboy causes the death of the bull, the rancher finds out, various individuals attempt to resuscitate the bull, the bull comes back to life and all celebrate. The festival ends with music and dancing.

This chapter outlines social customs that demonstrate the importance to Brazilians of life in social relationships. But for the lower and middle socio-economic ranks, which means a majority of the population, there is another feature of cultural identity that must be mentioned before closing, and that is the belief in miracles. This belief in the sudden apparition of good luck, big winnings, or a way to get ahead can be seen as a means of coping with the fatalism of Catholicism, expressed in the often heard expression *Se Deus quiser* (if God wishes it), and from the rigidity and authoritarianism of a social class structure that has survived almost unchanged for several hundred years. Brazilians seem susceptible to the utopian visions of politicians promising a better tomorrow and to extraordinary, even mystical occurrences. Gambling on the *jogo do bicho* (animal lottery) is one way to win big, especially when the gambler dreams of a number or an animal the night before. This *palpite* (tip) serves to orient gambling choices, but dreams are signs used in making other decisions as well. Although the animal lottery is illegal, it has been practiced widely in Brazil since the late nineteenth century and is responsible for generating enormous profits. Some of those profits return to the people who place their bets and collect their winnings through an informal network of verbal transactions. Religion is another area in which the search for possible benefits leads to practicing several different religions in order to ask each for favors and make promises for payment if they are received. Salvation from the difficulties of life and the pursuit of all available avenues to find it are powerful antidotes to the hardships of Brazilian reality. Living in community and believing in miracles are characteristics that make Brazilians a hopeful and energetic people who treat others with enthusiasm, humor, and generosity.[2]

NOTES

1. A musical movement launched in Rio de Janeiro in the 1950s that transformed popular music and at the same time made an important contribution to jazz in the United States. Characterized by its intimate lyrics, colloquial language, and beautiful harmonies, its most famous figure was Antônio Carlos Jobim, composer of *Garota de Ipanema*.

2. It has been a privilege to contribute this chapter and to honor the career, friendship, and family of my first mentor.

7

Print Media and Broadcasting

Mark A. Dinneen

PRINT MEDIA

THE YEAR 1808 marks the beginning of the Brazilian press. Until then, the Portuguese colonial authorities had forbidden the printing of books, pamphlets, and newspapers in the territory. In 1808, however, the Portuguese court fled Lisbon to escape the invading French armies of Napoleon, and established itself in Brazil, and the royal printing house was set up in Rio de Janeiro soon afterwards. It produced the first newspaper to be printed in Brazil, called the *Gazeta do Rio de Janeiro* (Rio de Janeiro Gazette). Published for the first time on September 10, 1808, its role was limited to extolling the monarchy and conveying government information. Three months earlier, the first copies of another newspaper in Portuguese, the *Correio Braziliense* (Brazilian Post), had circulated illegally in Brazil, but it was printed in London and did not focus primarily on Brazil; many historians do not consider it to have been a Brazilian paper. Its creator, Hipólito da Costa (1774–1823), is nonetheless often referred to as the founder-figure of the press in Brazil. Having spent three years in prison in Portugal, accused by the Inquisition of disseminating freemasonry, he went into exile in London, where he used his monthly newspaper to convey penetrating analyses of political events in Europe and the Americas. For many of its readers in Brazil, it represented their first contact with high-quality journalism. Costa finally closed the paper in 1822, after it had been in circulation for 14 years.

Based in Rio de Janeiro, the Portuguese monarchy still maintained firm control over publishing, and restricted what could be produced. In 1811, it granted permission to Manuel Antônio da Silva Serba to establish the first private print-works in Brazil, and with it the right to produce a newspaper, the *Idade d'Ouro do Brasil* (The Golden Age of Brazil). The following year, the country's first magazine, *As Variedades ou Ensaios de Literatura* (Literary Miscellany or Essays), was published. Only in 1821 did a new and more dynamic period of press production begin. That year, Dom Pedro, who was left to govern Brazil as Prince Regent after his father King João VI had returned to Portugal, relaxed the restrictions and opened the way for much greater press freedom. New papers emerged with regularity. The majority were created to promote a particular political cause or the interests of particular group. There were, for example, papers which advocated Brazilian independence and others which campaigned against it. Some of the most important journalists of the period were also politicians, and their newspapers, though often influential at the time, were generally short-lived. Such was the experience of the major liberal politicians, Joaquim Gonçalves Ledo (1781–1847), whose *Revérbero Constitucional Fluminense* (The Constitutional Echo of Rio de Janeiro) was only in circulation for 1821 and 1822; Evaristo da Veiga (1799–1837), who published *Aurora Fluminense* (The Rio de Janeiro Dawn) from 1828 until 1835; and Teófilo Ottoni (1807–1867), whose *Sentinela do Serro* (The Sentinel of the Sierra) lasted only from 1830 to 1832. There was one particularly notable exception to this situation, however. In November of 1825 the *Diário de Pernambuco* (The Pernambuco Daily) was founded in Recife, and, still being published today, it proudly claims to be the oldest paper still in circulation in Latin America.

In the mid-nineteenth century the domination of political journalism began to wane, and newspapers expanded their coverage of other areas of interest. Fiction serialized in regular installments became a popular feature in some of them. Works by such outstanding writers as José de Alencar and Machado de Assis appeared in this form. In 1852, the first newspaper dedicated to women readers appeared. Appropriately called *Jornal das Senhoras* (The Ladies Paper), it contained items on art, literature, and fashion, complete with illustrations. Its founder, Violante Ataliba Ximenes de Bivar e Velasco, became the first woman in Brazil to take charge of a newspaper. During this period, the development of the press was aided by improvements to the distribution system for papers and journals. The introduction in 1844 of mail deliveries to private residences in some towns meant that individuals could subscribe to a newspaper and receive it regularly at home, and from the late 1850s onward, copies could be purchased from a growing number of street sellers in the large cities. A decade or so later, kiosks in Rio de Janeiro and São Paulo, the most important centers for the Brazilian press, added newspapers to the flowers, tobacco, sweets, drinks, and other items that they sold.

However, the basis for the modern Brazilian press was really laid between the 1880s and the 1920s. A steady increase in investment, the use of modern equipment imported from abroad, and a variety of technical advances, including the use of photography, enabled newspapers to be considerably more professional in their production, and provided them with much greater financial stability. The print media became a viable business that attracted the interest of entrepreneurs. The major Brazilian newspapers of today emerged in this period. One of them, *O Estado de São Paulo* (The State of São Paulo), which was called *Província de São Paulo* (Province of São Paulo) when it first went into circulation in January 1875, was created by a group campaigning for the establishment of a republic and the abolition of slavery. It was given its new name when the Republic was finally declared in 1889. In 1891 the *Journal do Brasil* (Newspaper of Brazil) was founded in Rio de Janeiro, followed by the *Folha de São Paulo* (Newspaper of São Paulo) in 1921 and *O Globo* (The Globe) in Rio de Janeiro 1925. All would acquire considerable prestige and influence during subsequent decades, with offices in major cities throughout Brazil and correspondents scattered overseas.

The growing influence of the press meant that newspapers became increasingly at risk of interference from government and from the hostility of groups opposed to their editorial lines. The first republican governments (1889–1895) closed down a number of papers in different parts of the country. The *Jornal do Brasil* was one of many that became embroiled in the political conflicts of the time. In December 1891, the famous writer Joaquim Nabuco (1849–1910) wrote some articles in the paper, which he had helped to found, advocating the restoration of the monarchy, and the newspaper's offices were attacked and pillaged by anti-monarchists baying for Nabuco's blood. The government announced that it could not guarantee the safety of pro-monarchist journalists, and Nabuco and some of his colleagues were obliged to sever their ties with the paper. In 1893, another famous figure, the writer and politician Ruy Barbosa (1849–1923), became editor of *Jornal do Brasil*, but his criticism incurred the wrath of the government. The paper was shut down for a lengthy period and Barbosa went into exile. Among the many other writers who also made a significant contribution to journalism during this period, the name of Euclides da Cunha (1866–1909) stands out. In 1887 he was sent as correspondent of *A Província de São Paulo* to northern Brazil to cover the dramatic war between messianic rebels and government troops at Canudos, in the interior of Bahia. Da Cunha used his reports on the savagery of the conflict and the eventual liquidation of the rebels as the basis for his masterpiece *Os Sertões* (Rebellion in the Backlands), which, published in 1902, has achieved a fame matched by few other Brazilian literary works.

Periods of severe repression would afflict the press in the twentieth century too, but they would not halt the steady growth and modernization of the industry. Another step in that process was the foundation in the 1920s of three companies that would play a major role in newspaper and magazine production during later decades: Folha de São Paulo (São Paulo Newspaper) in 1921; Diários Associados (Associated Newspapers) in 1924; and Organizções Globo (Globe Organizations) in 1925. The creation of the first trade unions for journalists in the early 1930s was an indication of the growing strength and organization of the profession in Brazil. Between 1937 and 1945, the dictatorship of Getúlio Vargas imposed tight restrictions on the press, but they did not significantly curb its economic expansion, largely because the regime dedicated substantial resources to newspaper publicity, disseminating government announcements and propaganda. It was nonetheless an extremely difficult period for newspaper editors and journalists. The press was muzzled. The regime's Departamento de Imprensa e Propaganda (Press and Propaganda Department), created in 1939, exercised strict ideological control over the media, and prohibited newspapers and magazines deemed unfavorable to the government.

The return of press freedom following the collapse of the Vargas dictatorship in 1945 stimulated the desire for a new phase of modernization in the newspaper industry. Many journalists and editors had visited Europe and the United States during the years of the World War II and they had learned much about newspaper design and production in the countries they visited. The changes that resulted were evident in such popular papers of the 1950s as *Diário Carioca* (Rio de Janeiro Daily), *Última Hora* (Latest News), and *O Globo* (The Globe). Greater emphasis was given to visual appeal—with, for example, more imaginative use of photographs and illustrations—and newspaper reporting became sharper and more concise. Copy desks were established to rewrite the reports submitted by correspondents in a lively but accessible form. Sunday supplements became common, and they frequently played a significant role in diffusing new developments in literature and the arts. To provide some of the new skills and training demanded by this process of transformation, the first regular courses of journalism were opened in Brazilian universities.

The 1950s was also a very fruitful decade for magazine production. Back in 1928, Diários Associados had launched Brazil's first magazine with a national circulation, *O Cruzeiro*, which was published weekly, and in the 1950s it was at the height of its popularity. In 1956, 570,000 copies of it were printed each week, which at the time was a record print run for a Brazilian magazine. The strength of *O Cruzeiro*, in addition to its high standard of writing and good quality photography, was the diversity of its subject matter. It included current affairs, political and social satire, society gossip, and news about the most celebrated Hollywood stars of the 1950s. Its popularity finally began to fade at the end of the decade, due to strong competition from other magazines that had appeared on the market. One of those was *Manchete*, another high-quality weekly, produced for the first time in 1952. It included some notable innovations, such as the chronicles of daily urban life written by well-known writers like Ruben Braga and Fernando Sabino. Equally popular were the satirical studies of Brazilian political and social life written by Stanislaw Ponte Preta, which made him one of the country's most celebrated humorists.

In 1950, an adventurous immigrant named Victor Civita founded the publishing company Editora Abril, and it proved to be an event of huge importance for magazine production in Brazil. Its first publication was a Portuguese version of the *Donald Duck* comic, and its success encouraged the company to launch a series of other titles. One of the best known was *Capricho* (Fancy), a magazine of romantic stories told through photographs, which went into circulation in 1952, aimed above all at young women. It appeared to be a failure at first, but a brainwave by Civita turned it around. Romance magazines of that type generally consisted of one chapter of the story, with future chapters being produced week by week, but Civita decided that each edition of *Capricho* would contain one complete story. As a result, sales climbed steadily, and it became one of the best-selling magazines in Latin America. Among Abril's other popular titles are *Manequim*, a fashion magazine launched in 1959; *Contigo*, created for women readers in 1963; and, most famous of all, *Veja*, a newsweekly launched in 1968. In the last decades of the twentieth century, *Veja* was the magazine with the highest circulation in Brazil, enjoying a comfortable margin over its rivals and attracting a massive advertising revenue. It provides detailed and incisive analyses of the latest political, cultural, and economic developments in Brazil and overseas. Its success has helped Abril to consolidate its position as Brazil's largest magazine publisher, and the company has gone on to diversify its activities in the media, acquiring interests in television, for example.

Veja's quality of production testifies to the technical advances that had been made in publishing in the 1960s, but once more, political circumstances undermined freedom of expression. The military regime that took power through a coup in 1964 imposed press censorship and closed down many publications of leftist or even liberal tendency. Restrictions on what was published increased still further with the government's infamous Institutional Act No. 5, introduced in 1968. Among other measures, it imposed absolute control over the media and subjected all publications to prior censorship. It was now dangerous for editors to publish articles that were critical of the regime. Violence against newspaper offices and staff were not uncommon. Many still managed to respond creatively to those conditions, however. A vibrant alternative press emerged, led by satirical magazines which used comedy as vehicle for expressing dissent. Given that direct political criticism was close to impossible, humorists had a major role to play in the dissemination of alternative ideas. By far the most significant of these publications was *O Pasquim* (The Rag), which first appeared in 1969. A large part of its success was due to the fact that it brought together some of Brazil's most talented cartoonists, such as Millor Fernandes (b. 1924), who contributed drawings to virtually all Brazil's major magazines; Ziraldo (Ziraldo Alves Pinto, b. 1932), whose work had become well-known in many newspapers in the 1950s; and Henfil (Henrique de Souza Filho, 1944–1988), whose black humor found its finest expression in his contributions to *O Pasquim*. Their cartoons poking fun at the government provided the most memorable element of the magazine, though there were also important sections of interviews, poetry, and discussion of alternative youth culture. Many expressed surprise that it was not closed down by the authorities, but its writers and artists became skilled at suggestion, symbolism, and indirect reference. Even so, some of them were arrested and imprisoned. The importance of *O Pasquim* to the Brazilian press during those years of intense oppression was enormous. Other satirical papers were launched in the 1960s and 1970s, but few managed to last so long, and none were of equal impact.

In the late 1970s there was a relaxation of press restrictions and new political papers were founded. Some were linked to particular political groupings, such as Hora do Povo (Hour of the People), which was produced by the Eighth of October Revolutionary Movement, and Convergência Socialista (Socialist Convergence), created by an organization of the same name. As freedom of expression was reestablished, and pressure mounted for a return to civilian rule, the Brazilian press enthusiastically took up its role in the political life of the country once again. In 1984, newspapers were fundamental in mobilizing the public for a huge popular campaign demanding that the president be chosen by direct elections. Military rule ended in 1985. As if making up for lost time, investigative journalists began probing all areas of government activity, exposing any misdemeanor or ineptitude. It was press reports on corruption in 1992, particularly in the magazines *Veja* and *IstoÉ*, that began the campaign to remove President Fernando Collor from office. An impeachment process was set in motion, and he was obliged to resign in December of that year. It confirmed that the press had fully recovered its political and social influence within the country.

Newspaper sales grew appreciably in the 1990s, and the same is true for magazines, with the appearance of a growing number of new titles catering to specialist interests. However, given the size of the Brazilian population, the potential for the expansion of readership is huge. Despite the large number of newspapers in circulation in 2000, only nine of them had daily sales of more than one million copies (Almanaque Abril, 2000, 240). The highest selling paper was *Folha de São Paulo*, followed by *Estado de São Paulo* and *O Globo*. They, together with *Jornal do Brasil*, are the newspapers that have the greatest impact nationally, although there are many others which are very influential at a regional level, such as *Zero Hora* (Zero Hour), in the southern state of Rio Grande do Sul, and *O Estado de Minas* (State of Minas), published in Belo Horizonte, in the state of Minas Gerais. São Paulo has maintained its position as the dominant center for the print media. The capital, Brasília, has still to produce a newspaper of national influence. The availability of Brazilian newspapers in electronic form was the most significant development of the 1990s. The first, *JB Online*, was launched by *Jornal do Brasil* in 1995, but the other major papers quickly followed.

RADIO

Brazil had already made a notable contribution to the development of radio many years before broadcasting began in the country in 1922. Following several years of scientific study in the early 1890s, a remarkable man by the name of Roberto Landell de Moura (1861–1928), a priest from the southern city of Porto Alegre, constructed one of the first radio transmitters, which he later patented in Brazil and the United States. According to some sources, Landell was the first in the world to transmit the human voice via electromagnetic waves. However, few at the time took his work seriously, least of all the Brazilian government, and it was only many decades after Landell's death that he began to receive some long overdue recognition.

It was on September 7, 1922, as part of the celebrations to mark the centenary of Brazilian Independence, that the first public radio transmission in Brazil took place. The broadcast was made in Rio de Janeiro, from a station installed by the Brazilian Telephonic Company and Westinghouse Electric, and it consisted of a speech by the president of Brazil, Epitácio Pessoa, live music, and discussion. The following year, Brazil's first radio station was established: Rádio Sociedade do Rio de Janeiro. A well-known anthropologist and university professor, Edgar Roquette-Pinto (1884–1954), was the main inspiration behind the project. Acclaimed as the "father of Brazilian radio," Roquette-Pinto saw the huge potential broadcasting had for education and for facilitating national integration. Other stations quickly followed in different parts of the country, all of them founded as amateur radio clubs or societies and financed by the subscriptions of their members, and all dedicated to the provision of educational and cultural programs.

There were already 29 stations operating in Brazil at the onset of the 1930s, but radio broadcasting expanded rapidly in the course of the decade, with the cities of Rio de Janeiro and São Paulo in the forefront. The launch of commercial broadcasting in 1932, when a law authorized advertising on radio, was the most significant factor in the process. As new stations competed ever more vigorously to widen their audiences, and so attract further advertising revenue, programming became increasingly oriented toward entertainment, with variety shows attracting the greatest numbers of listeners. One of the most successful was the Ademar Casé show, which began in 1932 on Radio Transmissora of Rio de Janeiro, and which incorporated light theater, stories, comedy sketches, and popular music. Such programs made their presenters national celebrities; launched the careers of many musicians, actors, and comedians; and created the first national idols of popular song, such as Francisco Alves and Carmen Miranda. Stations worked strenuously to discover new artists, and also contracted orchestras and paid major musicians to star in them. Audiences boomed for the most popular stations of the period, such as Rádio Record in São Paulo and Rádio Mayrink Veiga of Rio de Janeiro. The commercial radio of the United States provided the basic model for the owners of Brazilian stations, and U.S. influence was clearly evident in the production and style of programs. Despite the frequent articles and letters that appeared in the Brazilian press of the 1930s decrying the devaluation of radio's educational role, entertainment programming became firmly established as the mainstay of broadcasting during those years, with innovations such as shows with a live audience and quiz programs being introduced in the attempt to win over new listeners.

Recognizing the value of radio as a means of mass communication and its potential as a political instrument, the government took an increasing interest in broadcasting in the 1930s. At the same time as it sought to provide radio with secure sources of finance through commercialization, the Vargas regime also introduced censorship legislation and a law, in 1931, giving the government sole authority to concede broadcasting rights to interested companies. Vargas made considerable use of radio to strengthen support for his regime.

In 1935 his government created a program titled *Voz do Brasil* (Voice of Brazil), which all stations were obliged to broadcast in the evening. It imparted government news and propaganda, and promoted national culture. The program has continued in modified form right to the present, transmitting information on government business for half an hour each weekday evening, on all stations.

After Vargas established his populist dictatorship, the Estado Novo, in 1937, government influence in broadcasting was felt even more strongly. The process culminated with the expropriation in 1940 of Rádio Nacional, one of the country's leading stations. Founded in Rio de Janeiro in 1936, Rádio Nacional had developed into a vast organization broadcasting throughout the nation, and regularly producing high-quality programs that achieved the highest audience figures. The Vargas government converted it into an instrument for consolidating its political power, but the high funding that it received enabled it to contract the best radio artists, technicians, and program producers, and throughout the 1940s and 1950s, Rádio Nacional was regularly the station that attracted the largest number of listeners.

Other stations were established by both Brazilian and overseas companies. Powerful Brazilian businessmen who already owned newspapers and magazines became key figures in the development of commercial radio operations. The first major example was Francisco de Assis Chateaubriand, proprietor of Diários Associados, who, having founded Rádio Tupi in São Paulo in 1937— to which he later added other stations—created Brazil's first national media network. However, a far larger communications network would later be built by Brazil's best known media magnate, Roberto Marinho. The owner of *O Globo* (The Globe) newspaper, Marinho launched Rádio Globo in 1944, and then in the 1960s, as Chateaubriand had done the previous decade, used his experience with broadcasting to create a television network.

Popular music dominated the program schedules of the commercial radio stations during the first 10 years of their existence, but in the 1940s its supremacy was increasingly challenged by the radio soap opera, or *radionovela*. Adaptations of theater plays had long been broadcast, and had often been of a high standard, but the success that soap operas had achieved on radio in the United States soon attracted the attention of Brazilian producers. The first Brazilian *radionovela* was transmitted by Rádio Nacional in 1942. Titled *Em busca da felicidade* (In Search of Happiness), it enjoyed considerable success and was on the air for three years. Many listeners were absorbed by the show's realism. One of the actors, Amaral Gurgel, who played the role of a doctor, regularly encountered members of the public waiting for him at the studio to seek his medical advice. Soon many stations were dedicating a large part of their evening schedule to *radionovelas*, which attracted an increasing share of advertising revenue.

The importance of radio news reporting grew significantly after 1939 because of public demand for information about the progress of World War II. The most important news program in the history of Brazilian radio was undoubtedly *Repórter Esso*, on Rádio Nacional. It went on the air for the first time in August 1941, reporting on an attack on Normandy by German aircraft, and was broadcast regularly until 1968. The program was sponsored by the Esso oil company and produced by the advertising agency McCann Erickson. This system of sponsorship, by which an advertising agency created a program on behalf of a large multinational company, produced many popular programs on Brazilian radio, and later on television too (Sinclair, 1999, 65). Greater freedom for political discussion was possible on radio after the Estado Novo ended in 1945. Political and social satire also became popular. Perhaps the most notable example was the show *Pimpinela Escarlate* (Scarlet Pimpernel), on Rádio Mayrink Veiga, in which Paulo Silvino Neto mimicked the major political figures of the day, including Getúlio Vargas.

Sports commentaries, mostly soccer matches, began early on Brazilian radio. The first soccer commentary was broadcast in 1938, and was relayed by loudspeakers to thousands of listeners gathered in an esplanade in Rio de Janeiro. Such programs were soon among the most popular on radio, and a number of the commentators, renowned for their passion, became household names. A particularly memorable soccer commentary was transmitted by Rádio Record in 1948. The São Paulo club was playing against the Italian side, Fiorentina, in Italy, and Brazilian listeners were dismayed to hear Geraldo José de Almeida describe a crushing 8-0 defeat for their team. Next day, however, they learned that São Paulo had in fact won 1-0. The match had been played on April 1, and as an April Fool's joke Almeida had invented the whole commentary from his studio in São Paulo.

Radio enjoyed massive popularity in Brazil in the 1940s and 1950s, and its influence on public opinion, taste, and social customs was considerable. Popular music, also being promoted by an expanding recording industry, was another vital element of the phenomenon. Fan clubs were formed for the most popular singers, such as Emilinha Borba and Marlene (Victória Bonaiuti), and new artists were regularly promoted with great success. Each year the contest to elect the "king" and "queen" of Brazilian radio—the most popular and successful radio artists—was avidly followed by millions of listeners. Until the end of the 1950s, when programs of recorded music became dominant, variety shows before a live audience were often those that achieved the highest ratings. The most famous example was the César de Alencar show, broadcast throughout the country on weekends by Rádio Nacional, which became one of the most listened-to programs in the history of Brazilian radio. Tickets to see the show were regularly sold out two weeks in advance. Other programs helped to popularize music from overseas, especially that of U.S. artists such as Frank Sinatra and Bing Crosby, but the enthusiasm for national popular music did not wane. That was clearly demonstrated by the huge success achieved by a show launched on Rádio Tupi and Rádio Tamoio in 1947, called *O Pessoal da Velha Guarda* (Personnel of the Old Guard), which was clearly a reaction to the growing influence of American mass culture (McCann, 1999). Compered by an already well-known radio personality, Henrique Foreis Domingues, nicknamed "Almirante" (the admiral), the program presented performances of samba, chorinho, and other traditional rhythms, seeking to reaffirm the value and richness of Brazil's popular music tradition.

The rapid growth of television in Brazil in the 1960s meant that radio lost its preeminence as a provider of information and entertainment to the public, and the industry had to develop new ways of retaining listeners. In 1968 the first FM radio stations began broadcasting in Brazil, and by the 1990s they had become those with the highest audience figures. Most of those stations were dedicated principally to recorded popular music, though there were some notable exceptions, such as "Central Brasileira de Notícias" (Brazilian News Center), part of the Globo network, which became the first FM station devoted exclusively to news reporting. A significant feature of Brazilian radio in the last decades of the twentieth century was the emergence of new types of stations with objectives other than commerce and entertainment. Protestant churches, for example, created a number of stations for evangelical broadcasting. Community radio also became increasingly significant. Community stations were run by organizations on a nonprofit basis to provide programs to address the needs and interests of the residents of a local area. By opening up the airwaves to social sectors often marginalized from the mass media, they represented an important step toward greater democracy in broadcasting. However, illegal stations also proliferated in the 1980s and 1990s. Legislation required all stations to obtain a government concession in order to go on the air, but it was estimated that by 2002 there were as many as 10,000 pirate stations operating in the country (*Almanaque Abril,* 2002, 201). The cost of installing such stations was very low, and they could often attract significant advertising revenue. In 2000, the government responded by announcing new measures to identify them and close them down.

Statistics for the year 2001 confirmed the continuing importance of radio in Brazil: 88% of Brazilian homes had a radio set, and 2,965 stations were broadcasting in the country (*Almanaque Abril*, 2002, 200). However, only a small percentage of total advertising revenue in Brazil—as little as 5.1%—went to radio, which had evidently suffered considerably from competition with television in particular. The changing financial circumstances forced commercial radio networks to review the nature of the programs they provided, seeking to capture more young listeners, for example, by modifying the type of music played and the style of presentation. But radio has shown itself able to change and adapt in much more radical ways in order to find new listeners and new markets. In particular, developments in technology regularly present new opportunities. In the 1990s, the first Brazilian stations available via the Internet were launched, and satellite links were used to connect radio stations in Brazil with others in Argentina, Chile, Uruguay, and Paraguay.

TELEVISION

It was the media entrepreneur Francisco de Assis Chateaubriand, already mentioned for his experience with radio, who introduced television in Brazil in 1950. The first program seen in the country was broadcast in São Paulo on the night of September 18, and it launched Brazil's first television station, T.V. Tupi, which became the latest part of Chateaubriand's media empire. Since only a handful of Brazilians owned televisions in 1950, Chateaubriand imported several hundred sets in readiness for the broadcast. Some were sold to private buyers, and others were located in main squares and buildings in São Paulo, so that the wider public could witness the launch. In that first program, called *TV na Taba* (TV in the Village), there were live songs and comedy, and a discussion about the benefits that television could provide. Regular evening broadcasts, from 6 to 11 o'clock, were established, and in January 1951, Chateaubriand launched a second station, TV Tupi of Rio de Janeiro.

Improvisation was a striking feature of the early years of Brazilian television, largely because, until the arrival of videotape in 1962, everything, including the advertisements in which products were demonstrated to the viewers, had to be broadcast live. Technicians, cameramen, and presenters had to become adept at covering up for mistakes. Radio provided many of the first professionals to work in the Brazilian television industry. Some would enjoy long careers in the spotlight as popular television personalities. A notable example is Hebe Camargo, a successful radio singer who sang on some of the first television programs, and was still a popular host of interview shows in the 1990s. Another case was Lima Duarte, a radio presenter who became a well-known television actor in the early 1950s, and was still appearing in soap operas 40 years later. Radio also provided television with its most successful programs in the 1950s. *Radionovelas* were converted into *telenovelas*, the soap operas that would become such a salient feature of Brazilian television. TV Tupi broadcast the first Brazilian soap in 1951. Titled *Sua vida me pertence* (Your Life Belongs to Me), it was shown in two installments each week, and enjoyed considerable popularity. It also caused great commotion among the viewing public by including the first kiss to be seen on Brazilian television. Other programs imported from radio were *Repórter Esso*, which, launched on TV Tupi in 1953, remained the major news program on Brazilian television until the late 1960s, and the quiz show, in the form of *O Céu é o Limite* (The Sky's the Limit), also on TV Tupi, which, in the mid-1950s, was the television program with the highest viewing figures. The contestants accumulated prize money by answering questions on a specialist subject, and the show established a model for many future TV quiz shows.

The number of television sets in Brazil was low throughout most of the 1950s. According to one source, the figure had only reached 250,000 by 1956 (Sinclair, 1999, 64). Because public access was restricted, the advertising revenue attracted by television stations remained limited. As a result, it was cheaper to advertise on Brazilian television in the 1950s than on radio or in magazines. Television sets were manufactured in Brazil from 1951 onward, but they were very expensive for the large majority of Brazilians. Nevertheless, despite these limitations television expanded steadily as the decade progressed. New stations were founded regularly, not only where television was already strong, in São Paulo and Rio de Janeiro, with stations such as TV Paulista (São Paulo, 1952), TV Record (São Paulo, 1953), and TV Rio (Rio de Janeiro, 1955), but in the capitals of other regions as well. Notable examples were TV Paraná in Curitiba and TV Itacolomi in Belo Horizonte, both established in 1952; TV Rádio Clube de Pernambuco, in Recife in 1957; and TV Piratini in Porto Alegre in 1959. Twenty stations were operating in Brazil by 1960, and the number of sets in the country had risen to nearly 1.8 million (*Almanaque Abril*, 2001, 350).

Some significant technological advances were made as well. A soccer game was first televised in 1952, and in 1956 a match between Brazil and Italy became the country's first interstate broadcast. The game was played in Rio de Janeiro, but TV Tupi managed to broadcast it directly to viewers in São Paulo. In 1960, the inauguration of Brasília as the new national capital was followed by television viewers in such cities as Belo Horizonte, Rio, and São Paulo, thanks to government investment to ensure that the event could be transmitted to as many parts of the country as possible. As far as the production of programs was concerned, the introduction of videotape in 1962 was the most important innovation of the period. It meant that programs of all types could be recorded and edited, leading to a dramatic improvement in their quality.

It was against this background of ongoing technical development and a steadily expanding audience that TV Globo, soon to become Brazil's largest television network by far, was established in 1965. It became another branch of the huge media conglomerate being built by Roberto Marinho (1904–1998), the most powerful figure in the history of the Brazilian media. Several years before, Marinho had signed an agreement with the U.S. corporation Time-Life, which, in return for 30% of Globo's profits, provided Marinho with considerable investment and technical support to help create the new channel. The agreement ended in 1971, but it gave TV Globo a significant advantage over rival television companies during the 1960s. Globo grew rapidly, and by 1969 it was already the channel with the highest audience figures in Brazil. Another crucial factor was the close cooperation that existed between Globo and the military dictatorship which took power in Brazil in 1964. A major policy of the military government was to promote and sponsor the expansion of the mass culture industry, particularly cinema and television, as a means of controlling information and uniting the population behind its drive for rapid economic growth and modernization. Globo became an important instrument for realizing those objectives, and it benefited considerably through its support for the regime. It carefully tailored its programming to avoid conflict with the government, which imposed strict censorship and dealt severely with television professionals it suspected of propagating dissent. The most publicized case was that of Wladimir Herzog, newschief of TV Cultura in São Paulo, who was arrested by police in 1975 and died under torture.

Globo dedicated much effort to expanding its audience. One way was by taking advantage of the new telecommunications infrastructure, such as cable and satellite systems, that the government developed (Sinclair, 1999, 69). Another was to create programs that had mass popular appeal. Globo soon became a major producer of television programs. Again, it benefited from government policy, namely, the creation of incentives for Brazilian program production to counterbalance foreign programming (Sinclair, 1999, 69). Top managers, program producers, and artists were recruited from other television channels. A series of high-quality and innovative programs resulted. *Jornal Nacional*, which went on the air for the first time in 1969, became Brazil's most-watched news broadcast. Popular children's programs were created, and variety shows, such as the Sunday spectacular *Fantástico*, which was launched in 1973, enjoyed huge success. It was, however, the *telenovelas* produced by Globo that attracted most attention and won the largest audiences. Many were exported and shown in countries across the world. In addition to its attention to quality, Globo took the lead in the incorporation of technological development in broadcasting. It was TV Globo, for example, that led the way in introducing programs in color in the early 1970s. By the 1980s, the company had distanced itself from the military government, and new television stations were attempting to compete, but by then Globo was one of the largest television networks in the world and its dominant position was not seriously challenged.

Series imported from the United States proliferated on Brazilian television in the 1960s, but Brazilian production of entertainment programming remained strong. It relied above all on comedy, popular music, and *telenovelas*. A number of comedians obtained such a huge following that they enjoyed long careers as high-profile television personalities. None was more popular than Chacrinha (real name José Abelardo Barbosa de Medeiros), who defined himself as "the people's clown." He began as a radio presenter, and then, for nearly 30 years, hosted a number of successful television shows on several different channels, including Globo. His anarchic style of humor made him a controversial figure, but endeared him to millions of viewers. Another comedy star who established his television career in the 1960s was Chico Anísio, famous for his creation of over 200 larger-than-life humorous characters. His shows on TV Globo were still achieving high ratings in the 1990s, by which time he was one of the station's highest-paid artists. One particular comedy program that has a special claim to fame is *Adoráveis Trapalhões* (Adorable Fools), which began on TV Tupi in 1967. Featuring the antics of a comic quartet, it entered the *Guinness Book of Records* at the end of the 1990s as the longest-running comedy show in the history of television.

The boom of Brazilian popular music in the 1960s was considerably aided by certain television programs of the time. In 1965, TV Record launched two music shows that proved to be enormously popular with young viewers. One was *O Fino da Bossa* (The Best of Bossa), hosted by Elis Regina and Jair Rodrigues, which helped to popularize the work of such talented and original young singer–songwriters as Chico Buarque, Gilberto Gil, and Caetano Veloso. The other, *Jovem Guarda* (Young Guard), a Sunday afternoon show presented by Roberto Carlos, promoted a Brazilian form of rock and roll largely derived from American and British models. Broadcast in several large cities, it achieved an audience of almost three million in São Paulo alone. Another program shown in 1965 was even more significant for Brazilian popular music, however. In April, TV Excelsior broadcast the first Festival of Brazilian Popular Music, which took place in the town of Guarujá, in São Paulo state. Such was its success that further festivals were organized and broadcast annually for many years, with TV Record taking over the transmission. The festivals not only provided a focal point for a whole generation of singers and composers, and gave them huge audiences for their work, but also opened up rare television space for the expression of the dissent of 1960s youth culture.

Music and comedy have always been essential ingredients of the extravagant and ever-popular variety shows that have long dominated weekend programming on Brazilian television. Although originally modeled on American variety shows, they have developed their own distinct characteristics over the decades. They are a peculiar mixture of games involving members of the public, news items, interviews, and all kinds of entertainment. Their maximum expression is found in the Sunday spectaculars presented by the major networks. They can last for eight hours or more, and competition between them for viewers is fierce. Audience figures for all programs in Brazil are regularly produced by OBOPE (The Brazilian Institute of Studies of Public Opinion and Statistics), a private company established in the 1940s. The statistics it produces are closely scrutinized by the major television networks, which frequently alter their programming according to the information the figures provide.

It is for its *telenovelas* that Brazilian television is best known. They have dominated primetime evening viewing for decades, and, exported to numerous countries in Europe, Africa, Asia, and Latin America, they are the element of Brazilian television that has received most international acclaim. Many of the early *telenovelas* were written outside Brazil, such as *2.5499 Ocupado* (2.5499 Is Busy), broadcast by Excelsior in 1963, which was the work of the Argentine writer Alberto Migré. Following the story of a female prisoner, it was the first Brazilian soap opera to be shown on a daily basis and lasted for 43 episodes. The popularity of such programs was confirmed by *O Direito de Nacer* (The Right to Be Born), shown in 1965 by TV Tupi, which was the first *telenovela* to achieve a mass audience in Brazil. Written by the Cuban, Felix Caignet, it enjoyed similar success in many other Latin American countries, enthralling viewers with turbulent love affairs and family conflicts. Its high ratings encouraged all Brazilian TV stations to invest more in *telenovelas*. TV Tupi, Globo, and TV Excelsior were soon broadcasting three, or sometimes four, concurrently each week. Many Brazilian soap operas that were broadcast in the 1960s adhered to the formula that had proved to be successful elsewhere in Latin America, such as in Cuba and Mexico, and relied heavily on romance, melodrama, and exoticism. Those were the salient characteristics of the popular *telenovelas* produced by the Cuban, Gloria Magadan, for Globo, for whom she began working in 1966. Far-away locations such as Morocco and Japan generally provided the settings for her plots. At the same time, however, other writers were already creating soaps dealing with distinctly Brazilian social realities.

Typically, a Brazilian soap opera runs for about seven or eight weeks, though the precise length can vary according to its success. It has been a common practice for a new *telenovela* to go on the air once 12 or so episodes have been written, and for the rest to then be written in accordance with the viewers' reaction, which is gauged via audience research that is carried out. The development of characters and of the plot can thus be modified as the series continues, depending on the likes and dislikes of the viewers. This practice has sometimes produced bizarre results. One example occurred in *Redenção* (Redemption), which, consisting of 596 episodes, is reputedly the longest *telenovela* to have been shown on Brazilian television. Broadcast by TV Excelsior between 1966 and 1968, it focused on a mysterious doctor who inspired amorous feelings in three different women. The script writers confronted a difficult problem when, having killed off another female character of the series, audience research indicated that viewers were dismayed by the death and that ratings were likely to suffer. A solution was quickly sought. Forthcoming episodes were rewritten, with the doctor carrying out a heart transplant on the woman, who, although assumed by everyone to have died, was therefore miraculously restored to life.

Beto Rockfeller, shown on TV Tupi between 1968 and 1969, is often credited with having revolutionized the Brazilian *telenovela*. It relied on colloquial speech instead of the formal theatrical dialogue common in previous soap operas, and was innovative in terms of the filming techniques and style of acting employed. It also explored important aspects of Brazilian society. Beto, the protagonist, is set on achieving social status and financial prosperity, and, pretending to be a millionaire, uses his charm and skills of deception to enter São Paulo high society. The focus on an anti-hero and the dilemmas created by his behavior were also novel, and fascinated viewers. *Beto Rockfeller* launched a new era for the Brazilian *telenovela*, but it would be dominated by TV Globo. Despite the successes that TV Tupi and TV Excelsior had had with the genre, it was Globo, bringing together the best writers, directors, and actors, that for the next three decades produced the majority of the *telenovelas* that achieved the highest ratings. Successful *telenovelas* became an essential part of Globo's dominant position over its rivals. The station established a regular evening program schedule, showing three or four hour-long soap operas, one after the other, six days a week.

O Bem Amado (The Beloved), shown by Globo in 1973, was another landmark. Not only was it the first Brazilian *telenovela* to be broadcast in color, but it was also the first to be exported on a significant scale. It was shown in most other Latin American countries. The author was Alfredo Dias Gomes, one of Brazil's leading dramatists, and *O Bem Amado*, focusing on the squabbles and intrigues of small-town life, was adapted from one of his stage plays. It offers a good example of how the *telenovela* writer can engage the audience through reference to topical issues. In one episode the town's mayor conceals a microphone in the confession box in the church in order to listen in on the intimate revelations made by other townsfolk, a clear allusion to the Watergate scandal that had dominated international headlines shortly before. Dias Gomes wrote several other important *telenovelas* for Globo, most notably *Roque Santeiro* (Roque the Saint Maker), which he co-authored with Aguinaldo Silva. Satire and farce are used to discuss political corruption and the role of religion in Brazilian society. It was prepared for broadcast in 1975, but was censored by the military government and was only shown when the dictatorship ended 10 years later.

Some of Globo's most popular *telenovelas* have been adaptations of literary works. *Gabriela*, based on Jorge Amado's novel of comedy and social satire, *Gabriela, cravo e canela* (Gabriela, Clove and Cinnamon), was a huge success in 1975, and the following year *A Escrava Isaura* (Isaura the Slave Girl), an adaptation of a nineteenth-century anti-slavery novel by Bernardo Guimarães, reached an even larger audience, for it was exported to over 30 countries. Overseas markets for its *telenovelas* became increasingly important to Globo in the course of the 1980s. In Brazil itself, only occasionally did a *telenovela* by a rival network beat Globo's soap opera productions in the ratings. The capacity of the *telenovela* to generate discussion of important matters of public concern, as well as to entertain, was clearly demonstrated by *O Rei do Gado* (The King of Cattle), broadcast on Globo between 1996 and 1997. Through the story of landless rural agricultural workers, it focused national attention on the very sensitive issue of agrarian reform. Intellectuals, journalists, and politicians of all persuasions participated in a heated public debate on the series and the questions it raised. The author of *O Rei do Gado*, Benedito Ruy Barbosa, was also responsible for Globo's last big *telenovela* of the 1990s, *Terra Nostra* (Our Land). Shown in 1999, it was a lavish and costly production of vast scope, tracing the experience of Italian immigrants to Brazil, from the late nineteenth century to the end of the twentieth. The "Globo

Xuxa, or Maria da Graça Meneghel, dancing on her television show in July 1990. (AP Photo/Renzo Gostoli)

label of quality" tends to become a norm for all networks to follow. In 1984, Globo created the Casa de Criação Janete Clair, named after the network's most famous and popular *telenovela* writer, who died prematurely in 1983. This in-house creation center was largely responsible for the training of future screenwriters and served as a think tank until 1986.

Mention must be made of one other popular Globo program of the 1980s and 1990s, such was the huge impact it made. The *Xou da Xuxa* (The Xuxa Show) was first broadcast in 1986, and because of its success it was eventually shown for five hours each morning, six days a week. Xuxa (real name Maria da Graça Meneghel) began a modelling career as a teenager, and then hosted children's programs on TV Manchete in the early 1980s. Her show on Globo was primarily produced for children, but conquered adult viewers too. Tall, blond, energetic, and flirtatious, Xuxa has become a media icon, the focus of much press attention and even of academic studies analyzing how her charismatic image has been created and why it has proved so alluring to a mass audience. It has been argued that much of the appeal of her show derives from the fact that, by skillfully incorporating and manipulating diverse cultural elements, it symbolically reconciles the deep social and economic divisions within Brazilian society (Simpson, 1999). At the height of her popularity in the early 1990s, Xuxa was the highest-paid entertainer in Latin America.

In the early 1980s the Brazilian government granted television concessions to two new companies, in order to stimulate competition. The successful channels were SBT (Sistema Brasileiro de Televisão), launched in 1982, and TV Manchete, which went on the air the following year. SBT proved to be the most significant. Its owner is Sílvio Santos, one of Brazil's best known celebrities. He began work as a street seller in Rio de Janeiro, but in the 1960s he became one of Globo's biggest stars when he established himself as a popular variety show host. With SBT, he combined his roles as media entrepreneur and television personality. His 12-hour-long Sunday show competed strongly with rival shows on Globo, and SBT soon became Brazil's second-largest station. Globo's supremacy remained solid, however. Its profits far exceeded those of its nearest rivals, and, according to figures for 1999, its share of the national television audience was 56%, compared with 24% for SBT, 9% for TV Record, and 5% for Bandeirantes (*Almanaque Abril*, 2001, 234). Globo's capacity to produce almost all its own programming is one of the biggest advantages it has held over its competitors (Sinclair, 1999, 71). In 1996, Globo inaugurated Projac, the largest television production center in Latin America, situated just outside Rio de Janeiro.

In 1991, subscription television or "Pay-TV" was established in Brazil. The first station of this type was Televisão Abril, but it was soon facing strong competition from Globo. For several years "Pay-TV" expanded rapidly, but that had trailed off by 2000. Its cost was relatively high, and many viewers appeared unimpressed by the quality of programs it offered. By then, however, the development of digital television and interactive television in Brazil indicated that, as elsewhere, technological advance was promising to usher in a new era for television in the country.

REFERENCES

Almanaque Abril 2001. São Paulo: Editora Abril, 2001.
Capelato, Maria Helena. *Imprensa e história do Brazil*. São Paulo: Ática, 1988.
Enciclopédia Novo Século. São Paulo: Editora Abril Cultural, 1988.
Fernandes, Ismael. *Memória da Televisão Brasileira*. São Paulo: Proposta, 1982.
Mattelart, Michéle and Armand Mattelart. *The Carnival of Images: Brazilian Television Fiction*. Westport, CT: Bergin and Garvey, 1990.

McCann, Bryan. "The Invention of Tradition on Brazilian Radio." In *The Brazil Reader: History, Culture, Politics*, ed. Robert M. Levine and John J. Crocitti. Durham, NC: Duke University Press, 1999, pp. 474–482.

Simpson, Amelia, "Xuxa and the Televisual Imagery." In *The Brazil Reader: History, Culture, Politics*, ed. Robert M. Levine and John J. Crocitti. Durham, NC: Duke University Press, 1999, pp. 343–347.

Sinclair, John. *Latin American Television: A Global View*. Oxford: Oxford University Press, 1999.

Skidmore, Thomas E., ed. *Television, Politics, and the Transition to Democracy in Latin America*. Washington, DC: Woodrow Wilson Center Press, 1993.

8

Cinema

Jon Tolman

Cinema Novo is a phenomenon of new peoples everywhere and not a privilege of Brazil. Wherever one finds filmmakers prepared to film the truth and oppose the hypocrisy and repression of intellectual censorship there is the living spirit of Cinema Novo; wherever filmmakers of whatever age or background, place their cameras and their profession in the service of the great causes of our time there is the spirit of Cinema Novo.
—Glauber Rocha in "An Aesthetic of Hunger," 1965[1]

FILM AND SOCIETY

CINEMA IS A hybrid medium of the twentieth century that combines features of the narrative, theater, photography, and painting (or pictorial representation). Because it has always cost a great deal to produce films, questions of market and marketability rapidly developed an intrusive role in how films were made. The appearance of film coincides with the growth of mass consumer markets in the Western world and film quickly became a popular consumer good in the dense urban societies that characterized the twentieth century. It is only in the latter half of the twentieth century that film became regarded as an artistic medium and was given serious attention by intellectuals and academe. Today "movies" are the stuff of the classroom and their analysis is common in newspapers and television, another twentieth-century medium that combines the artistic with mass-market appeal. Regarding both media, conservative critics constantly carp at their shallowness, lack of social values, and seductive allure because they have supplanted such traditional entertainments of the elite as reading, theater, opera, and other manifestations of fine art.

At the beginning of the century, filmmaking was a hobby for a small elite and international group of pioneers, including several Brazilians, but as its popular appeal was revealed, it quickly developed into an industry. With industrial production and mass marketing came economies of scale and intense international competition. For decades, film industries in First World countries like the United Kingdom, France, Italy, and Germany were able to compete with Hollywood, but gradually the polish and sophistication of its productions and the development by the United States of a juggernaut distribution system have forced film in these countries to depend on government subsidies and other measures, like nationalistic legislation, to survive. Ironically, at the end of the century, Hollywood cannibalized itself, producing a system of production so expensive and technology-dependent that it seemed only able to produce blockbusters or expensive failures. In the shadow of the giant studios a new market for independent and foreign (especially slick, "Masterpiece Theater" European-look productions) has grown up, returning us to the situation before Hollywood ate the world.

If industrialized First World societies have been unable to resist the allure and power of Hollywood, imagine the plight of Third World countries. Small markets, language difficulties (subtitle translations are a sure way to destroy the market for a foreign film), lack of access to capital markets, and the ability of the U.S. film industry to use its international clout to price its products more affordably to consumers in poor countries have made it nearly impossible for filmmaking to thrive in all but a few places. Some exceptions to the general rule of failure (or sporadic production) are Mexico, which grinds out hundreds of potboilers a year for the gigantic Spanish-language market of Latin America and, increasingly, the United States; and India, which has a vigorous film industry that is confined to the subcontinent. Both Mexico and India occasionally produce films that escape the ghetto, where the majority of their productions languish. This is also true of the United Kingdom, France, Italy, and Germany. For *Life is Beautiful* (Italy) to have won an academy award in 1998 is remarkable, but it is nothing short of miraculous that a Brazilian film, *Central Station*, was also in the running for an award (for best actress).

THE BEGINNINGS OF BRAZILIAN FILM

Affonso Segreto, who amazed audiences in Rio de Janeiro and São Paulo with short documentaries, introduced filmmaking to Brazil in 1898. The medium did not become commercially viable until industrialization brought electricity to the capital. Exhibition halls sprouted wherever there was power, and local entrepreneurs began to supply the demand for product, mainly news and documentaries. Segreto began making re-creations of famous crimes, and it was not long until comedies (musical and burlesque) began to appear. Films were made about the country's growing obsession with soccer and Carnival. An adaptation of Antônio Carlos Gomes' opera, *O Guarani* (1870) was wildly popular. There was no lack of subjects. This growth of film accompanied a campaign to make Rio de Janeiro a modern city, with wide avenues, electric lights, running water, and other features of First World urban life. Cultural life flourished during this Belle Époque period. Intellectuals and artists were particularly taken with film, and film metaphors became a staple (it was equated in the popular imagination with modernity, along with the Model T Ford) of the avant-garde literary movement of the 1920s and 1930s (*modernismo*).

In 1911, Brazilians welcomed a delegation of American businessmen, who realized the potential of the Brazilian market for U.S. films. The United States quickly moved to dominate the local market with American and European films that were far more sophisticated than the local product. Brazilian filmmaking became an auxiliary to foreign imports, a situation that continued until the 1940s, when a local entrepreneur and exhibitor, Luis Severiano Ribeiro, purchased Atlântida, an existing studio. In the intervening two decades, Brazilian filmmakers produced, on a sporadic basis, dozens of films, experimenting with foreign techniques and methods. Two figures stand out as significant to modern students of film: Humberto Mauro and Mário Peixoto.

Mário Peixoto directed a silent avant-garde film in 1930, *Limit (Limite)*, which was seen by few viewers at the time, but which nevertheless gained almost mythical status as a daring, experimental film. A young man of 18, Peixoto was knowledgeable about European avant-garde techniques and his work used multiple points of view, symbolic montage, and different time lines, centering around two women and a man adrift in a small boat (static images of enclosure, thirst, and desperation) played against images of movement (walking, train wheels, sewing machine wheels, montages of beaches and storms) and imprisonment (handcuffs, a prison, a loveless marriage, meaningless drudge work). Each of the protagonists has a reason for seeking freedom but each has somehow come to be imprisoned on the boat, from which the only escape is death. The film, even today, is a stunning visual and symbolic exploration of freedom and limits. Although withdrawn from circulation by Peixoto himself, a partial restoration is now available on videotape, allowing contemporary viewers to validate Sergei Eisenstein's opinion that it was "an extremely beautiful film which one should submit oneself to right from the very first moments, as to the agonizing chords of a synthetic and pure language of cinema."[2]

Humberto Mauro (1897–1983) is Brazil's outstanding silent filmmaker. He began his career with a five-minute film about a kidnapping, *Valadião, O Cratera* (1925). From 1925 to 1933 he made four films set in his native Minas Gerais. Mauro moved to Rio de Janeiro in 1930 to work for the Cinédia studio, where he made several films, including *The Voice of Carnival* (*A Voz de Carnaval*), which was Carmen Miranda's debut as a film star. Mauro finished his masterpiece, *Raw Ore* (*Ganga Bruta*), in 1933, about a man who kills his bride on their honeymoon and his subsequent attempt to rehabilitate himself. The film used an Expressionist, Realist style that made a deep impression on several young men who would later become Cinema Novo filmmakers, when they saw it at a retrospective showing in 1961. Mauro went on to work for the Instituto Nacional do Cinema Educativo (National Institute of Educational Cinema) and produced and directed some 240 documentary films. He made his last film in 1974, *Oxcart* (*Carro de Boi*), about his childhood in Minas.

Luís Severiano Ribeiro decided that imitation was the way to beat Hollywood, so he built up his Atlântida studio into a vertically integrated operation that concentrated on producing what had become a national subgenre, the *chanchada*, a kind of musical comedy. The *chanchada* made stars of several Brazilian actors, including Carmen Miranda, Oscarito, and Grande Otelo, and lasted well into the 1950s. In the 1960s *chanchadas* gradually developed into a soft-core porn genre, the *pornochanchada*. Usually quickly produced, low-budget films made in São Paulo's red-light district, they were the unexpected result of nationalistic decrees during the dictatorship (1964–1985) which required cinemas to show "national" content.

INTIMATIONS OF HOLLYWOOD

During the first half of the twentieth century, São Paulo slowly grew into the industrial heartland of the country, a process that led to the city's becoming a cultural center as well. There was wealth in abundance and an enlightened elite that was aware of the avant-garde movements in Europe. It was no accident that Modernism burst forth on the country from São Paulo. As the world entered the long struggle that culminated in World War II, the isolation this event provoked in Brazil sheltered the growing industrial plant in the region surrounding the city. Rio de Janeiro entered a period of slow decline. This social, cultural, and economic shift was capped in 1960 when then President Juscelino Kubitschek inaugurated Brasília, in the interior, as the country's new capital.

In 1949 a group of Paulista industrialists, led by Francisco Matarazzo Sobrinho, founded the Companhia Cinematográfica Vera Cruz. This influential group recognized that the *chanchada* had developed into a legitimate Brazilian form, but wanted to elevate Brazilian production to the same level of sophistication as the imports. Vera Cruz contracted foreign technicians and producers, put actors on contract, built costly sets modeled on Metro-Goldwyn Mayer, and set out to compete with Hollywood. Between 1949 and 1954, the company produced 18 feature films before going bankrupt. While Vera Cruz was able to produce slick, sophisticated color films, it was unable to develop an international distribution system, and the internal Brazilian market could not generate sufficient income to support the company's inefficient and costly operation. The high point of Vera Cruz' production was Lima Barreto's *O Cangaceiro* (1953), about rural banditry, which won double gold palms at the Cannes Festival and went into worldwide circulation.

Following the demise of Vera Cruz, there remained a pool of talent, energy, and wealth in São Paulo, so quality films continued to be produced, but the younger generation drew the lesson that a Brazilian film industry would need protection from foreign competition to survive. They also rejected the big studio production system, developing instead a philosophy of reducing filmmaking to its essentials, simplifying production by using hand-held cameras and black-and-white film, using amateur or nonactors, and going into the streets and the interior of the country to find "authentic" Brazilians. As Glauber Rocha, one of the generation's theorists, said, "All you need is a camera in your hands and an idea in your head." They devised a name for their style of filmmaking: New Cinema (Cinema Novo).

CINEMA NOVO

The cinemanovistas were influenced by Italian Neorealism, by a Marxist intellectual milieu in the universities and among the intelligentsia, and by a developmentalist ideology that encouraged Brazilians to believe that they could bootstrap the burgeoning development of the Center-South into a countrywide prosperity that would finally bring Brazil into First World status. These young intellectuals had been deeply affected by the socialist-oriented Brazilian narrative of the 1930s that focused attention on the desperately poor Northeast (Jorge Amado, Graciliano Ramos, José Lins do Rego,

Rachel de Queiroz). They were also aware of the desperate poverty that seethed in the slums of every large Brazilian city. If the presidency of Juscelino Kubitschek (1956–1961) oversaw an amazing period of urban growth, economic development, and cultural diversity (bossa nova, painting, sculpture, the influential Concrete poetry movement, architecture, theater), it also brought the country's deficiencies in social and economic infrastructure into sharp focus. The building of Brasília through deficit spending and other grandiose projects led to an inflationary spiral that brought economic chaos to the country, exacerbated class and labor unrest, and provoked an intense right-wing reaction that culminated in the military coup of 1964.

Cinema Novo had its beginning in a film by Alex Viany in 1953, *Needle in the Haystack* (*Agulha no Palheiro*). Nelson Pereira dos Santos was an assistant director for the film, which depicted everyday Brazilians. He went on to make a breakthrough film, *Rio 40 Degrees* (*Rio 40 Graus*) in 1955, using Neorealistic techniques and a low-budget approach, and focusing on poor people in the streets of Rio. The film made an intense impression on the younger generation. Cinema Novo has been divided into phases or periods, the first lasting from 1955 to 1964, the second from 1964 to 1968, and the third from 1968 to 1972. The first period was one of intensely ideological films designed to raise the consciousness of the proletariat and the middle class. Generally, the films were also intensely unpopular with the public; none was a success at the box office. This was a moment when the United States was convinced that the Soviet Union was attempting to repeat its success with Cuba in South America. The Kennedy government was deeply suspicious of the Brazilian left and encouraged the developing right-wing movement that led to the coup in 1964. Two films stand out from this period: Nelson Pereira dos Santos' *Barren Lives* (1963—*Vidas Secas*), and Glauber Rocha's *Black God, White Devil* (1964—*Deus e o Diabo na Terra do Sol*).

Barren Lives is set in the drought-stricken Northeast and based on Graciliano Ramos' eponymous masterpiece of 1938. It chronicles one cycle of drought that takes a poor cowboy and his family from a desperate existence (the film opens with the family on the road fleeing from drought) to a slightly less desperate one when rains come bringing relief. The family secures a precarious existence on a ranch as sharecroppers. They are exploited and mistreated by the owner of the ranch and people in the nearby small town. At the end of the cycle, the drought returns and the family once again leaves, seeking a better future. The film is characterized by an intensely realistic and innovative cinematic technique, symbolic use of the soundtrack, and profound acting, albeit by a largely amateur cast.

Black God, White Devil is also set in the backlands of the Northeast, but Rocha develops his film as an allegorical study of the effect of religious messianism and banditry on the populace. Messianism is an abiding feature of popular culture in the Northeast and often involves a kind of naïve socialism (God will reward the suffering poor with the lands of the undeserving rich and establish a system of justice). Rural banditry (*cangaço*) is a violent response to an unjust social situation, but the *cangaceiros*, by serving as paid killers by one faction or another, only perpetuate the system.

After 1964, the military regime imposed censorship and persecuted the left, but its ideas continued in the universities and among the intelligentsia. Disillusioned with the failure of democratic populism (the government of João Goulart, and to some extent, Kubitschek before him), the cinemanovistas and other intellectuals engaged in a pessimistic analysis of their failure. The finest film to emerge from this short period is Glauber Rocha's *Land in Anguish* (1967—*Terra em Transe*). Set in a mythical Latin American country, Eldorado (to elude the censors), the film portrays the rise of a populist dictator and the powerlessness of intellectuals to affect the course of events. Like all of Rocha's films, *Land in Anguish* works along two different lines of inquiry, one allegorical and moral, the other political.

The cinemanovistas were aware that their films were unpopular and they developed a strategy to gain better distribution in the face of imports by founding their own distributor (Difilm) in cooperation with producer Luiz Carlos Barreto. At the same time, they began making comedies and films based on popular novels like Walter Lima Jr.'s *Plantation Boy* (1965—*Menino de Engenho*) and Leon Hirszman's *Girl from Ipanema* (1967—*Garota de Ipanema*). Also at the same time, hard-line military conspirators launched the coup of 1968, a sharp turn toward outright dictatorship, with a suspension of civil rights, very strict censorship, persecution, and exile of writers, filmmakers, intellectuals, and students.

TROPICÁLIA

The reaction of filmmakers to this situation was to move further toward allegory and to reach back to the exuberant "Cannibalist" phase of Modernism. Cannibalism (1928) was one of the first attempts by a dependent culture (or former colony) to formulate an ideology that accounted for foreign cultural influences but provided a mechanism for originality: digesting the foreign, as the Tupi-Guarani Indians had done to the Portuguese and French colonizers. Variously called *Tropicália* and Cannibalism, its adherents pronounced themselves free to use foreign elements in any way they saw fit, "putting foreign cultural influences in a blender" is the way one critic has described it. In film this attitude produced the first commercially successful contemporary products, movies that Brazilian audiences liked and that had some market appeal in the United States and Europe.

The first big hit during this period was Joaquim Pedro de Andrade's *Macunaíma* (1969), a wild, grotesque film version of the eponymous modernist narrative by Mário de Andrade. The main character, played by *chanchada* superstar Grande Otelo, portrays the life of a Brazilian everyman, "a hero with no character whatsoever," as Andrade defined him. A tragicomedy blending popular culture, folklore, a parody of urban guerrilla warfare, brilliant technicolor, and comedy, the film typified the Tropicália mind-set. Other films produced during the period include Glauber Rocha's *Antonio the Killer* (1968—*Antônio das Mortes*). Like Rocha's other films, this is a moralistic, ideological allegory, centered around the main character, a paid assassin. The film ranges from the streets of Rio de Janeiro to the backlands, and incorporates contemporary political commentary with its historical precedents in massacres and other violent episodes in Brazil's past. The third great film produced during this time is Nelson Pereira dos Santos' *How Tasty Was My Little Frenchman* (1971—*Como Era Gostoso o meu Francês*). This film is based on the memoirs of a German adventurer, Hans Staden, who participated in the ill-fated French Huguenot attempt to settle what was to become Rio de Janeiro in the sixteenth century. Staden also was instrumental in the literary Cannibalist movement previously mentioned. The film is literally about cannibalism (the Frenchman of the title gets eaten) but also about nationhood and the lies that underwrite the foundation myths of the country.

By 1971–1972, Cinema Novo was finished, with several directors driven into exile, and government harassment of intellectuals reaching a peak. There was an underground film movement that produced some memorable but little-watched films, especially Rogério Sganzerla's *The Red Light Bandit* (1968—*Bandido da Luz Vermelha*) and Júlio Bressane's *Killed the Family and Went to the Movies* (1970—*Matou a Família e Foi ao Cinema*). Directors like Nelson Pereira dos Santos and others, who escaped government persecution, sought out foreign funding, usually in France or Italy. It was during this time that *pornochanchada* had its heyday.

The years between 1972 and 1985, when the authoritarian regime relinquished control, were marked by a gradual lessening of tension and restoration of civil rights. The regime never was able to establish its legitimacy and the euphoria produced by the very high economic growth rates of 1967–1973 had almost no impact on the country's suffering poor or its middle

class. On the contrary, during these years, there was massive foreign investment in the country but the gap between rich and poor widened considerably.
The huge foreign loans floated by the regime during the world petroleum
crisis of 1973 led to a new inflationary spiral that was only brought under
control during the first term of President Fernando Henrique Cardoso
(1995–1998). An amnesty for exiles in 1968 was followed by the gradual
return of filmmakers, composers, politicians, and writers.

In this period, several cinemanovistas produced memorable films, and in
the 1980s and 1990s a number of new players emerged on the cinema scene.
One cinemanovista director not previously mentioned was Carlos Diegues,
whose *Xica da Silva* (1976), about a slave woman whose beauty and charm
allowed her to briefly become the "Queen of Brazil," was followed by *Bye
Bye Brasil* (1980). *Bye Bye Brasil* showed that a perceptive questioning of
modernization, the great quest of Brazil in the twentieth century, could go
hand-in-hand with a rollicking and enjoyable film. In *Bye Bye Brasil*, the
viewer follows the misadventures of a travelling sideshow as its corny, tawdry
routines are made obsolete by the advent of television. Who wants to pay to
see a striptease, a cheap magician, and a strong-man act, when you can watch
TV for free? Desperately seeking places where TV has not penetrated the
hinterland, the troupe flees to the interior along the Trans-Amazonian Highway, one of the military regime's costly boondoggles. Diegues followed *Bye
Bye Brasil* with a lavish production (to that time the most costly film ever
produced in Brazil), *Quilombo* (1984). *Quilombo*, loosely based on the runaway slave kingdom of the same name, Quilombo dos Palmares, was panned
by the Brazilian critics, but well received internationally. The film might best
be approached as sort of intellectual musical comedy, with its phantasmagoric
sets, brilliant musical score, dance, and panoply.

BRAZILIAN FILM AT THE END OF THE TWENTIETH CENTURY

In spite of its repression of intellectuals, artists, and filmmakers, the military regime accepted the notion that a national film industry could not
survive without government subsidies, and created the Instituto Nacional do
Cinema (INC) in 1966. The INC was replaced in 1969, at the height of
repression, with Embrafilme, and in 1975 the regime created Concine to
distribute Brazilian films. Operating through loans, subsidies, and other incentives to production, Embrafilme gradually became bureaucratized, and,
given Brazil's penchant for clientilistic relationships, increasingly inaccessible
to all but a small group of filmmakers. In spite of its problematic status
(paradoxically, the requirement that cinemas show Brazilian products led

Embrafilme to finance a large number of *pornochancadas*), Embrafilme did permit Brazilian filmmaking to grow under reasonably stable conditions, but after 1990, when Embrafilme, Concine, and the Fundação Brasileira de Cinema were abolished as part of the Collor government's scorched-earth policy toward culture, film production plummeted to its lowest levels in the century. The following period led some pessimistic students of cinema to conclude that the industry was finished in Brazil. (In part this nadir was also the result of the economic crisis that affected all of Latin America in the 1980s and 1990s: production costs soared and capital became scarce.)

The gradual recovery of the economy under Itamar Franco and Fernando Henrique Cardoso (the famous *real* currency plan that brought a halt to galloping inflation), followed by new legislation designed to stimulate cultural activity in various areas through a system of tax incentives and other mechanisms (the Lei do Audiovisual in 1993; the Lei Rouanet; and the creation of a new distribution company, Riofilme, for example) gradually led to a resurgence in production. Investments in film alone since 1994 total more than 500 million *reais*. The Ministry of Culture had as its goal getting financing of some 100 films in production per year by 2000. The goal was substantially achieved, and the Brazilian film industry seems to have consistently produced a significant number of internationally competitive films in the period beginning in 2001–2002. Nonetheless, it is undeniable that subsidization is probably the only way that a Brazilian film industry can be viable today.

Among the dozens of other worthwhile films that were produced up to the 1990s, I shall mention only those likely to be available to American audiences, either in 16mm or video formats. Nelson Pereira dos Santos has made many good films, but one of his undeniable masterpieces is *Prison Memoirs* (1984—*Memórias do Cárcere*), based on the experiences of Graciliano Ramos, who was imprisoned during the Estado Novo of Getúlio Vargas.

Rui Guerra produced many films during and after Cinema Novo, some masterpieces, and almost all inaccessible in the United States, but his *Eréndira* (1982), based on a script by García Márquez, is widely available. *Eréndira* tells the story of a young woman who burns down her grandmother's house, and as penance is forced by the old woman to support them through prostitution. Since both Guerra and García Márquez delight in phantasmagoria and magic realism, the film is a rich, Tropicálist extravaganza.

Hector Babenco, like Guerra, an immigrant to Brazil, has produced many noteworthy films, several available in the United States. His *Pixote* (1980—*Pixote, a Lei do mais Fraco*) is a savage expressionistic indictment of the way

Brazil treats its street children. Using a cinema verité style and combining real street children with actors, the film follows the disastrous adventures of a group of street children who escape from a reformatory. The boys become involved with Sueli, a prostitute in Rio, who becomes the lover of one of the boys and a substitute mother figure to Pixote. The fact that the boy who plays Pixote (the word means "street child") was brutally murdered by police in São Paulo a few years after the film was made lends special poignancy to it. A feature-length documentary about the life of the boy who plays Pixote is now available in the United States in LAVA: *Who Killed Pixote?* (1996— *Quem matou Pixote?*) by José Joffily.

The Kiss of the Spider Woman (1985— *O Beijo da Mulher Aranha*), a postmodern critique of political and sexual repression, won William Hurt an academy award for best actor. *At Play in the Fields of the Lord* (1991— *Brincando nos Campos do Senhor*) is also an international coproduction that features well-known U.S. actors (Tom Waits, Tom Berenger, Daryl Hannah) together with several Brazilian stars. The film perplexed American and European audiences with its hostile portrait of the effect of foreigners on the Amazon, and was not a commercial success.

The Hour of the Star (1985— *A Hora da Estrela*), Suzana Amaral's moving adaptation of Clarice Lispector's eponymous novella, won many international awards. The film narrates the hapless attempts of an ignorant, slovenly, backwoods girl to fit into modern urban São Paulo. Avoiding Lispector's philosophical introspection on being and circumstance, the film adopts an almost Neorealistic stance toward its heroine, who is portrayed unflinchingly in her most intimate moments. That Macabea, the main character, is able to secure the affection and concern of audiences is a triumph for actress Marcélia Cartaxo.

Perhaps the most hopeful development at the end of the century was the emergence of Walter Salles Jr. as a major player in Brazilian film. He produced and directed two good films (*Exposure*, 1991— *A Grande Arte*, and *A Foreign Land*, 1995— *Terra Estrangeira*), and two superb films, *Central Station* (1998— *Central do Brasil*) and *Behind the Sun* (2001— *Broken April*). His *Midnight* (1999— *O Primeiro Dia*) is a short, experimental film that does not quite come together. *Exposure* and *A Foreign Land* explore detective fiction and film noir respectively. *Exposure* is based on a best-selling novel by Rubem Fonseca (A Grande Arte), and develops in the hard-boiled detective mode, using as its main character Fonseca's intriguing lawyer-detective, Mandrake. *A Foreign Land*, shot in black and white, follows two young Brazilians who immigrate to Portugal in reaction to the confiscation by the Collor regime of all personal savings accounts (an unsuccessful attempt to stop in-

Vinicius de Oliveira and Fernanda Montenegro in a scene from the movie *Central Station*, 1998. (KOBAL Collection, Sony Pictures Classics, Picture Desk)

flation). Alex (Fernanda Torres) makes a precarious living as a waitress. Paco agrees to be a courier for a "businessman" and comes to Portugal with a violin full of Brazilian diamonds. He meets Alex and they attempt to run with the diamonds.

Central Station has won innumerable awards, including a Golden Bear for direction, and a Silver Bear for Best Actress (Fernanda Montenegro) at the Berlin International Film Festival. It was nominated for Best Actress and Best Foreign Film at the U.S. Academy Awards, but did not win; in consolation, it did win Best Foreign Film from the Golden Globe Awards. Fernanda Montenegro's compelling performance as Dora, the selfish and bitter letter writer, has won near universal praise. The story develops as a road film, with Dora and Josué, an orphan she has reluctantly fostered, setting off from the claustrophobic atmosphere of public housing and Rio's Central Station to the vast hinterlands of the Brazilian Northeast in search of the boy's father. Their adventures along the way to their destination force Dora to confront her inhumanity and to surmount her selfishness. Josué learns to trust a woman he believes is responsible for his mother's death, and gains himself a family.

Behind the Sun is also set in the Northeast, but focuses on a long-standing feud between two families, one rich, the other poor. The story is narrated by the youngest of three sons, who during the film gains a nickname, Pacu. His family has not bothered to give him a name, because in the logical sequence of the vendetta between the families he will be assassinated. Tonho, the middle brother, is expected to avenge his older brother's death, but is convinced to break the cycle of violence by Pacu and an attractive circus performer who comes to his city. Although the situation fits perfectly into traditional rural Brazilian mores, the script was adapted from an Albanian novel by Ismail Kandaré. *Behind the Sun* won a Young Golden Lion award at the 2001 Venice film festival, and was nominated for best foreign film in 2002 by the Golden Globes and in 2001 by the National Board of Review in the United States.

Salles has created his own film distributorship and, with his international connections, is having success in fostering new filmmakers. A notable success is *City of God* (2002—*Cidade de Deus*) by Fernando Meirelles, which received a 2002 Academy Award nomination for best foreign film. *City of God* has received enthusiastic reviews in Europe and the United States. Roger Ebert considers the film a classic. A combination of innovative cinematography, ingenious soundtrack, and captivating story, the film is set in one of the worst slums of Rio de Janeiro, Cidade de Deus. The film's narrator is an aspiring young photographer, the only person in his generation in the slum to escape the cycle of poverty, violence, drug trafficking, and death endemic to Rio's *favelas*. As in Salles' own films, Meirelles uses a cast made up largely of nonactors, young people from the *favela*, and extracts convincing, moving performances from them.

Other notable films produced up to 2002 include *How Angels Are Born* (1996—*Como Nascem os Anjos*) by Murilo Salles, also an exploration of the violence bred in Rio's slums and of its impact on larger society; *Four Days in September* (1997—*Que é Isso, Companheiro?*) by Bruno Barreto, based on Fernando Gabeira's best-selling novel about an incident during the military dictatorship when the American ambassador was kidnapped by leftist guer-rillas; *Perfumed Ball* (1997—*Baile Perfumado*), by Lívio Ferreira and Paulo Caldas, an engaging historical fiction that narrates the encounter between famous outlaw Lampião and a Lebanese immigrant filmmaker who travels to the Northeastern backlands to interview him; *The Oyster and the Wind* (1997—*A Ostra e o Vento*) by Walter Lima Jr., a fantasy in which a lonely young woman on an island develops an infatuation with the wind; *Me You Them* (2000—*Eu Tu Eles*) by Andrucha Washington, a fairly standard sexual comedy involving the theme of polyandry; and *Brave New Land* (2001—*Brava Gente Brasileira*) by Lúcia Murat, which narrates a conflict between Brazilian Indians and Portuguese colonists.

Brazilian film at the end of the twentieth century and at the beginning of the twenty-first displays energy, diversity, and creativity. The past two decades have seen the emergence of several distinguished female directors and a thriving documentary segment, as well as a vigorous art video movement based in film study departments at various universities.

SOURCES

The best and most easily available general study of Brazilian cinema is Randal Johnson and Robert Stam's *Brazilian Cinema* (New York: Columbia University Press, 1995). Johnson is the author of *Cinema Novo x 5: Masters of Contemporary Brazilian Film* (Austin: University of Texas Press, 1984), and *The Film Industry in Brazil: Culture and the State* (Pittsburgh: University of Pittsburgh Press, 1987). Stam has published *Tropical Multiculturalism: A Comparative History of Race in Brazilian Cinema and Culture* (Durham, NC: Duke University Press, 1997). Among the few remaining sources for VHS rentals is LAVA (Latin American Video Archives), 124 Washington Place, New York, NY 10014, phone-212-263-0108, fax-212-243-2007, e-mail: imre@igc.org; Web: www.lavavideo.org/lava/. Facets Video is another, but more limited source of Brazilian films: 1517 W. Fullerton Avenue, Chicago, Illinois 60614; phone-1-800-331-6197; e-mail: sales@facets.org; Web: www.facets.org. Facets now has a good collection of subtitled DVD versions of contemporary films, and more than 50 VHS films available at quite modest prices.

NOTES

1. Quoted in Randal Johnson and Robert Stam, eds., *Brazilian Cinema* (New York: Columbia University Press, 1995), p. 70.

2. Quoted by Robert Stam, "On the Margins: Brazilian Avant-Garde Cinema," in Randal Johnson and Robert Stam, eds., *Brazilian Cinema* (New York: Columbia University Press, 1995), p. 309.

9

Literature

We had heard of Camões, but that was about all. As for nineteenth-century Eça de Queiroz, the Portuguese Balzac, he was inaccessible and unknown. Is it strange, then, if the Brazilian Machado de Assis, one of the great writers of all time, is not even a name to the majority of us?
—Samuel Putnam, *Marvelous Journey*, pp. vii–viii

IT MAY SEEM paradoxical to consider literature the most distinguished of the arts in a society which until very recently has been largely illiterate. But Brazilian society is one in which there has always existed great esteem for the humanities, for encyclopedic education, and for the people who create works of art. Brazilians read poetry a great deal more than Americans—what is more, they are fond of reciting both poetry and prose in public, a practice which has all but disappeared from American culture. In addition, writers in Brazil are almost always something more than writers, given the near impossibility of living by the pen alone, and thus people who produce literature are often also journalists, civil servants, politicians, diplomats, or professors. Because they are so frequently professionals in more than one endeavor, writers are attributed extraordinary influence as men and women of ideas and as makers of language. Their influence is so great that they are frequently interviewed in the daily press and asked to give their opinions on the current status of Brazilian diplomacy or the latest controversial bill before Congress, a situation which in the United States is nearly unthinkable. It might be fair to say, in fact, that Brazilian writers may be as influential in what they say as in what they write.

Literature is also the art form most closely coinciding chronologically with developments in Europe. When Dom João VI arrived in Brazil in 1808, the Neoclassical period in literature was almost at an end, but the corresponding architectural form had not yet reached Brazil, and only did so in short order because of the intervention of the monarch. Literature is also the art form in which novelty and innovation most quickly reach the public, in part because of the very prestige authors enjoy, and in part because, unlike painting or sculpture, literature is a daily feature of newspapers. Indeed, most papers carry at least one daily column on literature and at least one daily feature which is essentially literary. Until recently, many of Brazil's best known literary works originally appeared in part or in entirety in a newspaper.

Brazil inherited a long and enduring literary legacy from Portugal, which is often considered a country with a literary culture much grander than such a tiny country should possess. Students of the Luso-Brazilian literary tradition are fond of pointing out that many of the important names in these literatures would be among the most famous writers in the world if only they had written in one of the languages of recognized literary prestige such as English, French, or German. They are unknown only because they chose to write in Portuguese.

The concept of what is and what is not literature is not the same in Brazil as it is in the United States. Many members of the Brazilian Academy of Letters have earned seats for writing sociological treatises or scientific studies, but such works are considered as "literary" as novels or poetry. More important, however, is the fact that since literature appears as some sort of discourse rather than as graphic or affective representation, it is the most ideologically transparent of the arts, allowing almost immediate analysis of the esthetic positions of those who produce it, which makes it the art form that most easily lends itself to a study of intellectual history.

A complete overview of all of Brazilian literature would occupy a volume larger than this one. Since it is such a rich literature, a framework of limitation has been adopted which focuses on the great writers and their principal works. The names and titles included are by and large those included in a consensus "Brazilian canon," that is, the authors and works that are generally held to constitute the best and the most representative in the national literature.[1]

THE COLONIAL PERIOD (1500–1830)

Early colonial Brazil was a harsh environment with sparsely settled and widely separated Portuguese outposts in which survival itself was by no means assured and in which the Portuguese faced hostile Indians, hostile Europeans, and a hostile environment. Even with the advent of sugar cultivation and the foundation of the first royal city there was little time for leisure—certainly not the kind of culture which would be likely to produce great works of literature. Strangely, this rather barbaric situation altered the character of Brazilian literature but did not preclude its existence.

There are some curious uncertainties involved in the discussion of literature in colonial Brazil. First, since most early authors were Portuguese by birth, it is not at all easy to claim any of these writings as part of a "Brazilian" body of work. Second, most of the existent literature was produced in the shadow of esthetic currents in Portugal, at least in theory, making it a kind of satellite form. Third, most of the body of works we have today were either didactic or reports to the crown or the head of a religious order about conditions in the colony, which somewhat complicates the application of the term "literature." No one has proposed adequate solutions to these problems, but the tendency has been that in the case of writers considered to be of good quality, both Portugal and Brazil claim that author as part of the national literary patrimony. The second problem is easier to deal with, because the unusual circumstances of Brazilian society meant that the "classical" and "baroque" writing of sixteenth-century Portugal were by and large impossible to produce in Brazil. Finally, the use of the term "literature" for didactic treatises and reportage can be justified both on the basis of the imaginative nature and esthetic ambitions of the works.

Didactic Works

The major didactic works were all produced by Jesuits, six of whom landed with Tomé de Souza in 1549. The Jesuits were responsible for most of the education that took place in the colony until their expulsion in 1759. Obviously, "education" in the context of this untamed settlement consisted largely of instruction in the rites of the Roman Catholic Church, which means that most of the efforts expended by the Jesuits in colonial Brazil were directed toward catechizing both the Indians and the Portuguese colonists. The three most important Jesuit writers of the early colonial period were Manuel da Nóbrega, Fernão Cardim, and José de Anchieta. The last of these produced a considerable body of work, consisting of letters, a history of the

Jesuit order, a Tupi grammar, and sermons. Anchieta also wrote an extensive collection of poetry and drama, most of which was used by members of his order as pedagogical tools for the instruction of Indians and colonists. His literary works are unpretentious and rather anachronistic, since they are rather medieval in form and content, seemingly unaffected by the innovations of the Portuguese Renaissance.

Lay Literature

The other major contributors to early Brazilian literature were laymen, such as Pero de Magalhães de Gândavo (*Tratado da Terra do Brasil*—Treatise on the Land of Brazil); Gabriel Soares de Sousa (*Notícia do Brasil*—Report on Brazil); and Pero Vaz da Caminha (*Carta a El Rei D. Manuel*—Letter of Pedro Vaz de Caminha to King Manuel), a letter written to King Manuel of Portugal by a notary who accompanied Pedro Álvares Cabral on his voyage of discovery to Brazil. One of the few early documents available in English, it is a fascinating document of the meeting of two worlds, as in this description of the first meeting with Brazilian Indians:

In appearance they are dark, somewhat reddish, with good faces and good noses, well shaped. They go naked, without any covering; neither do they pay more attention to concealing or exposing their shame than they do to showing their faces, and in this respect they are very innocent. . . . There were also among them four or five young women just as naked, who were not displeasing to the eye, among whom was one with her thigh from the knee to the hip and buttock all painted with that black paint and all the rest in her own colour; another had both knees and calves and ankles so painted, and her privy parts so nude and exposed with such innocence that there was not there any shame. (Letter of Pedro Vaz, 10–11, 20–21)

The only other notable example is *Dialogues of the Great Things of Brazil* by Ambrósio Fernandes Brandão, written in 1618 and first published in a historical review in 1883. A fine exemplar of the genre, it is fascinating as a window into the mind of the early Portuguese colonist, particularly in regard to its extensive discussion of the otherness of native populations and the exotic nature of the native plants and animals. Its author remarks on such oddities as the hammock and the habit of the daily bath, both of which are integral parts of modern Brazilian culture. He also includes a long passage on the barbaric custom of cannibalism, which was adopted by modern Brazilian writers as a sort of quirky symbol of Brazilianness.

Most of the lay literature produced during the colonial period is today referred to as *ufanismo*, a term based on a book published in 1901 by Afonso Celso, entitled *Porque me ufano de meu país* (Why I Boast about My Country). Most of these works combine a kind of awe at the newness of everything found in Brazil with a scarcely veiled message that the recipient of the missive encourage more Portuguese colonists to come to this land of wonders. Most also contain allusions to gold, or hints that it might not be far off.

History and Epic

Two other writers in the early colony produced works of some interest. Frei Vicente do Salvador, a Franciscan priest, wrote the first known history of Brazil. His *História do Brasil* was completed in 1627. It was not printed until 1889, and even then was only a fragment of the original, since many chapters had been lost in the intervening two and a half centuries. Bento Teixeira was a layman who is known for his short epic poem *Prosopopéia*, first published in 1601. Likewise incomplete, this poem is interesting in part because of its evident Renaissance character. It was clearly modeled on the Portuguese epic poem *Os Lusíadas*, by the great Luís de Camões. Although chronologically the date of the poem corresponds to the Portuguese Renaissance, his is the only work overtly influenced by the open-mindedness and impartiality of Renaissance thought and the formal models of Renaissance verse. Teixeira also occupies a unique place in Brazilian literary history because he is thought to be the first important writer born in Brazil, a distinction still open to controversy.

The Baroque Period

The writer who truly merits the fame of being Brazil's first native son to produce great works of imaginative literature is one of the writers of the Baroque period, Gregório de Matos (1623–1696). Born in Bahia into the family of a wealthy planter, Matos went to Coimbra to study law and later became a judge in Lisbon. He returned to Bahia in 1681 and became notorious for the scathing satires he wrote about both the great and the lowly. A true bohemian, he earned the epithet "Boca do Inferno" (Hell's Mouth) for his disorderly conduct and even more disorderly verse. Because of his truculent attacks on the populace he was finally sent into exile in Angola for 10 years, returning to Brazil to spend the last year of his life in poverty. Since there were no printing presses in Brazil, his works circulated either in copies made by admirers or by word of mouth. His complete work, totaling seven volumes, was finally published in 1969. His *Complete Poems* is one of the three volumes of poetry included in the national canon.

Matos' poetry is divided into four categories: religious, satirical, lyrical, and erotic. Although some critics have downplayed his importance because of the close similarities between his verses and those of the Spanish poets Góngora and Quevedo, such borrowing was not considered illicit at the time. Fond of the conceits and wit characteristic of the Baroque period, he is probably at his best using those weapons to skewer clergymen, adulteresses, and a whole panoply of other social types of the Bahia of his time, as in this sample regarding an avaricious businessman:

> The money-grubbing merchant,
> When he extends his cash in hand,
> Be it what he buys or sells,
> He takes two hundred percent;
> No ass is he not to think
> That in a place like Lisbon
> They would throw him in the clink;
> But once his money is gone,
> Says he, honor means more
> And so does respect for the Law:
> Such is but justice, bidden by the King.
>   (Matos, "Satirical," *Borzoi Anthology*, 141)

The dominant voice in Brazilian prose of the Baroque period is that of the Jesuit Padre Antônio Vieira (1608–1697). Although he disliked the rhetorical excesses of the Spanish Baroque writers, the complexity of imagery and the fondness for antithesis and paradox give his prose a very Baroque cast.[2] Best known for his sermons (14 volumes), he is also noted for his letters and for his historical significance as a social and political critic of the important events and policies of his time. He was horrified at the brutal treatment of the Indians by the Portuguese and took pains to point out his views to the crown. He was also traumatized by the Dutch occupation of Brazil (he was 16 when they invaded Bahia) and became involved in the foundation of the company that would eventually be instrumental in the ouster of the foreigners. Because he was unfailingly outspoken he naturally drew the attention of the Holy Office (Inquisition), which for a time prohibited him from preaching. But he eventually regained the favor of both the pope and the king. Late in life he raised objections about the treatment of black slaves similar to those he had raised about the Indians, but his thinking on both counts was well ahead of the times as far as the reality of the labor situation in Brazil is concerned.

Neoclassicism (1750–1830)

Literature during the colonial period really began to flourish in the so-called Neoclassical period, when Brazil underwent a huge economic boom, accompanied by burgeoning activity in all the arts. It took the Portuguese almost two centuries to discover gold in Brazil, but when they finally found it they found a great deal of it. As a kind of bonus for the lateness of the discovery, they found diamonds along with the gold. The discovery of such riches transformed the colony fundamentally and very rapidly. People poured into the mining areas of Minas Gerais and beyond, not only from other parts of Brazil but also from Europe, and soon the sleepy colonial town of Rio de Janeiro, the port city nearest the wealth, was transformed into a boom metropolis because of the "new road" built between Minas and the coast. The gold boom coincided with new poetic ideas from Portugal, mainly the Arcadia Lusitana[3] of 1756, but ideals of the European Enlightenment and radical political ideas from the American and French Revolutions had profound impact on Brazilian thought. One of the principal new ideas was the concept of man as the master of his own destiny, which had important political implications, but it arrived accompanied by the Enlightenment notion of a return to Greek and Roman classicism, which gave the revolutionary politics a somewhat eccentric aristocratic cast.

The Neoclassical literature produced by the so-called Minas School (also called "Arcadism") is not really a cohesive body of work, because it lacked both a leader and a consistent esthetic doctrine. The single ideology which seems to inform the writers of the period was a rejection of the excesses of the ornate Baroque style, particularly the sometimes labyrinthine stylistic games of which Baroque writers were fond. The peak of influence of the Arcadian poets also coincided with new liberal ideas brought from abroad, and most of the major poets of the movement were involved in the Inconfidência Mineira (1789–1792), an intrigue generally regarded as the first organized independence movement in Brazil. The plot was discovered, and several of the prominent writers of this important movement spent their last days in exile in Africa. One implicated his co-conspirators and committed suicide.

Brazilian Arcadian writers are a paradoxical lot, because although most embraced the libertarian philosophies then coming into vogue, they were also beholden to a rather artificial esthetic which led them to write idealistic pastoral poems about picturesque shepherds—in a country in fact peopled by slaves, smugglers, and savages. The foremost exponent of the Arcadian ideal was Tomás Antônio Gonzaga (1744–1810). Born in Portugal, Gonzaga went to Brazil at the age of nine. He returned to Portugal to attend the University of Coimbra, from which he graduated in 1767. He returned to Brazil and became a magistrate in Vila Rica (Minas Gerais), where he became friends with Alvarenga Peixoto and Cláudio Manuel da Costa, two other principal poets of the age. He was imprisoned in 1789 for his participation in the Inconfidência and exiled to Mozambique in 1792. He died in 1810 a prosperous businessman. He is known principally for his *Marília de Dirceu*, a book of lyric poems which most perfectly represents the Arcadian ideal, and for his probable authorship (possibly with Cláudio Manuel da Costa) of the *Cartas Chilenas*, a book of 13 letters satirizing the governor of Minas Gerais. The book is considered one of the best political satires of the century.

Although there is contradiction and artificiality involved in writing pastoral poetry in the milieu of colonial Brazil, Gonzaga's poetry embraces ideas never before seen in Brazilian letters and some which existed only through happenstance. Like the early Jesuit works, his Neoclassic poetry is consciously accessible, meaning that it avoids the playful and at times opaque word play found in baroque art. This accessibility also implies that it is written with a public in mind—at least a public much broader than the narrow group of friends for whom the baroque writers wrote. It also embodies, for the first time, a set of values which might be identified as bourgeois conceits: the value of work, independence, self-reliance, and an anti-heroic tone that is quite novel. If it still contains elements of fatalism and focuses on the transitory nature of life, it is nevertheless much more a poetry of the immediate and the real than most previous literature.

Gonzaga is probably the writer who most clearly exemplifies the change in esthetic and political ideas the Neoclassical age embraced. Most of his fellow Arcadians shared his somewhat artificial view of the ideal of a pastoral life, but they also embraced to a degree the truly radical notion of inclusion—an esthetic posture that presupposed a broader audience for literature and a political philosophy that promoted not only independence but also active participation in the political process.

Although some of the notions of the Arcadian writers were on the liberal side, subsequent generations considered them tepid, and their insistence on an Edenic pastoral existence and an idealized view of love and labor made them appear out of step in a world undergoing rapid changes. By the early nineteenth century the Arcadian ideals of harmony and equilibrium were replaced by a new set of values which came from Europe but were given an unmistakable Brazilian character. Not surprisingly, the new esthetic coincided historically with independence and an entirely new role for Brazil in the context of the Portuguese Empire.

LITERATURE SINCE INDEPENDENCE

Romanticism (1830–1880)

The new ideals were those of the romantics, who promulgated an artistic style and a way of life which dominated most of Western civilization by the second decade of the nineteenth century. Although something of a tardy arrival in Brazil, Romanticism became the esthetic that would define Brazilian thought for most of the century. Germany and England were important sources of Romantic innovation, but France was the immediate source of most of the important ideas of romanticism in Brazil, since it was usually in French translation that Brazilians had access to writers like Goethe, Byron, and Scott. Romanticism also coincided historically with a powerful sense of nationalism that began with independence, and it offered much to a people just coming into being as a new nation and a separate culture.

Literary historians like to divide the Romantic period into a given number of generations, but since there is no unanimity on how many there were or on what to call them, it is probably more useful to discuss what the romantics had in common rather than what differentiated them. Romanticism was first and foremost characterized by centering on the self, on the "I." This single feature suggests several corollaries. First, the "I" can be construed merely as the ego of the writer, but it may be used by extension to refer to the writer's region or, more importantly, his country. The "I" also suggests subjectivism, a turning away from the objectivity and tranquility of the Classical period. In fact, much of Romantic writing might be viewed in modern terminology as bipolar, with emotion as central and an alternation between ecstasy and melancholy the norm. Because it is self-centered, Romanticism is also preoccupied with dreams, with faith, and with nature, particularly personal feelings about surroundings or natural phenomena as reflections of subjective states. Finally, because Romanticism was so subjective, it eventually became preoccupied with both the past (which derived from the European historical novel) and the present (which reflected social and political agendas associated with Romanticism).

Poetry. Early Romantic writers combined a sort of pantheistic religiosity with patriotic overtones to produce a new literary form and tone, but it was with Antônio Gonçalves Dias (1823–1864) that Brazilian Romanticism, and

Brazilian literature, really came into its own. Gonçalves Dias is the author of the immortal "Canção do Exílio" (Song of Exile), a lyric poem known by heart by every Brazilian schoolchild and a milestone so important in Brazilian literature that it has been rewritten, put into song, and parodied by generations of Brazilians. Only 24 lines long, and written when the poet was a mere 20 years old, it is a shameless ode to patriotic sentiment, with the presence of God and Brazilian scenery guaranteeing its universal appeal to Brazilian readers.

Gonçalves Dias also cultivated dramatic and epic poetry, and it is in these genres that he became a sort of spiritual father of what would come to be known as "Romantic Indianism." Except for some marginal examples which can be found in the earlier chronicles, Indianism was never really a genre in Portuguese literature, and it came to be one in Brazil by reason of part of the esthetics of Romanticism and the unique conditions in the New World. One important thread of European Romanticism was a preoccupation with the past, partly because of the exoticism implicit in such an endeavor and partly as an attempt to recreate a glorious national history. The Brazilians faced a dilemma that all American writers of the period had to wrestle with. It was easy for a Portuguese writer to situate characters in the remote past and to create dramatic heroes and heroines, because Portugal did in fact have a long and exciting history. But for Brazilians the recreation of a glorious past would imply making heroes of the Portuguese, an ideologically impossible construct in the Brazil of the nineteenth century, given the recent separation of the country from the motherland and the incredibly strong anti-Portuguese sentiment of the population. A second possibility would have been to write heroic works about African slaves, but this option was eliminated almost automatically for the very reason of the condition of servitude of this population. The third option was to use the Indian as material for heroic historical drama and fiction, which was exactly what happened. Although the Indian had also been subjected to servitude and was at this juncture not numerically even a very important part of Brazilian society, the Indian became, by process of elimination, the focus of much of the poetry, and later on the prose, of Brazilian Romantics.

Gonçalves Dias had studied at the University of Coimbra, where he read the Portuguese Romantics, including the historical novelists. But he also read Chateaubriand's *Atala*, which in some ways was a model for Brazilian Indianists. Although Chateaubriand had little or no real knowledge of Indians, his romantic portrait of the noble savage became an irresistible inspiration to Brazilian writers, and two of Gonçalves Dias' longer and most important works are the foundation stones of what would become an important part of Romantic expression in both poetry and prose.

Brazilian Romantics also produced a great deal of poetry that is more in line with what we now consider typical of the period. The best example is probably Álvares de Azevedo (1831–1852), dubbed by critics "the Brazilian Byron." His poetry contrasts with that of Gonçalves Dias first because of an almost complete lack of Brazilian nature as a theme, but also because of his penchant for the lugubrious, the exotic, and the macabre. He was an incredibly prolific writer for one who died so young (he died of the traditional Romantic disease of tuberculosis at the age of 21). He was also one of several notable writers of the period to obsess, in verse, about the unattainable Romantic love object, a theme which eventually became a cliché for Romantic poets. Although the poets of this "ultraromantic" school produced works which have little that could be identified as essentially Brazilian, they were nonetheless accomplished writers, some of them of great talent, who produced some of Brazil's most beloved verse.

At least one other Romantic poet deserves mention in this brief survey. Antônio Federico de Castro Alves (1847–1871) was a most eloquent voice in a country fond of eloquence. He was the foremost exponent of the "Condoreirismo," so-called because its exalted themes and rhetoric recalled the dramatic flight of the Andean condor. Most importantly, Castro Alves was known as the poet of Brazilian abolition, largely because of the immense popularity of his poem "O navio negreiro" (Slave ship), published in 1868. A dramatic and pictorial work, the poem was perfectly suited for public readings by Brazil's intellectuals, who by this point felt that the institution of slavery was a disgrace and a source of national shame. This is another clear example of literature as an arm of political and social action, which in many ways would be characteristic of Brazilian literature thenceforth.

The Novel. It was, though, in the novel that Brazilian romantics would produce works that would most directly address the problem of Brazilian identity. The salient figure in the Romantic novel in Brazil was José de Alencar (1829–1877) from the northeastern state of Ceará. Alencar authored some 40 volumes of prose, drama, and essays, but his novels, which number about 20, are his best-known works. The two most famous ones are *O Guarani* (1857) and *Iracema* (1865), though many others are still popular in Brazil. Alencar did in fiction what Gonçalves Dias had done a generation earlier in poetry, and since he was so prolific it is fair to say that he did it in a more complete fashion. Like Gonçalves Dias, Alencar was an amateur ethnologist and linguist, and he used his knowledge of Brazilian indigenous peoples both to inform his countrymen about native peoples and to create new symbols of the essence of Brazil. Again, like Gonçalves Dias, he is still revered in Brazil, and many know entire passages of his work by heart.

The best example of his work is the shamelessly romantic *Iracema* (*Iracema*, 1886). Published in 1865, it was reprinted *annually* for a century, and by now the number of editions probably surpasses the number of years of the book's existence. It is set in the early colonial period in Alencar's native Ceará and deals with the romance of a Portuguese soldier, Martim, and the beautiful Indian maiden Iracema. Along with the problems of the mixed union, there are other taboos and transgressions, a protracted war between Indian tribes, and the eventual demise of the lovely Iracema. Romanticism is known, of course, for its corny plots, but this one might easily be the storyboard for a modern soap opera. At least some of the perennial appeal of the book is that from the first page (the story is told in flashback), the product of the Portuguese/Indian union, the son Moacyr, is present. Moacyr is not important as a character since he is not at all developed, but as a sign he is of utmost importance, for what Romantic representation of the new Brazilian nation could better symbolize the blended culture of colonial Brazil?

Alencar's novels are not only immensely popular with Brazilian readers; they are also landmarks in the history of the culture. His prose is richly poetic, but it also expands literary language beyond the academic stuffiness of the Portuguese model. Whereas the Portuguese looked to the Middle Ages for historical inspiration, Alencar used both the Indian and other Brazilian types, including the *gaúcho* (gaucho) and the *sertanejo* (peasant), as the foci of his fictions. The result was that Brazilian fiction for the first time had as a central preoccupation representatives of the national reality, expressed in a language for the first time "incorrect" because it reflected some of the real differences between Portuguese and Brazilian vocabulary and usage. Alencar viewed the role of the writer as that of seer or prophet, but the somewhat didactic note this occasioned did little damage to his appeal. Part of the reason it had so little negative effect on his reputation was that Brazil was no longer simply an agrarian patriarchy, but was moving toward a pre-industrial society. Several factors contributed to a quantum leap in the size of the reading public, among them the rise of an incipient middle class, the increase in educational level, the growth of the publishing industry, and, for the first time, the presence of female readers.

Alencar was aware of at least some of the liberties he was taking in writing Indianist novels. When *Iracema* appeared, Amerindians amounted to less than 7% of Brazil's population, a percentage which was declining rapidly, making the fabrication of fictions based on the Indian a rather dubious project, but Alencar sensed that the reading public would consider the Indian somehow genealogically important. He also guessed, correctly, that readers would not be irritated by the frequent use of similes, especially those equating characters with some natural phenomenon (Iracema is the "honey-lipped virgin" and her father, the shaman, is "wise as the anteater"). In fact, though the speech of characters borders on an almost Tarzanesque dialect, the truly massive infusion of Brazilian flora and fauna appears to contribute an element of the charm Brazilians find in the novels. Alencar also knowingly titled *Iracema* as a "legend of Ceará," making it probable that he was aware of the appeal the story might have as an origin myth or a creation myth.

Controversy still exists as to whether the fact that "Iracema" is an anagram for "America" was intentional or not. What is incontrovertible is that *Iracema*, despite its shameless conventionality, is a paean to miscegenation in a historical period in which racial mixture was thought to be degrading and debilitating, yet another measure of its lasting importance.

Several other members of Alencar's generation were also very popular at the time, and a few remain so. One is Joaquim Manuel de Macedo (1820–1882), whose sentimental novel *A Moreninha* (1844) (Little Brunette) is still widely read. Another is Alfredo d'Escragnolle Taunay, Viscount of Taunay (1843–1889), whose *Inocência* (1872) (*Innocencia*, 1889) remains a favorite. In each it is possible to identify features of an incipient Realism, which would succeed Romanticism as the esthetic of the last part of the century. Another novelist of the generation, Manuel Antônio de Almeida (1831–1861) is often identified as author of Brazil's first Realist novel. *Memórias de um Sargento de Milícias*, first published in 1854–1855 (*Memoirs of a Militia Sergeant*, 1959), lacks the sentimental and idealized character of the typical Romantic novel, but it is in fact not much more than a novel of urban customs with an overlay of mild satire, which makes it look somewhat picaresque.

Drama. Brazilian theater also emerged during the Romantic period. Although Anchieta had written drama as early as the sixteenth century, his plays were *autos* (short religious plays) in the medieval mold, and were essentially didactic works used as teaching tools in the conversion of Indians. Not until the nineteenth century did anything that might be taken as a national theater begin to emerge. Alencar and many of the other Romantic novelists and poets wrote drama, but the founder of Brazilian theater is generally held to be Luís Carlos Martins Pena (1815–1848), a *carioca* who wrote almost 30 plays, most of them comedies of manners about the Brazilian lower and middle classes. Martins Pena was best known as a satirist of social types— the priest, the judge, the unscrupulous politician—and institutions such as government and marriage. His are not particularly notable plays except as social documents, but as such they are interesting, and they have historical importance as the first plays in Brazil to attract large audiences.

Realism-Naturalism-Parnassianism (1880–1910)

The latter part of the nineteenth century was dominated by new ideas which were so novel and so revolutionary that literature could not escape their effects. Among the most important theories were Darwinism and Positivism, the former for its emphasis on biology and the notion of the evolution of things and species toward some perceived betterment, the latter for its emphasis on scientific method and the application of science to solve the problems not only of species but of societies.

In Brazil it is not particularly useful to separate Realism and its satellites into discrete movements. Realism and Naturalism, always in relative dosages, characterized the prose of the period; Parnassianism was principally poetic. Realism was an attempt to avoid the subjectivism implicit in the prose of the Romantics and to replace it with an objective and disinterested view of humans and society. Naturalism added to this scientific view a preoccupation with understanding the perversities of human existence, and it thus placed relatively more emphasis on such things as heredity and race, often in a negative light. The more orthodox Naturalists viewed beings, including humans, as products of both heredity and environment, which precluded the idealized concept of free will as a factor in determining character. Both rejected the ornamental style of Romanticism in favor of a sober, more "truthful" prose, which at times verged on the coarse.

Prose. Most of the prose of decidedly Naturalistic writers has not traveled well into subsequent generations. Some, like Júlio Ribeiro, are remembered for introducing scandalous new themes into Brazilian literature—his *A Carne* (Flesh) was the first Brazilian novel that included powerful erotic scenes. Another, Adolfo Caminha, is still remembered for having introduced the theme of homosexuality into Brazilian prose in his *Bom Crioulo* (1895) (Good Black Man). The only clearly Naturalistic writer who is still widely read is Aluísio Azevedo (1857–1913), whose *O Cortiço* (1890) (*A Brazilian Tenement*, 1976) is probably the best representative of the genre. Azevedo is compared to both Balzac and Zola, respectively the most famous Realist and the most famous Naturalist of French prose, yet another indication that the two schools are not easy to separate in Brazil. *O Cortiço* is interesting for its introduction of a motif which has often been echoed in later works—the industrious and simple immigrant (in this case a Portuguese) who comes to Brazil and is seduced by the sensual temptations of the tropical milieu, which here includes the *mulatta, cachaça* (Brazilian rum), and samba. Since it is a Naturalistic novel, the treatment of this motif is a bit heavy-handed. In later novels the theme is treated with something closer to Brazilian nonchalance.

Another Realist-Naturalist with a title in the canon is the rather eccentric Raul Pompéia (Rio de Janeiro, 1863–1895). As Harold Bloom realized when he arrogated to himself the task of compiling something as ambitious as a Western Canon, the task is arduous and full of pitfalls, because any canon in any literature is an invitation to combat from some quarter. In the case of Pompéia, even his many admirers express reservations about him, and most claim that he is unclassifiable. Essentially a one-work author, he published *O Ateneu* (The Athenaeum) in the newspaper *Gazeta de Notícias* in 1888. Really an adult memoir recalling the rigors of boarding school, it is generally viewed as a psychological autobiography or simply a rancorous diatribe against the sadistic headmaster and the protagonists' malevolent colleagues. Some suggest that it be read as an allegory on the monarchy with Pedro II as the headmaster and his staff as the government bureaucracy, but there seems little evidence to support such a reading. It may be that the novel's popularity is that the coming of age motif in novels about boarding schools or military service strikes a note of recognition with most readers. Whatever the case, the reputed pictorial style does little to save the novel from being a bitter and sometimes spiteful caricature.

The more conventional Realists (that is, those not preoccupied with the somewhat lugubrious themes of Naturalism) produced a considerable body of work which today seems rather dated. Most of them tended to view the "real" Brazil as that which was immediate and local, and the result of this was a flourishing regionalistic movement in prose which was a dominant note in the late nineteenth century. Probably the best-known conventional Realist was Affonso Arinos de Melo Franco, known simply as Affonso Arinos, noted principally for his volume of what might have been short stories entitled *Pelo Sertão* (1898) (Through the Backlands). This book probably has both the best and worst features of this historically important tendency. The stories are interesting principally from an anthropological or historical perspective, because one of the clear intentions of this fiction is the documentation of the local, including speech patterns, customs, and folkways. This genre is comparable in many ways to Spanish *costumbrismo* (which also existed in Spanish America), a kind of fiction which seems to have been inspired as much by a desire to record the picturesque as to tell a good story. Arinos is also known as the author of a novel, *Os Jagunços* (1898) (The Bandits), one of the first works of fiction based on the dramatic events of Canudos.

Other regionalists include Valdomiro Silveira and Monteiro Lobato in São

Paulo, Simões Lopes Neto and Darci Azambuja in Rio Grande do Sul, José Veríssimo in Amazonas, and Gustavo Barroso in Ceará. Although their works were important and popular at the time of their publication, they are another example of a literature which has not traveled well, and their lasting contribution to the national literature is diminished by their exaggerated specificity.

Poetry. In poetry, the reaction against the perceived excesses of Romanticism manifests itself in an "objective" kind of verse that today is called Parnassianism. Although these two characteristics of Parnassianism—anti-Romanticism and Realism—would seem to be new and revolutionary features of verse, Brazilian Parnassians often wrote poetry that was neither revolutionary nor all that new. Often there are Romantic echoes in this poetry, and the view of reality is at times quite mannered. The real difference between the effusion of the Romantics and the Parnassians seems to be more a question of style and form than in substantive matters, because one facet of Parnassianism—"socialist" poetry—was in fact one facet of Romantic verse.

Parnassians reacted against what they perceived as the rhetorical excess of Romantic verse and the "looseness" of its form. In place of the hyperbole of the Condor they preached the pristine and classical lyric of Mount Parnassus. Some Parnassian poetry has the sense of detail of Realistic fiction, and some is quite political in its opposition to the clergy and the monarchy, but the principal trend is art for art's sake, which eventually merely produces a mannerism different from Romanticism but not notably more realistic; merely an example of moderation carried to the extreme.

The three principal poets of Brazilian Parnassianism were Alberto de Oliveira, Raimundo Correia, and Olavo Bilac, often referred to as the "Parnassian Trinity." They all emphasized elegance over expressiveness and precision of grammar and form over inspiration. Coinciding chronologically with *modernismo* in Spanish, these poets also demonstrated a fondness for viewing poetry as parallel to sculpture, in which the artist seeks to produce a perfect and plastic reality. Parnassian poetry is also noted for its formal precision, which makes the sonnet a favorite form, but they also introduced other challenging forms into Brazilian poetry, such as the Malaysian pantoum. Of the three members of the "trinity," Bilac remains the most popular today, probably because he was the only one of the group who never completely abandoned the sensuality and eloquence of Romantic verse.

Symbolism, 1890–1920

In Spain and Spanish America, Parnassianism and Symbolism achieved something of a fusion, resulting in what is called *modernismo* in Spanish. The term *modernismo* in Portuguese refers to what is called *vanguardismo* in Spanish, roughly the equivalent of "literary modernism" in English. In Brazil, Symbolism can be regarded as either an island in a sea of Parnassianism or an appendix to it. Symbolism shares with Romanticism a focus on the ego and on inspiration and the view of the poet as seer, but it is, like Parnassianism, a very literary school, although its inspiration is music rather than sculpture. Symbolists view a poem as a totally new entity, independent of the social milieu, in which the poet expresses something never said before or something which until the poem existed was impossible to say. Symbolists are fond of archaic and even invented words and view literary language as essentially enigmatic and imprecise.

Amazingly enough, in a society as subtly racist as Brazil's, the most famous member of this most literary of literary movements was João da Cruz e Souza (1861–1898), the son of slaves. Known as "the Black Swan" or "the Black Dante," Cruz e Souza was a great "pure" poet who wrote about a transcendent reality in a country that preferred eloquence and declamatory verse. Another Symbolist of importance was Augusto dos Anjos (Paraíba, 1884–1924). Author of a single volume of poems with the intriguing title of *Eu* ("I"), Augusto dos Anjos was one of Brazil's most pessimistic, and most imaginative, poets. His poems (mostly sonnets) are striking for the perfection of form and for the incongruous use of scientific and erudite vocabulary in a form normally associated with amorous lyric. The most Baudelarian of Brazilian poets, his fondness for the lugubrious is tempered by an essentially Romantic posture which has made him relatively popular.

Two Misfits

There are two Brazilian writers who defy all the parameters literary history likes to impose. Chronologically, their most important works should be either late Romantic or Realist-Naturalist, but none of the labels seems to fit.

Joaquim Maria Machado de Assis (born Rio de Janeiro, 1839–1908), is probably the most revered writer in Brazilian literature. The son of a mulatto house painter and his Portuguese immigrant wife, Machado, as he is known, never left Brazil but was the most cosmopolitan and sophisticated of writers. In the latter two decades of the nineteenth century he wrote novels that contained features normally associated with the modern, or even the postmodern, novel. As literary historian Susan Sontag has so eloquently put it:

Imagine a writer who in the course of a moderately long life, in which he never travelled farther then seventy-five miles from the capital city where he was born, created a huge body of work . . . author of a profusion of novels, novellas, stories, plays, essays, poetry, reviews, political chronicles, as well as reporter, magazine editor, government bureaucrat, candidate for public office, and founding president of his country's Academy of Letters . . . managed to write a sizable number of novels and stories deserving of a permanent place in world literature, and whose masterpieces, outside his native country, which honors him as its greatest writer, are little known, rarely mentioned.[4]

Indeed, Machado was such an extraordinary writer that neither Spanish America nor the United States can boast of having produced a writer his equal. He wrote in every genre, but it is in his voluminous collections of short stories and in his 10 or so novels that Machado excelled. He is the only writer with two books in the national canon, and a third and fourth received at least one vote. The two solidly in the canon are *Dom Casmurro* (1900) (*Dom Casmurro*, 1966) and *Memórias Póstumas de Brás Cubas* (1881) (*Epitaph of a Small Winner*, 1952).

A supremely ironic writer, Machado is held to be responsible for the introduction of "English humor," meaning "understated" in the Brazilian novel. His novels are characterized by an economy of expression rare in Brazilian letters and a linguistic precision unusual in any literature. He was also technically an incredibly inventive and original writer. None of his books uses the conventions of Romantic or Naturalistic or even Realistic fiction, though in a sense they are realistic in a way the Realists never imagined. His plots are simple but his narrative strategies are elaborate, ranging from the tongue-in-cheek implausibility of "The Psychiatrist" (a short story) to the downright perversity of the narrator in *Brás Cubas*. The narrator of this novel subverts the conventions of narration from the outset, since he is already dead as he begins to compose his memoir, and throughout the novel he persists in inventing theories to explain both the transcendent and the trivial. He writes chapters to himself and chapters the reader is instructed to insert into another chapter; he comments on his own lack of profundity, and muses about the defects of the book. Three short chapters, reproduced here in their entirety, may give some sense of the contrariness of the narrative process:

55. The Venerable Dialogue of Adam and Eve:

Brás Cubas

. . . ?

Virgília

. . . .

Brás Cubas

. . . .
. . . . . .

Virgília

. . . . . !

Brás Cubas

. . . . . .

Virgília

. . . .
. . . . ? . . . .
. . . .

Brás Cubas

. . . .

Virgília

. . . .

Brás Cubas

. . . .
. . . .
. . . . ! . .
. . ! . . . .
. . . . !

Virgília

. . . . ?

Brás Cubas

. . . . . !

Virgília

. . . . . !

136. Unnecessary:

And, if I am not greatly mistaken, I have just written an utterly unnecessary chapter.

139. How I Did Not Become a Minister of State:

. . . .
. . . .
. . . .

(Machado de Assis, *Epitaph of a Small Winner*, 110, 202, 205)

If this all sounds and looks like a modern novel, it's because it is. When Machado wrote *Memórias Póstumas de Brás Cubas*, F. Scott Fiztgerald,

William Faulkner, and Ernest Hemingway were not yet born; when he wrote *Dom Casmurro* they were, respectively, four, three, and two years old. But these two novels are not only the product of a mind profoundly engaged with human foibles; they are technically as daring, as modern as anything in our fiction of the twentieth century, anachronisms of amazing proportions.

The other misfit in this period was Euclides da Cunha (born Rio de Janeiro, 1866–1909). Trained in the army as a civil engineer, he was twice dismissed from the service, once for insubordination (before the Republic existed) and once for his journalistic attacks against government policy regarding political prisoners. He wrote several books, but only one of them, *Os Sertões* (1902) (*Rebellion in the Backlands*, 1947), is responsible for his stature as a national icon. Unlike Machado, who wrote much and in many genres, da Cunha's fame rests on a single work. It is the only volume unanimously included in the national canon.

Like Machado, he belongs chronologically to the Realist school, but there is very little in the book that would relate it to that or any other school. In fact, it is almost impossible to categorize it. He spent most of his adult life alternating between two professions, engineering and journalism. In 1897 he wrote two articles on the Canudos campaign for the prestigious daily *O Estado de São Paulo*, and later that year the paper sent him north to cover the story. He wrote 23 articles on the story and then returned south to São José do Rio Pardo in the interior of São Paulo where he wrote *Os Sertões* while overseeing the construction of a bridge. There is an annual week-long celebration in the town to honor him.

The book is in part a superb example of journalism, but it is more than that. It is also a military history, a treatise on geography and geology, and an anthropological study. It is also a terrific story, one which seems to strike a chord of response in most Brazilians, even if they find the prose too tortuous for their liking.

Although it reads like a novel, da Cunha had no literary pretensions and in fact wrote the book as an attack on a government which first failed to educate its population and then turned on that uneducated population to exterminate it for its failure to behave. Despite his evident racist attitudes, certainly a product of the time, da Cunha was both a humanist and a man of science, and his analysis of Brazil as a schizophrenic culture with a feudal, rural interior and a cosmopolitan, developed coast anticipated many later analyses.

Before Modernism

In 1913, Machado, Euclides da Cunha, Aluísio Azevedo, and Raimundo Correia were gone. Only Augusto dos Anjos and, more importantly, Olavo Bilac were still around as emblematic figures the Modernists would use to show people what was wrong with the "old" literature. Only one canonical work was produced in the time between the deaths of the great nineteenth-century writers and the Modernists: *O Triste Fim de Policarpo Quaresma* (1915) (*The Patriot*, 1978), by Lima Barreto (born Rio de Janeiro, 1881–1922). Lima Barreto was a mulatto, a journalist, and a public servant. He was also one of Brazil's most outspoken social critics of the period, and he viewed the novel as an ideal arm in his private war with bureaucrats, militarists, and snobs. He led a dissolute life and died an alcoholic at the age of 41. The hero of *The Patriot* is a quixotic figure, rabidly xenophobic, who wishes, among other things, to establish Tupi as the national language, an ambition that sounds nothing short of absurd but which in fact was promoted for a time by a small group of Brazilian intellectuals.

Modernism, 1922–1945

Like other vanguardist movements in Latin America, Brazilian Modernism initially appeared as a sometimes confusing conjunction of assorted European literary and esthetic movements, including but not limited to Italian Futurism, Cubism, Surrealism, and Dadaism. Brazil was unique in Latin America in that its Modernism can conveniently be seen as a movement which began at a specific point in time, because its proponents held a week-long happening in São Paulo in 1922 called the "Semana de Arte Moderna" (Modern Art Week). The Semana so agitated the Brazilian intelligentsia that it marks a definitive rupture with the past and the beginning of something really new, though at the time it was not clear exactly what it was. In most Spanish American countries vanguardism appeared with individuals or with small groups, but in no country was there a point at which the national consciousness about the new was as clearly marked as it was in Brazil.

The year 1922 was a date of great significance in Brazil: It marked the centennial year of independence, the founding of the Brazilian Communist Party, the Copacabana Revolt, and Modern Art Week, all of which were watershed social, political, and esthetic events in the transformation of Brazil into a modern country. Modern Art Week itself was not just a literary event; it was an intellectual turning point that changed the way Brazilians thought about themselves, and it had repercussions in all the arts and even in the social sciences.

At the center of Brazilian literary Modernism were two extraordinary writers, Mário de Andrade (1893–1945) and Oswald de Andrade (1890–1954). Not related, they were both *paulistanos* (from the city of São Paulo), and their work embodied complementary facets of the movement.

Mário de Andrade was an essayist, literary critic, musicologist, poet, novelist, folklorist, and writer of short stories. The guru of Brazilian Modernism, he not only wrote some of its monumental works, he was also Modernism's leading theoretician and a kind of intellectual godfather to a generation of Brazilian writers. His most famous book of poetry was *Paulicéia Desvairada* (1922), translated as *Hallucinated City* (1968), but he is most famous for his fanciful, and canonical, novel *Macunaíma* (1928) (*Macunaíma*, 1984). It is almost impossible to summarize the plot of this book, which his author dubbed a "rhapsody," but it deals with the adventures of the title character ("the hero without character") in search of a talisman and his own identity. Born a black Indian in the Amazon forest, he turns white through magic and travels to São Paulo to confront giants, sorceresses, and streetcars, until he is at last transformed into the Great Bear constellation. Like *Iracema*, it is a myth of origin, but here the myth is transformed into a study of the quirks and foibles of Brazilian popular culture rather than being an attempt to write a pretty tale about days of yore.

Oswald de Andrade is generally thought of as exemplifying the "frivolous" side of Modernism. Although he was a theatrical and sometimes ostentatious figure, he produced two of Modernism's most important manifestoes, and he was an inventive and sometimes daring poet. He also wrote two vanguardist novels, *Memórias Sentimentais de João Miramar* (1924) (*Sentimental Memoirs of John Seaborne*, 1972) and *Serafim Ponte Grande* (1933) (*Seraphim Grosse Pointe*, 1979). His works are all aggressively vanguardist, irreverent, and funny, and they are all examples of the esthetic and stylistic distance that exists between the Modernists and the Realists and Parnassians. His "Manifesto Antropófago" (1928, Cannibal Manifesto) is at once a humorous and a bellicose positioning of the new writers as devourers of both foreigners and predecessors in an attempt to produce "poetry for export." The most famous line in the manifesto is "Tupi or not Tupi, that is the question," a pithy motto which, with Mário de Andrade's "We don't know what we want, but we know what we *don't* want," serves as an encapsulation of this so-called destructive phase of Modernism.

The Northeast Regionalist Novel

Modernism's attacks against the sculptured verse of the Parnassians and plodding prose of the Realists naturally produced reactions. In 1926, Gilberto Freyre (Pernambuco, 1900–1987), the famous sociologist and cultural historian published his "Manifesto Regionalista" (Regionalist Manifesto), which took the Modernists to task for their excessive and artificial cosmopolitanism. Since, as Freyre reasoned, the Modernists were attempting to create a new Brazilian literature, they should look not to France and Italy for inspiration but at the authentic Brazil, which he identified as a Brazil of the interior. Today some passages of the manifesto sound merely eccentric (as when he criticizes the cuisine of Rio as too cosmopolitan, that of the North as too Indian, and that of Bahia as too African, leaving by process of elimination the only true Brazilian cuisine to be that of Pernambuco), but his Region-Tradition movement did spur a reexamination of some of the Modernists' pretensions. A spin-off of his movement was the appearance of a new novelistic form which dominated the literary scene in Brazil in the 1930s, the Northeast regionalist novel.

The 1920s had been characterized by increasing political polarization. With the exception of *Macunaíma*, the dominant literary forms were poetry and manifestoes. The political scene shifted radically in 1930 with the imposition of Getúlio Vargas' paternalistic dictatorship, and the genre of the day was the novel, specifically the novel of social protest. Two canonical works emerged from this movement, *Vidas Secas* (1938) (*Barren Lives*, 1965) by Graciliano Ramos and *Fogo Morto* (1943) (Dead Fires) by José Lins do Rego.

The two most popular writers in the 1930s were José Lins do Rego (Paraíba, 1901–1957) and Jorge Amado (b. Bahia, 1912–2001), who alternated producing best-sellers for most of the decade. Amado was a member of the Brazilian Communist Party and made that obvious in his early novels, and though Ramos eventually joined it as well (in 1945), the other members of the generation, including Lins do Rego, were thought to be revolutionaries and subversives. But Lins do Rego was really a memorialist, and it is difficult if not impossible to find any sectarian political views in his famous "Sugar Cane Cycle" of novels. He is really Brazil's novelist of decadence, specifically the decadence of the planter class which dominated the landscape of the old sugar belt in the Northeast. The five novels of the cycle culminated in *Fogo Morto*, in a sense both a revision and a recapitulation of his portrait of a vanishing culture, a culture for which he often seems to demonstrate considerable affection. Unfortunately, only a fragment of this novel is available in translation (*Borzoi Anthology*, 446–458), but the first three novels of the cane cycle are available under the title *Plantation Boy* (1966).

The other canonical literary work from the Northeast generation is by Graciliano Ramos (born Alagoas, 1892–1953). Like the other "leftist" writers of his generation he was persecuted by the Vargas government's Departamento de Imprensa e Propaganda, a secret police organization. He was imprisoned for nearly two years in the mid-1930s. He wrote an eloquent prison memoir about the experience, and, like other members of the generation, saw his books burned in public ceremonies. *Barren Lives* is thought by some to be his most politically revolutionary work, but it is not easy to find in it any references to a particular ideology. It is the story of a cowhand, Fabiano, his wife Vitória, their two nameless sons, and their unforgettable dog Baleia, whose necessary execution at the hands of Fabiano provide some of the most moving pages in the book. Driven from his place of work by the drought, Fabiano seeks and finds work on another ranch. He is exploited by his boss and by the police in town, and at the end of the narrative the drought returns and the cycle begins again. Told in a spare, almost skeletal style, *Barren Lives* is a depressing but compelling depiction of an important part of Brazil's dispossessed, a picture as accurate today as it was 50 years ago.

Since Freyre's writings were important for this generation of novelists, it is legitimate to mention that he himself contributed a volume to the canon, the monumental study of Brazilian culture *Casa Grande e Senzala* (1933) (*The Masters and the Slaves*, 1946). Almost overnight it became a kind of guidebook for Brazilians to think about their culture and its author became a major contributor to the national mythology. In *Casa Grande*, Freyre draws a picture of the "miscible" (a scientific term for "easily mixed") Portuguese explorers spreading Portuguese culture throughout Africa and India by producing mestizo children and then finding themselves in tropical Brazil surrounded by nude women, with predictable results. When the Indian population began to decline, it was replaced by African slaves, to whom Freyre again attributes uncommon lust. Finally, he argues that the very institution of slavery, which had so agitated the abolitionists in the nineteenth century, was in Brazil a more benign, almost fraternal, institution. Many of Freyre's ideas have been attacked by a generation of revisionist historians, but the importance of his ideas cannot be denied, and the appealing quality of much of his thinking has left a lasting legacy in how Brazilians view themselves.

Festa

Freyre's regionalists were the first to react against the Modernists of Rio and São Paulo. The second was a conservative group associated with the magazine *Festa*, which found the primitivism and frivolity of Modernism unattractive. Some claimed to be "spiritualists," not in the sense of affiliation with a religious movement but in the general sense of restoration of the Catholic tradition in poetry. Some of the poets affiliated with this group have become relatively famous, but only because they went their own way and produced works independent of the vague ideology of this movement. One poetess, Cecília Meireles, who was originally involved with this group, wrote the important *Romanceiro da Inconfidência* (1953), a collection of poems about the first political conspirators in Brazil.

After Modernism

The Canonical Poets. Although the Andrades both produced a large body of very interesting poetry, it remained for two writers marginal to the movement to produce the poetry that would become Brazil's canonical poetry of the twentieth century. The first was Manuel Bandeira (Pernambuco, 1886–1968). Bandeira began his long career as a Symbolist, a note which would never entirely disappear from his work. During Modern Art Week his poem "The Toads," an attack on the pretensions of Parnassians, was read, but he already had two books of poetry in print prior to the event, and he had expressed reservations about Modernism for some time. His first book of poetry with a Modernist bent was *Libertinism* (1930), and he went on to have a distinguished career as an essentially independent Modernist, borrowing new forms from successive generations of poets but never losing his own unmistakable voice. Essentially a lyric poet, his poetry was personal and often sentimental, occasionally tinged with irony. He was prolific and wrote on a great many themes, but in general his poetry seems to alternate between the trivial and the transcendent. He wrote sonnets, haikus, Concrete poems, ballads, and free verse, sometimes in the same book. And he wrote a lot about death—tuberculosis cut short his career as an architect when he was only 17, and the expectation of imminent death is often a presence in his verse, though he wrote for half a century. The preoccupation with death has led some critics to consider him a "poet of evasion," in which he flees from the painful realities of daily life either by evoking his childhood or focusing on his own personal earthly paradise, which he called Pasárgada.[5]

The other canonical poet of the twentieth century offers an interesting contrast to the immensely popular and generally accessible Bandeira. He is Carlos Drummond de Andrade (Minas Gerais, 1902–1987). Drummond, as he is known, published his first book of poetry, *Alguma poesia* (Some Poetry) in 1930, well after the Modernists had undertaken their dismantling of the academic literary establishment. The date is important, because it meant that he was one of the first modern poets in Brazil who had nothing to prove—form and language had already been relieved of the weight of tradition, and Drummond was free to proceed as he wished without the necessity of issuing manifestoes either in prose or in verse. He was a product of Modernism but not one of its makers.

A sense of this difference can be seen in a comparison of Bandeira's "Poetics" and Drummond's "In the Middle of the Road," both from around 1930. Bandeira's poem is discursive, prosaic, and opinionated. Drummond's is composed, low-key, and intellectual. In fact, the major difference between the two is that poetry for Bandeira derives from inspiration and personal experience, while for Drummond the approach is always cerebral and analytical. There is also a contrast in their evolution as poets—Bandeira began as an accomplished poet who experimented with different styles, but in Drummond there is a visible maturation from the early to the later works. Another contrast is one of origin—though Bandeira spent most of his life in Rio, he always considered himself a Northeasterner, a part of that mellow, tropical culture that seems to define the Brazilian psyche. Drummond was from Minas Gerais, a theme and a constant presence in his verse. Minas is the state thought to produce the most introspective, self-absorbed people, who never look you in the eye and always have a second agenda. In addition, Drummond could never forget the Scottish heritage suggested by his name, a starker and darker view of the world that contrasts sharply with the warmth of Bandeira's vision.

Drummond was also a poet of incredible range and depth. Less accessible than Bandeira, he was still much revered, and a large segment of the Brazilian intelligentsia put him forth as a candidate for the Nobel Prize. As different as they were, both were quintessentially Brazilian poets and both should be considered among the major figures of twentieth-century poetry.[6]

The Generation of 1945. The closing date for Modernism is somewhat arbitrarily set at 1945, at least in part because it was the date of Mário de Andrade's death. But 1945 also marked the end of both World War II and the Vargas dictatorship and is thus a major date of closure in Brazilian culture. It also marks the beginning of a new generation of Brazilian poets (called, in fact, the generation of 1945), whose principal exponent was João Cabral de Melo Neto (b. Pernambuco, 1920–1999). He was a major influence in subsequent poetic movements and is recognized as the poet who in a sense reinvented the metaphor as a core element in poetry. Like Drummond he is a cerebral poet, but he is very different in his sequences of striking and sometimes dense metaphorical chains, which constitute a unique kind of poetic discourse which is nevertheless still rooted in the social reality of the Brazilian Northeast.

Concretism. Another important poetic movement after Modernism was Concretism, an international movement in which Brazilian poets were prominent. An attempt to reinvent language in terms of its components and to avoid the tradition of poetic discourse, its influence can be found to some degree in later works by both Bandeira and Drummond.

Fiction. In fiction the first canonical post-Modernist work is the trilogy *O Tempo e o Vento* (1949–1961) (*Time and the Wind,* 1969) by Érico Veríssimo (born Rio Grande do Sul, 1905–1975). *Time and the Wind* is an epic history of Rio Grande do Sul. Chronologically, Veríssimo belongs to the same generation as José Lins do Rego and Graciliano Ramos, but he produced his best work after the polarization of the 1930s had dissipated, and the work is a remarkably dispassionate history of the region told as a chronicle of two families. Thought to be a "natural" novelist and the author most influenced by writers from the United States, Veríssimo's greatest novel is unusual in Brazil as a portrait of the middle class, and he differs from a long tradition in his country by being a regional writer without being a regionalist.

The work of fiction highest on the list in the canon is *Grande Sertão: Veredas* (1956) (*The Devil to Pay in the Backlands,* 1963) by João Guimarães Rosa (Minas Gerais, 1908–1967). A true original, Guimarães Rosa belonged to no school and often bewildered both his critics and his numerous fans. *Grande Sertão* is comparable in several ways to Machado's *Brás Cubas* in the nineteenth century—it is a work really without peer in its century. It was written by a novelist of no particular generational or ideological affiliation, and it is, though in a different way, an examination of the human soul. Unlike Machado's work, however, it at least appears to be a regional work, though the term is applicable only in the most tenuous fashion. Guimarães Rosa wrote seven volumes of fiction—the others are stories which range in size from the micro-text to the longest of short stories—but in no major language are more than three volumes available in translation. The reason for this was that he wrote in a perplexing and inventive Portuguese which even his countrymen find difficult to penetrate. The translations are all thus only attempts of greater or lesser success in rendering this dense prose into another code system.

It is also a structurally complicated work, a 500-page, chapterless monologue delivered by a retired gunslinger to an educated city man whose speech is never registered. A work of immeasurable suggestivity, it has been the subject of volumes of criticism, and the fascination with it seems not to have yet abated.

The most recent work in the literary canon is *Gabriela, Cravo e Canela* (1958) (*Gabriela, Clove and Cinnamon,* 1962) by Jorge Amado. Amado published his first novel in 1931 and 24 novels during his lifetime. For many

years not only one of Brazil's most popular novelists but also its most notorious Communist, Amado wrote his early works in line with the social
protest of his fellow Northeasterners of the generation of 1930. Some but
not all of these works were blatantly sectarian, and in some the "solution"
proposed by the Communist Party is quite evident. *Gabriela* was the first
work produced after his rather unpleasant break with the Party, a break which
brought new life to his career. It won dozens of prizes in Brazil and abroad
and was one of the few Latin American novels to attain best-seller status in
the United States. The story takes place in the port city of Ilhéus in southern
Bahia and chronicles the search of the Syrian-born Nacib for a new cook for
his bar. He finds Gabriela, a *retirante* (refugee from the drought) who brings
customers to the bar and love to his bed. This is the immigrant-seduced-by-
the-tropics of *A Brazilian Tenement*, here told with tongue in cheek. It is
also a story of betrayal and revenge, and the progress of the city is a major
theme. It is so rich in Brazilian language and lore that it was used for a time
by the Peace Corps to teach not only language but social mores for Brazil-
bound volunteers. And with such a plot it of course made a wonderful soap
opera and subsequently a successful movie. Like its author it is quintessentially Brazilian, and it is not thus surprising that two other Amado works
received votes for canonization, *Os Velhos Marinheiros* (1961) (*Home Is the
Sailor*, 1964) and *Mar Morto* (1936) (*Sea of Death*, 1984).

The Short Story. There are no short stories in the Brazilian canon, but a
few volumes did receive votes, and it has been a remarkably vigorous genre
in Brazil for the last century or so. One reason for its vigor is economic—
since it is difficult and expensive to publish books in Brazil, writers often try
short fiction (published in newspapers) as a way of earning both some money
and a reputation. An early master of the genre was Machado de Assis, who
published several volumes of short stories during his life. Others that appeared in newspapers or magazines are still being collected. His "The Psychiatrist," a classic tale of madness and sanity in a small town in Brazil,
received one vote for the canon. More of his stories can be found in *The
Devil's Church and Other Stories*.

João Guimarães Rosa's *Sagarana*, also available in translation with the same
title, also received a vote. This volume of nine tales was instrumental in
demolishing one of the cherished dichotomies in Brazilian fiction, because
although they are all stories firmly rooted in rural Brazil, they were written
with a variety of sophisticated narrative strategies that remove them from the
confines of the picturesque so often found in regionalistic fiction. Another
volume of his short stories available in English is *The Third Bank of the River
and Other Stories*.

Also important was Clarice Lispector's *Laços de Família* (1960) (*Family Ties*, 1972), a major work by one of Brazil's most famous woman writers. Although they are not precisely feminist stories, the narratives of *Family Ties* are all told from a female perspective and all produce their principal effect through the interpretation of events by female protagonists. Very little happens in Lispector's narratives, in fact, which is one reason her short stories, not her novels, were nominated, since the technique of interiorization is one that dims the effect of the story in a long narrative.

Another vote went to Jorge Amado's *Os Velhos Marinheiros* (1961) (*Home Is the Sailor*, 1964), which consists of a long narrative and a short story, "The Two Deaths of Quincas Wateryell." It is Amado's only short story, a funny and touching story of magic and death in Bahia, and one which has become a favorite in Brazil.

Finally, one vote was cast for Rubem Fonseca's *O Cobrador* (The Collector, 1979). Fonseca (Minas Gerais, b. 1925) is author of 22 volumes of prose, both short stories and novels. The most recent writer to be nominated for the canon, he began writing in the 1960s. This volume of short stories was one of the 400-plus works banned by the military dictatorship in the 1970s. Fonseca is noted for his detective fiction and for his often graphic portrayals of violence and crime in urban Brazil.

Drama. Drama has been an important genre in Brazilian literature since European contact, beginning with Anchieta's *autos*. In the nineteenth century the comedy of manners of Martins Pena and the *revista* (review) of Artur Azevedo were the most popular works by national writers, but none of these plays has the kind of esthetic ambitions expected of great art. But in the twentieth century a vibrant and multi-faceted theatrical literature and numerous original and innovative theatrical groups emerged.

Oswald de Andrade published two vanguardist plays in 1937 (*O Rei da Vela* and *A Morta*), though they were so challenging neither was actually staged until 1967. Numerous other writers, including Gianfrancesco Guarnieri, Ariano Suassuna, Jorge Andrade, and Joracy Camargo, have produced an impressive body of dramatic literature. Probably because an original Brazilian theatrical literature lacks the long tradition of poetry and narrative fiction, the only plays receiving votes for the canon were *Vestido de Noiva* (1943) by Nelson Rodrigues and *O Pagador de Promessas* (1960) by Alfredo Dias Gomes. Both plays are watershed events in Brazilian theatrical history, but many other plays and many other playwrights deserve attention.[7]

THE BRAZILIAN LITERARY CANON

NOVELS

Author	Title, date	Translation date
Jose de Alencar	*Iracema*, 1865	1886
Machado de Assis	*Memórias Póstumas de Brás Cubas*, 1881	1952
Raul Pompéia	*O Ateneu*, 1888	—
Machado de Assis	*Dom Casmurro*, 1900	1953
Lima Barreto	*Policarpo Quaresma*, 1915	1978
Mário de Andrade	*Macunaíma*, 1928	1984
Graciliano Ramos	*Vidas Secas*, 1938	1965
José Lins do Rego	*Fogo Morto*, 1943	1977 (fragment)
Érico Veríssimo	*O Tempo e o Vento*, 1949–1961	1969
João Guimarães Rosa	*Grande Sertão*, 1956	1963
Jorge Amado	*Gabriela*, 1959	1962
POETRY		
Gregório de Matos	*Poetry*, 1882–1943, 1969	1977 (fragments)
Manuel Bandeira	*Poetry*, 1917–1966	1989
Carlos Drummond de Andrade	*Poetry*, 1930–1970	1967, 1980, 1986
ESSAY		
Euclides da Cunha	*Os Sertões*, 1902	1947

Source: Rinaldo Gama, "Biblioteca nacional," *Vega*, Ano 27, no. 47 (23 de novembro de 1994): 108.

The creation of a literary canon is unquestionably an undertaking subject to a number of vagaries—the selection of who the judges will be, the personal tastes of the judges, the relative popularity of given authors at the time the question is asked, and political considerations of several varieties. This is not, then, a perfect list, and anyone familiar with Brazilian literature will wonder about the inclusion of some works and the absence of others. At least it provides a finite list in a very rich literature.

The scheme above does invite some interesting commentary. First, there is only one canonical volume from the colonial period and there are three from the nineteenth century. The other 11 are all products of the twentieth century, one indication that Brazilian literature has become what it is only recently. Second, of the 15 works on the list one is unavailable in English and we have only fragments of two others. Of those partly or entirely translated the *average* time span between publication in Brazil and publication in

English is over 31 years. Another curious fact, not apparent on the list, is that there are seven other works in the canon, most of which are historical or sociological studies about Brazilian society. Only two of them are available in English—Freyre's *The Masters and the Slaves* and *The Economic Growth of Brazil* by Celso Furtado. These two facts provide at least some sense of the relative attention Anglophone culture pays to the rest of the world. In contrast, American, and recently even Spanish American novels and nonfiction are translated and published in Brazil usually within a year of their release in the original language, merely one indication that Brazilians know the United States a great deal better than Americans know Brazil. And it is not as if the works produced in Brazil are in any sense inferior. Most of the books on this list would do any culture proud. The fact that they are so little known and so tardily translated makes the Brazilian novel one of the best-kept secrets in the hemisphere.

The editors of *Veja* noted two other features of the canon that merit comment. One is that the Brazil portrayed in the canon is much more rural than urban, which is easily explained by the fact that until very recently Brazil was a rural country. A future canon should prove to be more urban, but the present one is a reflection of the weight of history on the national identity. The second observation by the editors is that a preponderance of the works shows a preoccupation with national identity, an attempt to define what Brazil is and who Brazilians are. Despite the fact that Brazil was almost a century and a quarter old when the pilgrims landed on Plymouth Rock, it is for a variety of historical reasons (the principal one being the long colonial experience) a young culture, one that to this day is asking questions about what it means to be a Brazilian.

Given the inherent subjectivity of the procedure involved in the creation of the Brazilian canon—no criteria for the selection of panel members was provided, and none for the selection of the canonical works—it is probably wise not to take this canon as flawless. One telling way to broaden it somewhat might be to include works and authors which fell slightly short of the canon. In one way that broadening merely reinforces the reverence in which some authors are held. Gonçalves Dias, José de Alencar, Machado de Assis, Jorge Amado, and João Guimarães Rosa all received votes for works not in the canon, a clear indication of the importance of this handful of authors in the perception of the critics. But it is also interesting to consider authors who missed the cut completely. There are, for example, no women writers in the canon, but Clarice Lispector received votes for two different works of fiction and the poet Cecília Meireles received votes for a book of poetry. João Cabral de Melo Neto, the luminary of the Generation of 1945, received votes for four different collections of poetry, but none got enough votes to enter the canon.

Another weakness of a canon such as this one is a temporal one. The most recent novel on the list was published in 1958, which gives the altogether erroneous impression that Brazilian literature has not been very dynamic for the last few decades. Exactly the opposite is true, but canon formation is a glacial process which almost always slights the new. The omissions occasioned by the slowness of this process obviously include younger writers, but many important dramatists, woman writers, and poetic movements simply do not appear.

NOTES

1. Until very recently it was possible for a writer to make up his own canon and claim it as legitimate. But in response to Harold Bloom's controversial *The Western Canon* (New York: Harcourt Brace, 1994), the editors of Brazil's most popular newsmagazine, *Veja*, decided to approach fifteen of the most influential intellectuals in the country with a request for a list of the twenty works they considered most appropriate for the Brazilian canon. A total of twenty-two works—eleven novels, eight sociohistoric or literary studies, and three volumes of poetry—make up this consensus canon. I will refer to this list periodically throughout the chapter. Rinaldo Gama, "Biblioteca nacional," *Veja*, Ano 27, no. 47 (23 de novembro de 1994): 108–112.

2. Samples of both his sermons and letters can be found in *The Borzoi Anthology of Latin American Literature*, vol. 1, ed. Emir Rodríguez Monegal, asst. Thomas Colchie (New York: Alfred A. Knopf, 1977), pp. 131–138.

3. Following the massive Lisbon earthquake of 1755, an organization, Arcadia Lusitana, was established to renovate Portuguese letters by imitating the classical perfection of the Greeks and Romans.

4. Susan Sontag, "Afterlives: The Case of Machado de Assis," *The New Yorker*, May 7, 1990, p. 102.

5. Until recently, translations of Bandeira's poetry could be found only in fairly reduced numbers in anthologies of Latin American or Brazilian verse. An excellent and representative anthology of his work, with notes and bibliography, is now available in *This Earth, That Sky: Poems by Manuel Bandeira*, trans. with notes and intro. Candace Slater (Berkeley: University of California Press, 1989).

6. Translations of Drummond's poetry can be found in various anthologies of Latin American and Brazilian poetry. The first volume-length anthology, with an introduction, is *In the Middle of the Road: Selected Poems of Carlos Drummond de Andrade*, comp., ed., and trans. John Nist (Tucson: University of Arizona Press, 1965). More recent collections are *The Minus Sign: Selected Poems*, trans. Virgínia de Araújo (Redding Ridge, CT: Black Swan Books, 1980) and *Travelling in the*

Family: Selected Poems of Carlos Drummond de Andrade, ed. Thomas Colchie and Mark Strand, with addl. trans. Elizabeth Bishop and Gregory Rabassa (New York: Random House, 1986).

7. A fine overview of recent Brazilian theater is David George's *The Modern Brazilian Stage* (Austin: University of Texas Press, 1992).

10

Art and Architecture

If there had been no other reason, the existence of Art-Nouveau would
have been sufficient to justify Modern Art Week.

—Mário de Andrade[1]

INDIAN ART

ART AND ARCHITECTURE existed in Brazil long before the Portuguese came
to the New World. Several important archeological sites date early forms of
art back several thousand years. Most of the surviving artifacts are utilitarian
objects, such as stone and bone projectile points and axes, but Amerindians
in Brazil also made utilitarian pottery, much of it decorated with geometric
designs. They also made things of little immediate practical use such as zoo-
liths (animal figures) and amulets (charms), most frequently in the form of
frogs. They also made statuettes, most often in human form but also occasionally in animal representations. There are also several sites in Brazil in
which petroglyphs (paintings and engravings on rock) are found. Some of
the best preserved are in caves. Like prehistoric petroglyphs found in Europe,
the ones in Brazil usually depict animals and people. In other sites funeral
urns, some quite stylized, have been located. Not many other kinds of early
art survived in Brazil because the artistic media of the Amerindians are
ephemeral—cloth and feathers and basketry do not survive for long.

When the Portuguese came to Brazil they found the descendants of those
early artists still engaged in the arts, but their arrival had a profound effect
on Indian art. The most notable change came in the almost immediate elim-

ination of the art of making stone tools, since the metal ones brought by the Portuguese were much more efficient and, to the Indians, more beautiful because of that efficiency. The European presence also had an effect on ceramic art, because previously the notion of transporting or collecting pieces of pottery (mostly painted human or animal figurines and Venus figures) had not been necessary. With ceramics suddenly transformed into an economic commodity, artisans needed a way to preserve their work, so they began firing their pottery, a practice rarely followed before European contact.

Since there were a great many cultures in Brazil there is great variety from group to group, but in no case was a social organization more complex than that of a tribe, so there are also similarities. The Amerindian culture of Brazil was largely a classless society and a society of leisure. They hunted and fished and tended crops, but since they did not work for a wage, that still left hours in every day to do other things, and the result was that most of the population was involved in the production of some kind of art.

Aside from ceramics and tools, Brazilian Indians produced a great variety of basketry, and many made beautiful woven fabrics, usually dyed with extracts from native plants. They made mats, sieves, hammocks, and *tipitis* (woven basketry devices for extracting the toxins from manioc root). Painting was also widely practiced, but since the canvas for most painting was the human body it has not survived. As Pero Vaz da Caminha mentioned in his letter to King Manuel, bodies dyed partly black were common, but red and other colors were also used. In addition to simply painting part of a torso red or black, Brazilian painters also put elaborate geometric designs on their subjects, many of which can be found in identical form on such objects as mats and fans, suggesting some kind of ritual significance.

The human body was in fact the object of a great deal of artistic attention. Many groups used ear plugs, nose plugs, or lip decorations, and most had very elaborate haircuts. Some groups bound the heads of infants and some filed their teeth. The body was also where necklaces (an almost universal artifact) were worn. Some necklaces are body length, and often they are made with feathers, animal teeth and claws, mother of pearl, shells, and, after the Portuguese arrived, beads. Genital decoration of various forms was also practiced, including penis sheaths for the men and tiny garments made of shells or beads to cover the female genitals. These were called *tangas*, the term currently used for the string bikini. Most groups made combs, bracelets, belts, and arm and leg bands of a variety of materials.

Another very unusual art form which was widespread was feather art. The tropical environment is home to hundreds of species of birds with the most varied plumage, and many Indian groups used this abundant supply of feathers of every color imaginable to create feather cloaks, headdresses, and crowns of extraordinary variety and sophistication. Equally elaborate are the masks made by many groups. Some masks simply cover the face, but many have horns and ears or require the use of a full body costume as part of the disguise. Almost all Brazilian Indian masks are representations of spirits or deities, and all have ritual significance. In some of the larger villages as many as 50 masked figures might dance in a single ritual.

In architecture, Brazilian Indians constructed everything from small wind-breaks and awnings to the gigantic *malocas* (longhouses) of the upper Xingu. In the case of the larger structures, common in many groups, the construction of a new common house may have taken months and involved the entire community in the collection of palm fronds, vines, and beams. A move to a new *maloca* became necessary when game and crops in the old one were no longer sufficient. The new site was chosen with great care and the construction was overseen with care and with attention to ritual necessities. Often *malocas* had interior panels, themselves adorned with painting and geometric designs. A medium-sized one may have been 80 feet long, 30 feet wide, and 20 feet tall, while the large ones on the Rio Negro could have been 150 feet long, 45 feet wide, and 40 feet tall.

Some villages constructed smaller houses for the various clans and subclans around the central longhouse, all oriented on a precise North-South axis. Such settlements often had separate housing for women, likewise oriented, close to the central *maloca*.

Although many groups of Amerindians in Brazil still produce artistic ar-tifacts of all kinds, the impact of native art was until very recently minimal, since the Portuguese either suppressed or ignored the accomplishments of the first Brazilians. For all its richness, the one kind of art the Portuguese most sought in the Indian repertoire was worked gold, so common in Mexico and Peru. They found none.

THE SIXTEENTH CENTURY

The principal artistic manifestation of Brazil's first century as a colony was architecture. Brazil was still an untamed outpost, and the principal activities of its inhabitants were defense against foreign intruders and the conversion of Indians. The result was that the most important buildings in early Brazil were fortifications and churches, with some civil buildings being erected when Tomé de Souza landed in 1549 with a royal mandate. The style of the century was Mannerist, a not terribly complicated form which was further simplified by necessity and by the lack of materials. The first buildings, both forts and churches, were constructed of *taipa*, a form of stucco adapted from the Moors. *Taipa* was usually an amalgam of earth and straw, but in coastal areas it was often reinforced with the addition of whale oil (whaling was a minor industry throughout the colonial period). There are very few remnants of early architecture—the materials themselves are perishable, and many buildings in Brazil were reconstructed various times to conform to current tastes.

Only late in the century were there stone buildings, and many of these were constructed in Portugal and brought piece by piece to Brazil, a kind of build-by-numbers system, and one which indicates the purely European character of Brazilian architecture. In fact, most architects who worked in Brazil had studied in Europe. One of the most famous was Francisco Dias (1538–1633), a Jesuit who had studied in Italy. Dias designed the Jesuit school and one of the principal churches in Olinda (Pernambuco); the Jesuit school in Rio de Janeiro; and the Jesuit school church in Salvador, today the cathedral. Most architects in early Brazil were, however, anonymous.

Much of the civil architecture consisted of "spontaneous" design, and adaptation of the Portuguese style to the climate and materials of the tropics. Many houses were made of baked clay bricks and thatch roofs, materials which are still used today in many parts of Brazil. Wood was often used for reinforcing beams, to build aqueducts, and to make such things as sugar crates; the type of wood varied from region to region. Wooden artifacts do not last long in Brazil's tropical climate, which besides being hot and humid is a favorable environment for termites. The only way to avoid the ravages of the climate and insects was to use more durable materials—among the few surviving early examples of painting are painted copper altarpieces brought from Portugal.

The Jesuits also engaged in an intensive campaign not only to catechize the Indians but to teach them skills, and by the end of the century there was an artisan class of Amerindians, many of whom probably created such things as *santos* (statues of Catholic saints) and altar decorations.

DUTCH BRAZIL

When the Spanish occupied the Portuguese throne in 1580, the Portuguese were left without the means to defend their American colony, and the Brazilians had to rely on their own resources to fend off the raids by the English, French, and Dutch. The Dutch attacked Bahia in 1624 and in 1630 took Recife, where they remained for a quarter century. The most important period of the Dutch occupation coincided with the governorship of Maurício de Nassau (1637–1644). Recife, now renamed Maurisstad, underwent a complete renewal, with a centralized downtown and hundreds of new buildings. The Dutch imported building materials from Europe but also plundered existing buildings for their stone, tiles, and bricks. Almost all the churches in nearby Olinda were demolished for building materials. Nassau also invited astronomers, naturalists, cartographers, and architects to Recife. More important were the "Nassau painters," of various nationalities, who were the first artists in Brazil to depict Brazilian nature and daily life in a non-Catholic style. The most important of them was the Dutchman Frans Post (1612–1680), who painted almost 150 Brazilian landscapes. Another was Albert Eckhout (1610–1666), who painted still lifes and portraits of Brazilian "types," including blacks and mulattoes. A third was the German-born Georg Marcgraf (1610–1644), an eclectic scientist and artist who published the first known volume of drawings of Brazilian natural history, a volume containing over 400 detailed depictions of Brazilian flora and fauna.

When Portugal retook the crown from Spain in 1640, it was finally able to organize sufficient ground and naval forces to expel the Dutch, though the struggle lasted almost 15 years, and the brief interlude of flourishing Dutch art came to an end. In addition to the invaluable documentary significance of Dutch art, the Portuguese got an unexpected dividend from the occupation—the beautifully planned and rationally organized city of Recife, which became a very important commercial center in part because of the excellence of its design. Unlike most cities in Spanish America, Brazilian cities were rarely planned out on a grid, the result being that most cities in Brazil grew by unplanned accretion. The typical Brazilian city consisted of an upper city and a lower city connected by tortuous, narrow streets, which not only made them look like such Portuguese cities as Lisbon and Nazaré, but also lent them a decidedly medieval character. Recife was the only Brazilian city of the colonial period whose urban design was not an anachronism.

THE BAROQUE

Once the Dutch were gone, Brazilian art and architecture again reverted to the Portuguese model, which at this point was the Baroque, a style that emphasized curves over straight lines, free ornamentation, and extravagant forms suggesting movement. The Jesuits so dominated the artistic scene that for a time "Baroque" became a synonym for "Jesuit," though many of the major churches still standing today were designed by Franciscans and Benedictines. When gold was discovered in Minas Gerais in 1696, a series of important changes took place in Brazil. Gold was a magnet for population, and with the shift of the population to southern Brazil the economic axis also moved from north to south. The huge amount of wealth generated by the gold rush also provided both money and leisure time, and Brazil underwent the most dramatic cultural resurgence of the colonial period.

Most of the best examples of Brazilian Baroque are found in Minas Gerais, although many Brazilian churches were remodeled and enriched by the gold from Minas. The most notable of these was the cathedral in Salvador, whose interior was completely redone with gilt leaf from the mines of Minas. Churches were the most important manifestation of Baroque art, both in architecture and in painting. Most of the great painting of the era is found on church ceilings or on ornamental retables.

One of the few important manifestations of Baroque art outside the churches were *chafarizes* (public fountains), which might be erected near a church but were often in public squares or at intersections of major streets. Many of these fountains can still be found in small towns in Minas, examples of a unique civic art which nevertheless retain much of the religious symbolism present in church art.

By far the most important figure of the Brazilian Baroque was Antônio Francisco Lisboa (1738–1814), known as "O Aleijadinho" (the Little Cripple). The son of a Portuguese artisan and builder and a black Brazilian slave woman, Aleijadinho was born in the provincial capital of Vila Rica do Ouro Preto. He began carving wood and stone at the age of 14 and continued the craft for most of his 76 years. Shortly after he turned 50 he contracted a debilitating disease (probably leprosy), which caused him to work under the most unpleasant circumstances. Unable to walk, he had to be carried to his work sites by assistants. His toes and hands atrophied so badly that he had to have his chisel and mallet strapped to the stumps of his hands.

He produced an immense body of work, the most important of which is in Ouro Preto, Sabará, São João del Rei, and Congonhas do Campo. His masterpiece is the Church of Bom Jesus de Matosinhos at Congonhas, where he carved 66 life-size figures in cedar that represent the Stations of the Cross (1796–1799) and 12 striking soapstone statues of the Old Testament prophets (1800–1805). His work is marked by remarkable control of space, a theatrical sense, and a combination of elegance and simplicity rarely found in the art of any period. Since his father and brother were both builders, he was born to the guild tradition, though his roots were not academic but popular, which lends a slightly medieval cast to his sculpture.

The transfer of commerce and culture to southern Brazil was also accompanied by a change in the patronage of the arts. Traditionally, the monastic orders had been the major patrons of the arts, but the expulsion of the Jesuits and the changes in the economy meant that artists had to find new support. In Minas Gerais this new support was almost exclusively from lay brotherhoods, which vied with one another to produce ever more elegant churches and monuments to honor their patron saints. Some of the great Baroque churches in Minas were built under the patronage of slave brotherhoods. Another noted sculptor of the period, in fact, was Francisco Chagas Salvador, popularly called "Cabra." He was a black slave and a member of the lay brotherhood of Carmo.

Minas was not the only area of Brazil affected by the shift of power and influence to the South. The first great transformation of Rio de Janeiro also took place during this period, largely under the direction of Valentim Fonseca e Silva (1750?–1818). An eclectic artist and builder, he was responsible for the creation of the Passeio Público and the construction of numerous churches, *chafarizes*, and houses. His contributions were not in the Baroque style, however, but rather a blending of Italian Mannerism and the somewhat extravagant Portuguese Manueline styles.

THE BRAGANÇAS

A radical change occurred in the early nineteenth century with the transfer of the court from Lisbon to Rio de Janeiro in 1808. The transformation of Rio from a colonial backwash to the seat of empire had immediate and profound effect. João VI found Fonseca e Silva's buildings provincial and not at all in keeping with the Neoclassical style then in vogue in Europe. The emperor invited a former secretary general of the French Academy of Fine Arts to organize a Royal Academy of Sciences, Arts, and Professions, and in 1816 a French Artistic Mission came to Brazil at the court's invitation to help modernize art in Brazil. He also took steps to ensure that the state, not the Church, became the principal patron of the arts by establishing artistic academies, sponsoring exhibitions, and providing scholarships for young artists to study abroad.

The French Artistic Mission and invited visits by other European artists produced a curious situation—much of the most famous art and architecture produced in Brazil in the early nineteenth century was produced by foreigners. Brazil's great Neoclassical architect, Grandjean de Montigny (1776–1850), and its most famous landscape artist, Nicolas Antoine Taunay (1755–1830), were both members of the French Mission. Another member of the Mission was Jean-Baptiste Debret (1767–1848), who directed the first two important art exhibits in Brazil in 1829 and 1830. He remained in Brazil for 15 years, and when he returned to Paris he published a three-volume

Voyage pittoresque et historique au Brésil, one of the most complete artistic documentaries of Brazilian life of the period.

Brazilian artists were important as well, but most of them were trained by the French and simply reproduced art which catered to the rather conservative tastes of the court. Brazilian art became a kind of satellite of French art, and many new modes and schools were adopted without any developmental coherence. In architecture, "neos" predominated, including neo-Florentine, neo-Renaissance, neo-Romanic, and even neo-Arabic and neo-Hindu movements, these again adopted in Brazil without any real immediate relevance to Brazil.

One clear trend to emerge from this seeming confusion was the increasing secularization of art. The state became the principal patron of the arts; and art ceased to exist solely for the ends of the Church. A case in point is one of the most famous Brazilian painters of the late nineteenth century, Pedro Américo (de Figueiredo e Melo) (1843–1915). Pedro Américo was fond of paintings inspired by Biblical motifs, but he became famous for his *Batalha de Avaí* (1888), a patriotic painting inspired by one of the battles in the Paraguayan War. Other painters earned a name for paintings in line with the Brazilian Indianist literature of the period, such as Vítor Meireles (1832–1903) in his *Moema* (1861) and his disciple Rodolfo Amoedo (1857–1941) with his *Marabá* (1882). Indianism was one of the only ideals in which literature and painting coincided chronologically. The subject matter of Brazilian painting in the nineteenth century became increasingly national. The best still life painters painted tropical fruits, and some of the best genre painters earned their popularity for painting the rural people of the interior. The most important of these was Almeida Júnior (1850–1889) from the state of São Paulo. Although he had studied in Paris, he is among the most original and personal of Brazilian artists of the period. He, too, painted Biblical scenes, but he is best known for his second phase, called "pintura caipira," literally "hillbilly painting," in which he portrayed rural life in the interior.

BEFORE MODERNISM

By the end of the century architecture was influenced by Art Nouveau, the first school preoccupied with the use of new materials in the construction of buildings. Not many examples remain because of the tendency to blend all new techniques into one or another of the new schools in vogue, but one example is the Vila Penteado in São Paulo (later the Faculty of Architecture of the University of São Paulo), designed by Carlos Eckman (1866–1940), and the ornate, iron-covered markets in Belém and Manaus. The tendency to blend architectural and painting styles became known as the "eclectic-academic" style, a sumptuous but not very clearly defined style Brazilians refer to as "wedding cake."

The prime representative of this last phase before Modernism was Eliseu D'Angelo Visconti (1865–1944), who painted panels for the ceiling of the Teatro Municipal and the National Library in Rio in a neo-Impressionist or neo-Symbolist style. Visconti also made drawings, magazine covers, posters, and window designs in a great variety of styles and techniques. Typical of the artists of the time, he had studios in both Rio and Paris and designed much of his Brazilian work in France. The mixture of Brazilian and European (mostly French) styles contributed to a lack of precise definition in Brazilian art and architecture. Many buildings were designed by Europeans and decorated by Brazilians, which further blurs the definition of national art at the turn of the century. The lines of influence are so diverse and the proliferation of genres and schools so great that critics have not yet been able to decide on what constitutes a Brazilian canon for turn-of-the-century art. The only esthetic norm was to make things "modern," which led to such perversions as the plastering over and painting of many old sculpted stone façades.

MODERNISM AND BEYOND

In the early twentieth century there were two important artistic exhibitions that would herald in a new direction in Brazilian art. The first (1913) was of the works of Lasar Segall (1891–1967), a Russian-born artist who immigrated to Brazil in 1924 and became a leading figure in Modernism. The second (1917) was of the works of Anita Malfatti (1896–1972). By this time many Brazilian intellectuals had been exposed to the European avant-garde (that is, the rebellious young artists, not the "masters" previous generations had gone to study). The Malfatti exhibition touched off a storm of controversy between conservative and radical critics and artists. Both Expressionism and Cubism were referred to by conservatives as "futurist," an epithet they considered pejorative, and their negative reviews in the press were answered by equally heated rebuttals.

Modern Art Week, held in São Paulo in 1922, consisted of three "festivals"—painting and sculpture, literature and poetry, and music. During the week an eclectic exhibition of painting, sculpture, and architectural design was shown. None of the art shown would have raised eyebrows in Paris, but the novelty of both the show and the presentations caused a scandal in Brazil. The most representative Brazilian painter of early Modernism was Tarsila do

Amaral (1886–1973). Tarsila was so closely affiliated with the intellectual leaders of Modernism that the first two phases have the same names as manifestoes and poetic movements led by the poet Oswald de Andrade. In the first, *Pau-brasil* (brazilwood), Amaral combined themes of the modern world—São Paulo—with rustic and picturesque themes based on rural life. In the second, *Antropofagia* (cannibalism), the central figures are mythic, tropical beings only tenuously based on any observed reality. Among her most famous cannibalist paintings are *Abaporu* and *Urutu* (both 1928), Cubist pieces in which perspective and proportion are eliminated to produce figures which only suggest human forms in a mythic, tropical space.

Many other Brazilian artists produced nativistic works in the 1920s, among them Emiliano Di Cavalcanti (1897–1976) and Vicente do Rego Monteiro (1899–1971). Di Cavalcanti's most famous work of the period is *Cinco Moças de Guaratinguetá* (1930), a tropicalized Picasso. Most of Monteiro's early work is characterized by a relative lack of color and an emphasis on geometrically designed large human figures which are reminiscent of some of the Mexican muralists. Similarly monumental forms are also found in sculpture, especially in the works of Vítor Brecheret (1894–1955), whose *Monumento às Bandeiras* (1936–1953), a group of 40 figures in the Ibirapuera Park, is now a São Paulo landmark.

The worldwide depression and the collapse of the Brazilian coffee market marked a profound change in all aspects of Brazilian life. Many artists affiliated with early Modernist movements began to paint more socially conscious works. Amaral's *Operários* (1933) is a fine example of the shift from the mythic space of the tropical forest to the grimy factories that were to most Brazilians a much more immediate reality. The 1930s also marked the emergence of a large number of cultural "clubs" and organizations that promoted the arts, some of them actually composed largely of members of the proletariat.

The most important painter of the next two decades was Cândido Portinari (1903–1962), probably the best-known Brazilian painter of the century. Portinari spent two years in Paris on a travel grant from 1928 to 1930 and returned to Brazil to paint and teach. In 1935 his *Café* won an honorable mention at the Carnegie International exhibition in the United States, and the government soon began awarding him commissions for murals in government buildings. He did murals for the Ministry of Education in Rio and the famous Pampulha Church in Minas Gerais. He then began to receive considerable international recognition and subsequently did murals both in the Hispanic Foundation of the Library of Congress and the headquarters of the United Nations in New York. The influence of the Mexican muralists is also evident in Portinari's larger work, but he was also an accomplished easel artist, and there the influences range from sixteenth-century Italian painting to Cubism. His *Espantalho* series in the 1940s and his portrayals of drought victims are both Surrealist and Expressionist. In the 1940s and 1950s he returned to murals, most of these with Brazilian historical themes. Three major art museums were founded in the late 1950s, the Museu de Arte de São Paulo (1947); the Museu de Arte Moderna (1948), also in São Paulo; and the Museu de Arte Moderna do Rio de Janeiro (1949). Accompanying this flourishing of venues to display art, a major phenomenon in the 1940s and 1950s was the decentralization of Brazilian art. Where once the Rio/São Paulo axis had been the only home for art and artists, such places as Fortaleza, Porto Alegre, Recife, and Salvador became important art centers. Antônio Bandeira (1922–1967), Brazil's foremost abstractionist, participated in an exhibition in Fortaleza in 1941. In Recife the Ateliê Coletivo was founded in 1952. Salvador became a mecca for artists of all kinds, among them Carybé (Júlio Páride Bernabó, b. 1911) for his paintings of Bahian types and Mário Cravo, Júnior (b. 1923) for his sculptures in wood and metal.

Such rapid change in the art world would suggest parallel modifications in architecture, but in fact it was the only art not immediately affected by Modernism. The first Modernist building in Brazil was the residence of Russian architect Gregory Warchavchik (1897–1972) in São Paulo. Warchavchik submitted plans for approval with the elaborately decorated exterior then in vogue, then built the house without the decorations, creating a national scandal. With time Brazilians became accustomed to the rather stark new design, and Warchavchik and his wife designed numerous residences and gardens in São Paulo. The couple also experimented with furniture, some of it art deco.

Brazilian architects were given further encouragement to create new styles with the visit of the famous Swiss architect Le Corbusier in 1929. Soon there was a "Modernist group" of Brazilian architects who came to dominate the field. The two most important members of the group were Lúcio Costa (1902–1998) and Oscar Niemeyer (b. 1907). They were awarded a contract to construct the new Ministry of Education and Health building, begun in 1935. They also designed the Brazilian Pavilion for the 1939–1940 World's Fair in New York, a project that brought them international acclaim. Juscelino Kubitschek, the future president and the principal force behind the construction of Brasília, was at the time mayor of Belo Horizonte. He commissioned Niemeyer to build a church in Pampulha, a suburb of Belo Horizonte. The artist commissioned to do the external murals was Portinari. One of Portinari's important decisions at Pampulha was to render the exter-

A typical mix of colonial and modern architecture in Brazil. (Author photo)

nal walls in *azulejos*, the blue-and-white tiles that go back hundreds of years in Portuguese tradition.

The Pampulha Church is an excellent example of modern Brazilian architecture. Niemeyer rejected the use of straight lines, then in vogue, in favor of curvilinear concrete slabs. During World War II, Brazilian architects had adapted to the lack of structural steel by using pre-stressed concrete, a necessity which they turned to advantage because of the plasticity of the material. Unlike American architecture, which is based on the use of steel frames, Brazilian architecture thus gained in the use of space and lightness.

The crowning achievement of Costa and Niemeyer, nevertheless, was Brasília. The driving force behind the construction of the new capital in the interior, and ideas several hundred years old was Juscelino Kubitshek, now president of the Republic. They won the competition based on Costa's detailed 23-paragraph proposal. It was to be a two-man city, designed in its entirety by Costa and with its buildings created by Niemeyer. Costa laid out the city in the shape of a cross, with the two principal avenues being the intersecting principal lines. He also laid out the streets with the ample use of the cloverleaf, so that no major street crosses another directly. Niemeyer designed the Plaza of the Three Powers with its striking bowl/dome combination for the Senate and House of Deputies, behind which stand the vertical office towers. Across from them is the Palácio do Planalto, the Presidential Palace, the design for which has evolved into a national icon, used in everything from new public buildings to the design of truck beds.

Brasília was a controversial architectural complex, but it still influenced generations of younger architects, who saw great potential in the plasticity and lightness of functionalism. Niemeyer's ideas were dominant especially in Rio and Bahia, but he was such a big target it was not long before a reaction set in. Functionalism's major antagonist was a professor at the University of São Paulo, Villanova Artigas (1915–1985), who developed an anti-individualistic, communal form called "brutalism," which favored the use of exposed plumbing and ventilation. In its most extreme form brutalism even made privacy an impossibility inside a structure.

Brasília focused international attention on Brazilian architecture, and the founding of the São Paulo Bienal in 1951 did the same for painting. In the middle and late 1950s there was another of those rare convergences of art and literature in the Concretist movement, founded in São Paulo by poets but soon attracting graphic artists because of its insistence on geometric and nondiscursive poetry. A neo-Concretist movement of similar configuration was formed in Rio de Janeiro.

The military takeover in 1964 is in some senses comparable to the Cultural Revolution in Communist China. Persons thought "deviant" (meaning leftist) were imprisoned or exiled, and the effect on the arts was profound. Artigas was arrested and Niemeyer was forced into exile, and many other artists were harassed or imprisoned by the government. The *cultura popular* movements of Rio and the Northeast were suppressed, and painters resorted to a variety of strategies to allow them to criticize the government without seeming to do so. One solution was Pop Art, which allowed the use of banal themes to allude to Brazilian problems. Another was the multi-media *Tropicália*, which used Brazilian tropical imagery in an increasingly vanguardist fashion to veil the implicit criticism. Other artists resorted to reviving the Brazilian Indian and popular festivals as metaphors for Brazil. Whether a result of self-censorship or not, nonrepresentational art, including Surrealism, became a major trend in the late 1960s and 1970s.

With democracy reestablished in 1985, art and architecture returned to a new version of eclecticism, with painting paralleling artistic trends in the United States and Europe, and architecture tending toward a "multinational" style. Art and architecture are both dominated by independents, who individualize and personalize their works and generally insist on making the cultural context of works unmistakably Brazilian.

POPULAR ART

Throughout the history of Brazil, folk artists have operated more or less at the margins of establishment art. Much less subject to the whims of new styles, popular artists today produce many artifacts that are not much different from those made 200 years ago. Among the longest traditions is the production of fired and painted figurines of people and animals, which can be seen to have an immediate connection with Indigenous art. Religious art of various kinds is also a tradition in Brazil, particularly the production of the images of Catholic saints and ex-votos, often miniature representations of parts of the body, which are offered by individuals to a particular saint or church for having a prayer answered. Ex-votos also appear in the form of small paintings, often on metal. Other traditional arts include the making of lace and the production of woven cotton fabrics, either for clothing or for hammocks. African influences can be found even in erudite art, but in popular art *candomblé* and its offshoots have produced a vast array of artifacts, from iron representations of the symbolic accoutrements of the *orixás* to representatives of the deities themselves. There is also a considerable amount of metalwork, including everything from tin to silver, for the ritual tools of religion and for body decorations that have religious significance, such as the *balangandãs* used by Bahian women on a *penca*, a necklacelike equivalent of the charm bracelet. Woodcuts are a popular form often used for the covers of *literatura de cordel*, a popular literature usually in verse which is sold in public markets. The woodcut is one of the many popular forms which has also been revived by erudite artists, another blending of the old and the new characteristic of much of Brazilian art.

NOTE

1. Cited in Walter Zanini, org., *História geral da arte no Brasil*, vol. 1 (São Paulo: Instituto Walther Moreira Salles, 1983), p. 471.

Glossary

Aldeias	villages
Amigos	friends
Autos	short religious plays
Bairro	neighborhood
Bandeirantes	slave mongers
Blocos	dancing groups
Branco fino	"fine white"
Caboclos	those of mixed Indian and white blood
Cafuso	black/Indian
Candomblé	religious rituals of African origin
Cangaço	rural banditry
Capitania	captaincy system
Cariocas	natives of Rio
Cassação	power to exclude people from political activity
Chafarizes	public fountains
Chanchada	musical comedy
Colegas	acquaintances
Creole	blend of two languages
Degredados	criminals expelled from Portugal

Desquite	legal separation that prohibited marriage
Fantasias	costumes for Carnival
Favelas	slums
Feitorias	trading post
Jeitinho	way or knack of getting something done
Malocas	longhouses of the upper Xingu
Mameluco	white/Indian
Marajás	overpaid public servants
Modernismo	literary Modernism
Negro retinto	"very dark black"
Parentela	extended family network
Patrão	person of wealth and prestige
Paulistas	natives of São Paulo
Plano cruzado	"cruzado plan" created new cruzado currency
Quilombos	runaway slaves
Radionovelas	radio soap operas
Real	Brazilian currency
Reino	kingdom
Santos	statues of Catholic saints
Sertão	sizable, inhospitable tracts of land
Taipa	form of stucco adapted from the Moors
Telenovelas	television soap operas
Tenentes	labor movement sympathizers
Terreiro	equivalent of a churchyard
Ufanismo	lay literature of the colonial period
Umbanda	blend of African and Indian ritual and spiritualist doctrines

Bibliography

Almanaque Abril 1997. São Paulo: Editora Abril, 1997.
Almanaque Abril 2000. São Paulo: Editora Abril, 2000.
Almanaque Abril 2001. São Paulo: Editora Abril, 2001.
Almanaque Abril 2002. São Paulo: Editora Abril, 2002.
Andrade, Carlos Drummond de. *In the Middle of the Road: Selected Poems of Carlos Drummond de Andrade*, comp., ed., and trans. John Nist. Tucson: University of Arizona Press, 1965.
Andrade, Carlos Drummond de. *The Minus Sign: Selected Poems*, trans. Virgínia de Araújo. Redding Ridge, CT: Black Swan Books, 1980.
Andrade, Carlos Drummond de. *Travelling in the Family: Selected Poems of Carlos Drummond de Andrade*, ed. Thomas Colchie and Mark Strand, with addl. trans. Elizabeth Bishop and Gregory Rabassa. New York: Random House, 1986.
Andrade, Oswald de. *Sentimental Memoirs of John Seaborne*, trans. Ralph Niebuhr and Albert Bork. *Texas Quarterly* 15, no. 4 (1972): 112–160.
Antonil, André João. *Cultura e Opulência do Brasil*. Salvador, Brazil: Progresso, 1995.
Ash, Russell. *The Top Ten of Everything 2002*. New York: DK Publishing, 2001.
Assis, Machado de. *Epitaph of a Small Winner*, trans. Eilliam L. Grossman. New York: Noonday Press, 1952.
Bandeira, Manuel. *This Earth, That Sky: Poems by Manuel Bandeira*, trans. with notes and intro. Candace Slater. Berkeley: University of California Press, 1989.
Bloom, Harold. *The Western Canon: The Books and School of the Ages*. New York: Harcourt Brace, 1994.
The Borzoi Anthology of Latin American Literature, 2 vols., ed. Emir Rodríguez Monegal, asst. Thomas Colchie. New York: Alfred A. Knopf, 1977.
Brandão, Ambrósio Fernandes. *Dialogues of the Great Things of Brazil*, trans. and

ann. Frederick Holden Hall, William F. Harrison, and Dorothy Winters Welker. Albuquerque: University of New Mexico Press, 1987.

Brasil A/Z (Larousse Cultural). São Paulo: Ed. Universo, 1988.

Burns, E. Bradford. *A History of Brazil,* 2nd ed. New York: Columbia University Press, 1980.

Cândido, Antônio and José Aderaldo Castelo. *Presença da Literatura Brasileira,* 3 vols. São Paulo: Difusão Européia do Livro, 1964.

Capelato, Maria Helena. *Imprensa e história do Brasil.* São Paulo: Ática, 1988.

Coutinho, Afrânio. *An Introduction to Literature in Brazil,* trans. Gregory Rabassa. New York: Columbia University Press, 1969.

DaMatta, Roberto. *O que faz o brasil, Brasil?* Rio de Janeiro: Rocco, 1991.

DeFiore, Ottaviano C. *Architecture and Sculpture in Brazil.* Albuquerque: University of New Mexico, n.d.

Degler, Carl. N. *Neither Black Nor White: Slavery and Race Relations in Brazil and the United States.* New York: Macmillan, 1971.

Eaken, Marshall C. *Brazil: The Once and Future Country.* New York: St. Martin's Press, 1997.

Enciclopédia Novo Século. São Paulo: Editora Abril Cultural, 1988.

Encyclopedia of Latin American History and Culture, 5 vols., ed. Barbara A. Tannenbaum. New York: Charles Scribner's Sons, 1996.

Fernandes, Ismael. *Memória da Televisão Brasileira.* São Paulo: Proposta, 1982.

Gama, Rinaldo. "Biblioteca nacional." *Veja,* Ano 27, no. 47 (23 de novembro de 1994): 108–112.

George, David. *The Modern Brazilian Stage.* Austin: University of Texas Press, 1992.

Greenlee, William Brooks, trans., intro., and notes. "Letter of Pedro Vaz de Caminha to King Manuel." In *The Voyage of Pedro Álvares Cabral to Brazil and India from Contemporary Documents and Narratives.* London: Hakluyt Society, 1938, pp. 3–33.

Harrison, Phyllis A. *Behaving Brazilian.* Rowlay, MA: Newbury House, 1983.

Hasenbalg, Carlos A. *Race Relations in Modern Brazil.* Albuquerque: University of New Mexico, n.d.

Hess, David J. and Roberto daMatta. *The Brazilian Puzzle.* New York: Columbia University Press, 1995.

Holm, John A. "Creole Influence on Popular Brazilian Portuguese." In *Pidgin and Creole Languages,* ed. Glenn G. Gilbert. Honolulu: University of Hawaii Press, 1987, pp. 406–429.

Holm, John A. *Pidgins and Creoles,* vol. 2. Cambridge: Cambridge University Press, 1988.

Hulet, Claude L. *Brazilian Literature,* 3 vols. Washington, DC: Georgetown University Press, 1974.

Johnson, Randal. *Cinema Novo x 5: Masters of Contemporary Brazilian Film.* Austin: University of Texas Press, 1984.

Johnson, Randal. *The Film Industry in Brazil: Culture and the State.* Pittsburgh: University of Pittsburgh Press, 1987.

Johnson, Randal and Robert Stam, eds. *Brazilian Cinema*. New York: Columbia University Press, 1995.

Kirsch, John. *Why Is This Country Dancing?* New York: Simon & Schuster, 1993.

Lemos, Carlos, José Roberto Teixeira Leite, and Pedro Manuel Gismonti. *The Art of Brazil*. New York: Harper & Row, 1983.

Levine, Robert M. *The History of Brazil*. Westport, CT: Greenwood Press, 1999.

Maior, Mária Souto. *Nomes Próprios Pouco Comuns*. Rio de Janeiro: Livraria São José, 1974.

Matos, Gregório de. "The Satirical and Popular Muse." In *The Borzoi Anthology of Latin American Literature*, vol. 1, ed. Emir Rodríguez Monegal, asst. Thomas Colchie. New York: Alfred A. Knopf, 1977.

Mattelart, Michele and Armand Mattelart. *The Carnival of Images: Brazilian Television Fiction*. Westport, CT: Bergin and Garvey, 1990.

McCann, Bryan. "The Invention of Tradition on Brazilian Radio." In *The Brazil Reader: History, Culture, Politics*, ed. Robert M. Levine and John J. Crocitti. Durham, NC: Duke University Press, 1999, pp. 474–482.

Moreira, Marcílio Marques. *The Brazilian Quandary*. New York: Priority Press Publications, 1986.

Mörner, Magnus. *Race Mixture in the History of Latin America*. Boston: Little, Brown and Company, 1967.

Nowell, Charles E. *A History of Portugal*. Princeton, NJ: D. Van Nostrand, 1952.

Putnam, Samuel. *Marvelous Journey: Four Centuries of Brazilian Literature*. New York: Alfred A. Knopf, 1948.

Rego, Stella de Sá and Marguerite Itamar Harrison. *Modern Brazilian Painting*. Albuquerque: University of New Mexico, n.d.

Rosa, João Guimarães. *The Devil to Pay in the Backlands*, trans. James L. Taylor and Harriet de Onís. New York: Alfred A. Knopf, 1963.

Simpson, Amelia. "Xuxa and the Televisual Imagery." In *The Brazil Reader: History, Culture, Politics*, ed. Robert M. Levine and John J. Crocitti. Durham, NC: Duke University Press, 1999, pp. 343–347.

Sinclair, John. *Latin American Television: A Global View*. Oxford: Oxford University Press, 1999.

Skidmore, Thomas E. *Black into White: Race and Nationality in Brazilian Thought*. Durham, NC: Duke University Press, 1993.

Skidmore, Thomas E., ed. *Television, Politics, and the Transition to Democracy in Latin America*. Washington, DC: Woodrow Wilson Center Press, 1993.

Smith, T. Lynn. *Brazil: People and Institutions*, rev. ed. Baton Rouge: Louisiana State University, 1963.

Sontag, Susan. "Afterlives: The Case of Machado de Assis." *The New Yorker*, May 7, 1990, p. 102.

Stam, Robert. "On the Margins: Brazilian Avant-Garde Cinema." In Randal Johnson and Robert Stam, eds., *Brazilian Cinema*. New York: Columbia University Press, 1995, pp. 306–327.

Stam, Robert. *Tropical Multiculturalism: A Comparative History of Race in Brazilian Cinema and Culture.* Durham, NC: Duke University Press, 1997.

Stephens, Thomas M. *Dictionary of Latin American Racial and Ethnic Terminology.* Gainesville: University of Florida Press, 1989.

Summ, G. Harvey, ed. *Brazilian Mosaic: Portraits of a Diverse People and Culture.* Wilmington, DE: SR Books, 1995.

Van Dyk, Jere. "Amazon, South America's River Road." *National Geographic* 187, no. 2 (February 1995): 3–39.

Vicente do Salvador, frei. *Historia do Brasil, 1500–1627.* Nova edição revista por Capistrano de Abreu. São Paulo and Rio: Editores Weiszflog Irmãos, 1918.

Wagley, Charles. *An Introduction to Brazil,* rev. ed. New York: Columbia University Press, 1971.

The World Almanac and Book of Facts, 1997. Mahwah, NJ: K-III Reference, 1996.

Zanini, Walter, org. *História geral da arte no Brasil,* 2 vols. São Paulo: Instituto Walther Moreira Salles, 1983.

Index

About the Author

JON S. VINCENT (Ph.D., University of New Mexico) joined the faculty of the University of Kansas in Lawrence in the fall of 1967, fresh from a Fulbright year in Brazil. Jon taught Portuguese, and occasionally Spanish, at Kansas until his premature death in 1999. He loved Brazil and its culture; one of his major publications was a book in the Twayne series on João Guimarães Rosa.

About the Contributors

MARK DINNEEN is Assistant Professor of Latin American Literature and Cultural History in the School of Modern Languages, University of Southampton, United Kingdom.

MARGO MILLERET is Professor of Spanish and Portuguese at the University of New Mexico, where she specializes in Brazilian and Spanish American theater.

JON M. TOLMAN is a retired professor of Portuguese and Brazilian studies at the University of New Mexico.